THE EVERYTHING

Stir-Fry Cookbook

Dear Reader,

My love affair with stir-frying began when I was still a teenager, when my Asian coworkers introduced me to Chinese cuisine. I soon began spending my weekends exploring Vancouver's Chinatown, shopping for the best soy sauce, rice wine, and other ingredients to use in stir-fry dishes.

The first stir-fries I produced were typical Chinese fare: chow mein, pork fried rice, lemon chicken. However, I soon found that stir-frying was perfect for making quick, healthy dishes for my family every night of the week, whether or not I was using Chinese ingredients. Better still, stir-frying was a great way to make quick and easy versions of classic dishes from around the world. Today, along with Quick Broccoli Beef (page 74), Stir-Fried Bok Choy (page 264), and other classic Asian dishes, I use my trusty wok to make everything from Chicken Cacciatore (page 45) to an omelet.

In this book, I hope to show you how stir-frying is a great way to prepare quick and easy meals with little time and effort. I hope you have as much fun learning about the art of stir-frying and preparing the stir-fry recipes contained in this book as I did in writing it.

Rhonda Lauret Parkinson

YTHING® Series

Editorial

Publisher	Gary M. Krebs
Managing Editor	Laura M. Daly
Associate Copy Chief	Sheila Zwiebel
Acquisitions Editor	Kerry Smith
Development Editors	Rachel Engelson
	Brett Palana-Shanahan
Associate Production Editor	Casey Ebert

Production

Director of Manufacturing	Susan Beale
Project Manager	Michelle Roy Kelly
Prepress	Erick DaCosta
	Matt LeBlanc
Design and Layout	Heather Barrett
	Brewster Brownville
	Colleen Cunningham
	Jennifer Oliveira
Series Cover Artist	Barry Littmann

Visit the entire Everything® Series at *www.everything.com*

THE EVERYTHING

STIR-FRY COOKBOOK

300 fresh and flavorful recipes
the whole family will love

Rhonda Lauret Parkinson

Adams Media
Avon, Massachusetts

To all my Chinese cooking instructors, who introduced me
to stir-frying and taught me to know my way around a wok.

An Everything® Series Book.
Everything® and everything.com® are registered trademarks of F+W Publications, Inc.

Published by Adams Media, an F+W Publications Company
57 Littlefield Street, Avon, MA 02322 U.S.A.
www.adamsmedia.com

ISBN 10: 1-59869-242-9
ISBN 13: 978-1-59869-242-6

Printed in the United States of America.

J   I   H   G   F   E   D   C   B   A

Library of Congress Cataloging-in-Publication Data
Lauret Parkinson, Rhonda.
The everything stir-fry cookbook / Rhonda Lauret Parkinson.
p.   cm.
(An everything series book)
Includes index.
ISBN-13: 978-1-59869-242-6 (pbk.)
ISBN-10: 1-59869-242-9 (pbk.)
1. Stir frying. 2. Wok cookery. 3. Skillet cookery. I. Title.
TX689.5.L38 2007
641.7'7—dc22

This book is available at quantity discounts for bulk purchases.
For information, please call 1-800-289-0963.

Contents

Acknowledgments

I would like to thank my husband, Anthony, for his support and encouragement. Thanks also to my agent, Barb Doyen, and my project editor, Kerry Smith, for their guidance throughout this project.

Introduction

THE ORIGINS OF STIR-FRYING, or chao, may date back as far as the Han dynasty (206 B.C.–A.D. 220). Chronic fuel shortages meant that people needed to find a way to cook food without using too much oil. Stir-frying—quickly stirring food in a pan that has been heated with just 1 or 2 tablespoons of oil—fit the bill perfectly. Today, stir-frying has become China's most well-known cooking technique.

Over time, stir-frying caught on in other parts of Asia. Thailand's signature dish, pad Thai, is a flavorful combination of stir-fried seafood, vegetables, scrambled egg, and noodles, finished with a tangy sauce. Stir-frying is also a popular cooking technique in Korea, which shares a northern border with China.

History credits Cantonese immigrants who worked on the American railroads in the mid-1800s with introducing North Americans to Chinese cuisine. Despite this early influence, stir-frying didn't take hold in North America until the health-conscious 1970s. Suddenly, it seemed that everyone was buying a wok and tuning in to watch TV-celebrity chefs like Stephen Yan prepare mouthwatering stir-fries in mere minutes. In California, skilled chef Madame S. T. Ting Wong and restaurateur Madame Sylvia Wu attained minor celebrity status.

Unlike wheat germ, cod liver oil, and other health-food fads that came and went, stir-frying has proven it has staying power. One reason why stir-frying has remained so popular over the years is that it is quick. In today's fast-paced society, many families find it difficult to fit family dinnertime into their hectic schedule, let alone spend hours preparing a meal. A stir-fry can make its way from stovetop to dinner table in as little as fifteen minutes.

Once you've tried a few dishes, you'll quickly find yourself falling into a rhythm—marinating the meat, then cutting and preparing the vegetables, then combining ingredients for a sauce while the meat continues to marinate. The total time for preparing dinner—from cutting and chopping to serving the final product—will nearly always be under thirty minutes.

Stir-frying is also healthy. The short cooking time means that vegetables retain more of their nutrients than they do when prepared using longer cooking methods. Furthermore, the amount of oil listed in the recipes is a general guideline only—the amount of oil you will actually need for stir-frying depends partially on the type of wok or skillet you are using and how well seasoned it is. Experienced Chinese cooks know that a properly seasoned carbon-steel wok develops its own nonstick coating after just a few uses. If you do decide to purchase a carbon steel wok, be sure to follow the instructions on how to season a wok (page 6).

Stir-frying is a great choice for vegetarians and anyone wanting to prepare a vegetarian meal. Studies show that the boundary between strict vegetarians and nonvegetarians is dissolving—even people who wouldn't classify themselves as vegetarians are choosing to incorporate one or two vegetarian dishes into their diet each week. Stir-frying makes this easy. Often it's just a matter of replacing the meat with tofu (skipping the marinating stage) and adding the tofu to the pan near the final stages of cooking.

Finally, stir-frying is easy. For anyone new to cooking, stir-frying is one of the simplest cooking techniques to learn.

Chapter 1

Stir-Fry Essentials

IN today's fast-paced society, many families barely have time to sit down to a meal together, let alone spend hours in the kitchen preparing it beforehand. So it's no surprise that fast cooking techniques like stir-frying are more popular than ever. The average time for stir-frying a dish is only five to seven minutes. Better still, stir-frying is one of the simplest cooking techniques to learn. All it takes are a few cooking tips and the right ingredients, and you're ready to start stir-frying!

The Art of Stir-Frying

At some point, you have probably watched an expert chef on a culinary television show stirring and tossing around a variety of exotic-looking vegetables and other ingredients in a bowl-shaped Chinese wok. You may wonder what exactly he or she is doing.

Basically, stir-frying involves cooking food at high heat in a small amount of oil. With a few exceptions (such as allowing beef to sear briefly when it is first added to the pan), it's important to keep the ingredients moving constantly during stir-frying. The constant stirring motion ensures that all the food comes into contact with the bottom surface of the pan, where the heat is most intense. It also keeps food from sticking to the pan.

Like stir-frying, sautéing also involves cooking food at high heat. The major difference between the two is that food is normally cut into bite-sized pieces before stir-frying, while sautéed food is left whole.

Getting Ready to Stir-Fry

While the technique of stir-frying is quite straightforward, there are a few basic principles that make the process of stir-frying go more smoothly. It's important to prepare all the ingredients ahead of time. As noted above, on average, it takes only five to seven minutes to stir-fry a dish. You'll be too busy stirring to have any extra time for chopping an onion or measuring out ingredients for a sauce to add at the end. Always double-check the recipe to make sure you have all ingredients prepared before you begin stir-frying.

Most stir-fry recipes call for meat, poultry, or seafood to be marinated prior to stir-frying. A marinade helps tenderize meat, and it's a great way to add extra flavor to a stir-fry. Always cut and start marinating the meat before doing anything else. Once the meat is marinating, you're free to complete the remaining prep work, such as chopping vegetables, preparing a sauce, and cooking rice.

Whenever possible, try to cut the stir-fry ingredients into uniform-sized pieces so that they will take approximately the same amount of time to cook. Many of the vegetables will need to be washed or rinsed prior to stir-frying. It's important to make sure vegetables are thoroughly dry before adding them to the stir-fry; wet vegetables won't cook properly and can cause the hot oil to splatter. To avoid this, you can wash the vegetables and leave them to drain earlier in the day (for example, in the morning before you leave for work), which gives them more time to dry.

Organization is key when it comes to stir-frying. Keep the sauces, prepared vegetables, and aromatics near the stove so that you'll be able to add them quickly when you start cooking. Have a colander or paper towels set out to drain the meat or seafood if needed.

The Basics of Stir-Frying

The process of stir-frying will unfold smoothly if you follow these basic guidelines:

- Make sure that all the ingredients for the stir-fry are near the stove, so that you can reach for them quickly.
- Add the oil to a preheated pan, tilting the pan so that the oil drizzles along the sides. Stir-fry ingredients don't just sit at the bottom of the pan, so the sides need to be oiled as well.
- Before adding the main ingredients, add the aromatics such as ginger and garlic to flavor the oil.
- If the stir-fry includes meat or poultry, add that first. Let it sear briefly, then stir-fry until it changes color and is nearly cooked through. (The beef should have no trace of pink and the chicken should have turned white.)
- When adding vegetables, add the thicker, denser vegetables first, as they will take more time to cook. Feel free to add a small amount of water or soy sauce if the vegetables begin to dry out during stir-frying.

Keep these instructions in mind as you try out the recipes in the following chapters.

Wok Versus Frying Pan

Selecting the wrong equipment can turn stir-frying from a quick and easy task into an exercise in frustration. The right equipment, on the other hand, will help ensure a successful result. When it comes to cooking equipment, the most important decision you'll need to make is what type of pan to use. Asian cooks traditionally use a wok for many types of cooking, from steaming to stir-frying. With its high, sloping sides and rounded or flat bottom, the wok's unusual design is perfect for stir-frying. Unlike with a standard frying pan, in a wok, you can stir and toss food with ease without worrying about it winding up on the floor. The wok bottom also rests directly on the heat source, allowing food to cook more quickly.

While most people prefer a wok for stir-frying, the frying pan has its fans as well. Unless you live near an Asian market, a good carbon steel wok can be hard to find. Furthermore, many cookware shops carry stir-frying pans that are specifically designed both for stir-frying and other types of pan-frying. The learning curve for stir-frying may be shorter with a frying pan—as with any other piece of cooking equipment, you will probably need to use the wok a few times to get used to it.

Here are a few basic features you should look for when choosing a frying pan for stir-frying:

- **Heavy material.** A frying pan made of cast iron or heavy-gauge aluminum (such as Calphalon's hard anodized pans) can handle heat without scorching. If you try stir-frying with a pan made of lighter material, such as Teflon, you may ruin the pan.
- **Deep sides.** While it won't have a wok's deep, sloping sides, a frying pan with deeper sides will make stirring easier.
- **A tight-fitting lid.** Even stir-fry recipes sometimes call for the food to be covered and briefly steamed or simmered in addition to stir-frying.
- **In the end, whether you use a wok or frying pan for stir-frying is really a matter of personal preference.** You may want to start out stir-frying with a frying pan, and wait to purchase a wok until you are sure you'd like to continue stir-frying.

A Stir-Fry Cook's Best Friend—the Wok

While a frying pan can be used, when it comes to stir-frying, there's really no substitute for a good wok. Definitely consider purchasing a wok if you're planning to stir-fry on a regular basis.

When purchasing a wok, factors to consider include the wok's size, design, and the type of material it is made from. Most important is whether the wok is made of a type of material that can handle high heat. While the original woks were made of cast iron, today the majority of Chinese chefs favor carbon steel. Carbon steel is lightweight, durable, and a good conductor of heat, so food cooks evenly. Better still, carbon-steel woks are inexpensive—a good wok can often be purchased for under $25.

How to Choose a Wok

Cast iron still has its fans, particularly since its conduction of heat is superior to carbon steel. However, the heaviness of cast iron makes it more difficult to drain food or quickly clean out the wok before stir-frying the next batch of ingredients.

Originally, all woks were round bottomed, designed to sink into the pit of a Chinese woodstove. While round-bottomed woks are still commonly used on gas stoves, their shape makes them a poor choice for Western electric stoves. Not only does the food cook unevenly, but the rounded wok can reflect heat back on the stovetop element, causing permanent damage. When stir-frying first took hold in the West, designers attempted to solve the problem by creating a collar for the wok to rest on that would be placed on the stovetop element. A more recent innovation is the flat-bottomed wok, which can sit directly on the stovetop element. However, some people still prefer to use a round-bottomed wok with a collar—the choice is yours.

While Chinese restaurants can use woks up to three feet wide, twelve to fourteen inches is a good size for most families. A larger wok won't fit comfortably on a Western stove, and it will be difficult to cook a meal for four people in a wok that is too small. However, college students or anyone living alone may prefer a smaller wok, between nine and twelve inches in diameter, particularly if space is an issue.

In theory, an electric wok seems like a great way to ensure even heating during stir-frying, while freeing up a stovetop element. In practice, however, electric woks may fail to generate enough heat for stir-frying (although they are good for keeping cooked food warm). Generally, higher-end electric woks tend to perform better than less-expensive models.

How to Season and Clean a Wok

A carbon steel wok must be seasoned in order to perform properly. Seasoning a wok replaces the sticky protective coating put on by the manufacturer with an oil coating that protects the surface, and it also helps keep food from sticking to the pan. Over time, the wok will develop its own nonstick coating and will require less oil for stir-frying.

The first step in seasoning a wok is to wash it in hot water and scrub it with a scouring pad to remove the manufacturer's coating. (Unless you need to reseason it at some point, this is the only time you should use a harsh cleanser on the wok.) Rinse the cleaned wok and dry it on a stovetop element over high heat. Once the wok is dry, remove it from the element, and use a paper towel to rub a small amount of oil around the inside. Heat the wok over medium-low heat for ten minutes, and use a clean paper towel to wipe off the oil. You will probably find black residue on the paper towel. Keep repeating the process—rubbing oil over the wok, heating, and wiping—until the paper towel contains no black residue.

When cleaning a wok, the two most important things to remember are to avoid using a scouring pad or abrasive cleanser and to dry the wok thoroughly. Scouring pads and harsh cleansers can remove the protective coating, and wet woks can rust.

Cooking Utensils

You're probably already familiar with many of the cooking utensils used in stir-frying: a sharp knife for cutting meat, measuring cups and spoons for measuring out ingredients, bowls for mixing everything together. You'll be putting all of these to use when preparing stir-fry recipes. However, you may also want to consider stocking up on a few less-common items, some of which are specifically designed for stir-frying.

- **Wok spatula.** A wok spatula has a wider base than a regular spatula, making it easier to lift and stir food during stir-frying.
- **Wok lid.** In addition to covering the food during simmering or steaming, the interior of the wok lid comes in handy for transferring food from the preparation area to the wok.
- **Mandoline.** A mandoline is a cutting tool that is handy for cutting vegetables into thin matchsticks (also called cutting the vegetables "julienne style").
- **Colander.** Investing in a good colander will keep you from going through an endless supply of paper towels to drain meat after stir-frying.
- **Cooking chopsticks.** Longer than regular chopsticks, cooking chopsticks are used for everything from stirring food and lightly beating eggs to separating long noodles in a pot of boiling water.
- **Slotted spoon.** Even stir-fries sometimes call for the meat to be immersed and cooked in hot oil, or for vegetables to be blanched before combining them with the other ingredients in the stir-fry. A slotted spoon makes it easier to remove the food from the hot oil or boiling water.

Don't worry if you can't find stir-fry utensils in a kitchenware store and a trip to an Asian marketplace isn't practical. Many Chinese cooking utensils are available on the Internet (see Appendix B, "Online Shopping Resources").

Essential Ingredients for Stir-Frying

There are a few basic ingredients that you'll want to keep on hand so that you can whip up a stir-fry on short notice. While some of these, such as rice vinegar or hoisin sauce, may be new to you, most are readily available in the ethnic or international section of local supermarkets.

Sauces and Seasonings

There are a number of sauces and seasonings that lend flavor to stir-fry dishes. Soy sauce is an indispensable ingredient in Asian cuisine, from Japanese shoyu to Indonesian kecap manis, which is a thick version of soy sauce sweetened with palm sugar. Since stir-frying is most closely associated with

Chinese cuisine (and to a lesser extent, Thai cuisine), most of the recipes in this book are made with Chinese soy sauce. The two main types of soy sauce used in Chinese cooking are light and dark soy sauce. Both are made from fermented soy beans. However, while light soy sauce (usually referred to in recipes simply as "soy sauce") is quite salty, the addition of molasses gives dark soy sauce a darker color and a richer texture and flavor.

If you can't find Chinese light soy sauce in the supermarket, Kikkoman soy sauce can be used as a substitute. Persons on a low-sodium diet may prefer to use Kikkoman, because Chinese light soy sauce brands are typically quite high in sodium. If you're not watching your sodium intake, be prepared to add a bit of salt (or a seasoning substitute) when using Kikkoman instead of Chinese light soy sauce in recipes.

Every meat marinade needs an acidic liquid to help tenderize the meat, and rice wine plays that role in Chinese stir-fry cooking. It is also splashed on meat during stir-frying, and it is sometimes added to sauces. Rice wine can be difficult to find without making a trip to an Asian grocery store. Fortunately, dry sherry makes an acceptable substitute.

Like rice wine, rice vinegar is made with fermented glutinous rice, but it goes through a more extensive fermentation process. Rice vinegar is frequently used in sauces, particularly in sweet-and-sour dishes.

Rice vinegar can often be found in the international or ethnic section of local supermarkets. If it is unavailable, try substituting a mellow flavored vinegar such as cider vinegar instead of regular white vinegar. With the exception of sweet-and-sour sauce, the sharply acidic taste of regular white vinegar is too harsh for most stir-fry recipes.

Chile paste is a spicy condiment made with chilies, vinegar, and other seasonings. If you're not a fan of handling hot chili peppers, chile paste makes a convenient substitute.

Made from toasted sesame seeds, Asian sesame oil has a wonderful nutty flavor. You'll recognize Asian sesame oil by its rich dark color—Kadoya sesame oil from Japan is a good brand. Sesame oil is used in marinades and added to stir-fries at the end of cooking for extra flavor. A little goes a long way though, so be sure to use it sparingly.

While not a stir-fry staple, another ingredient made from white sesame seeds is sesame paste. Used in Chinese cooking for more than 2,000 years, sesame paste lends a thick texture and nutty flavor to Strange Flavor Chicken

Salad (page 42), a popular restaurant dish. Many supermarkets do not carry sesame paste. Smooth peanut butter makes a convenient substitute.

Made by combining soybean paste with chilies, garlic, and other seasonings, hoisin sauce has a sweet and spicy flavor. In stir-frying, the thick brown paste is frequently added to sauces and sometimes to marinades as well. Hoisin sauce is sometimes called duck sauce because it is spread on the pancakes that are traditionally served with Peking duck.

While it is the most well known, hoisin sauce is not the only soybean-based sauce used in stir-fries (and Chinese cooking). Black bean sauce is made with soybeans that are fermented with garlic and other seasonings. Several popular stir-fries use black bean sauce or the fermented black beans themselves. Depending on where you live, finding black bean sauce may require a trip to the Asian grocery store or shopping online.

Essential Fresh Ingredients

Sometimes called the "holy trinity" of Chinese cuisine, garlic, ginger, and green onion have a particularly important role to play in stir-frying. Both garlic and ginger are added to the heating oil to help prevent an oily flavor from being imparted to the other ingredients. Green onion (also called spring onion) lends a mild onion flavor to stir-fries. It may be added to the oil with the garlic and ginger, stirred in with the other ingredients during stir-frying, or sprinkled on the dish at the end as a garnish. All three are sometimes added to marinades to give meat or seafood extra flavor.

Unless a recipe specifically calls for powdered ginger, always use fresh ginger in stir-fry dishes. You can peel the ginger or leave the peel on as desired. When using green onion in stir-fries, cut off the ends and cut the green onion on the diagonal into the size called for in the recipe. Normally, all of the green onion is used. However, you can also use only the green or white parts to enhance the appearance of the dish.

Canned Asian Vegetables

For many people, their first introduction to Asian vegetables came when they ordered a stir-fry dish made with bamboo shoots and water chestnuts. The popularity of these two vegetables stems partly from their easy availability—bamboo shoots and water chestnuts (along with baby corn and straw mushrooms) are readily available on local supermarket shelves. Always rinse canned Chinese vegetables after opening or blanch briefly in boiling water to remove any taste from the can. Like all canned vegetables, Chinese vegetables are heated to kill any bacteria before canning, so they need to be stir-fried only long enough to heat them through.

While canned vegetables are convenient, nothing beats fresh Chinese vegetables for flavor. Fresh water chestnuts have a sweet flavor that canned water chestnuts lack. Both water chestnuts and bamboo shoots are available year-round in the produce section of Asian markets. Feel free to use them in place of canned vegetables in any of the recipes.

Rice, Noodles, and Cornstarch

Stir-fries are frequently meant to be accompanied by rice. Rice is a staple grain in southern China, where it is frequently consumed at every meal. While long-grain white rice is the rice of choice throughout much of China, the type of rice you use is really a matter of personal preference. Feel free to use other types of rice, such as medium grain or healthy brown rice.

The main difference between white and brown rice is the level of processing that takes place. All rice is hulled, but in white rice the brown or reddish layers of bran underneath the hull are removed as well. Besides giving brown rice its darker color, these layers of bran are a rich source of B vitamins, making brown rice more nutritious than white varieties.

A number of popular stir-fries, including pad Thai, are made with noodles. While Asian noodles may not come in the variety of shapes that characterize Italian pasta, there is more variety in the basic ingredients used to make the noodles. In addition to standard wheat-based flour, Asian noodles are made from rice flour and mung bean starch. The unusual ingredients give these noodles specific properties: both are superabsorbent, soaking up the seasonings and sauce they are cooked with. They also puff up nicely when deep-fried.

Cornstarch, made from the starchy substance contained inside corn kernels, plays a major role in stir-fry cooking. It is used in marinades to seal in the other ingredients and protect foods from the hot oil, and added to sauces as a thickener.

While cornstarch is a popular thickener in North America, starches made from tapioca, arrowroot, and even water chestnut are used throughout Asia. When a recipe calls for a cornstarch and water mixture to thicken the sauce, feel free to experiment with replacing the cornstarch with one of these other starches. Just remember that each has slightly different properties: for example, tapioca starch thickens more quickly than cornstarch, and arrowroot starch will actually thin out again if overcooked.

Dried Ingredients

While they are more commonly found in long-simmering dishes such as soups and stews, dried ingredients are regularly used in stir-fries. Depending on where you live, it may require a trip to the Asian market or going online and surfing the Web (see Appendix B, "Online Shopping Resources," page 303) to buy them. But you will find it is well worth the effort to have these items in your culinary repertoire.

Dried Chinese mushrooms are ubiquitous in Chinese cuisine, lending a rich flavor that fresh mushrooms lack. Like other dried ingredients, dried mushrooms need to be reconstituted through soaking in hot water. The strained soaking liquid from these mushrooms is frequently added to the sauce.

Dried lily buds are the dried buds of unopened tiger lilies. The dried lily buds lend a yellow color and earthy flavor to soups and stir-fries. Also called golden needles because of their length (about three inches), dried lily buds are found in the popular restaurant dishes mu shu pork (see Restaurant-Style Mu Shu Pork, page 184) and hot-and-sour soup. Like dried mushrooms, the dried lily buds need to be reconstituted in water before using.

Dried shrimp are tiny shrimp that have been preserved in salty water and dried. The tiny shrimp add a strong salty flavor to dishes such as Shrimp and Spinach Stir-Fry (page 133).

Putting Together a Stir-Fry from Scratch

While you'll usually be following a recipe, sometimes it's fun to create your own stir-fry. At other times you'll want to adapt a recipe to use ingredients you already have on hand. When doing so, feel free to look beyond the Asian pantry. After all, Chinese cuisine has a long tradition of borrowing ingredients from other cultures. For example, chili peppers, which help give Szechuan cuisine its spicy flavor, are not native to China. Stir-frying is a great way to take advantage of the fresh fruits and vegetables in season in your area.

Most important is to choose ingredients that won't melt under high heat or fall apart under the constant stirring and tossing needed for stir-frying. Choose food that is firm and will hold its shape well. Quick-cooking shellfish are a great choice for stir-frying, as are firm-fleshed fish such as whitefish, cod, or salmon. When it comes to tofu, steer clear of silken and soft dessert tofus, and stick to tofus with a firm texture. Pressed tofu, which is regular tofu that has been pressed and drained to give it an even firmer texture, is perfect for stir-frying and saves you the work of draining the tofu. When it comes to meat and poultry, choose cuts that are tender and also quick cooking.

It's hard to imagine a vegetable that would be unsuitable for a stir-fry dish. Even lettuce, the staple salad ingredient in the West, is stir-fried with seasonings in Asia. Some types of vegetables will require a little extra care. Hardier, thicker vegetables are often blanched prior to stir-frying, and it's important not to overcook delicate vegetables such as mung bean sprouts.

While the growing popularity of stir-frying is making it easier to find ingredients used in stir-frying, sometimes you will need to make a substitution. Here are some common substitutions for ingredients used in stir-frying:

- **Water chestnuts.** While it won't have quite the same flavor, the southern vegetable jicama is similar in texture to fresh water chestnuts.
- **Dried mushrooms.** Fresh mushrooms will also give the dish a savory flavor, although the exact taste will vary depending on the type of mushroom.
- **Fish sauce.** Although it is made from soybeans instead of fermented fish, the texture and flavor of Chinese light soy sauce is very similar to fish sauce.
- **Oyster sauce.** Again, Chinese light soy sauce has a similar taste, although it lacks the depth of flavor and thick texture of oyster sauce.
- **Rice wine.** Dry sherry is the best substitute for rice wine in cooking.

- **Chile paste.** While it won't have the extra spices and seasonings found in chile paste, red pepper flakes will provide the same level of heat.

If you want to adapt a recipe that normally uses another cooking technique into a stir-fry, start by taking a careful look at the ingredient list. Will the ingredients hold up while being constantly stirred over high heat? Often, it takes only a few simple adjustments to transform a longer-cooking dish into a good candidate for stir-frying: using the right cut of meat, marinating the meat to tenderize it and add extra flavor to the dish, replacing dried herbs with fresh herbs that impart their flavor more quickly where possible, and reducing the total amount of liquid.

Common Cooking Problems

No cooking technique is completely foolproof. Here are solutions to the most common problems that can arise during stir-frying.

Food Sticking to the Wok

This is one of the most common problems in stir-frying. The usual culprit is a wok that hasn't been preheated. Never add hot oil to a cold wok—always heat the wok for at least thirty seconds before adding the oil. The wok should be nearly smoking, and you should be able to feel the heat when you place your hand two to three inches above the wok's bottom.

Burning the Aromatics

Flavoring oil with aromatics (such as garlic and ginger) is a well-known cooking technique, designed to prevent an oily flavor from being imparted to the food. When you're stir-frying, however, there is a danger that the garlic will burn, adding a bitter flavor to the dish. Following the basic steps for stir-frying and stir-frying quickly will take care of much of the problem. If you're still having difficulties, instead of stir-frying the garlic and ginger for ten seconds, try pressing down on the garlic and ginger with a spatula, forcing them to quickly release their flavor into the hot oil.

A Lumpy Cornstarch Mixture

Thickening a sauce with cornstarch is one of those techniques that seems like it should be simple but can go wrong very quickly if you don't follow the correct steps. Never add the cornstarch directly to a sauce heating in the wok or skillet. The cornstarch will not combine properly with the hot liquid, and the sauce will be lumpy. Instead, prepare a cornstarch slurry by dissolving the cornstarch in a small amount of cold water. Pour the slurry into the heated sauce and stir until the sauce thickens. You can also add the cornstarch to the sauce before it is heated, whisking in the cornstarch to combine it with the other ingredients.

Keep in mind that no matter how thoroughly you stirred it, it takes only a few minutes for grains of cornstarch to separate out of the slurry and settle on the bottom of the bowl. Always remember to stir the cornstarch and water mixture before adding it to the sauce.

chapter **2**

Marinades and Sauces

Serves 3 to 4

1 tablespoon dry sherry,
   Chinese rice wine, or
   white cooking sherry

1 tablespoon light soy sauce

¼ teaspoon Asian sesame oil

2 teaspoons cornstarch

Easy Chicken Marinade

*Use this simple but flavorful marinade with 1 pound of chicken breasts cut into
1-inch cubes. Be sure to add the cornstarch last so that it seals in the other flavors.*

Place the chicken cubes in a bowl and add the marinade ingredients.
Marinate the chicken in the refrigerator for 30 minutes. Use as called for in
a stir-fry recipe.

Yields ½ cup

3 tablespoons soy sauce

3 tablespoons water

1 tablespoon oyster sauce

2 teaspoons red wine vinegar

2 teaspoons granulated
   sugar

¼ teaspoon garlic salt

Simple Stir-Fry Sauce

*Add this simple sauce in the final stages of stir-frying. If you like, thicken the sauce by
adding 1 teaspoon cornstarch dissolved in 4 teaspoons water. Add the cornstarch and
water mixture directly into the sauce in the wok or skillet, stirring quickly to thicken.*

Combine the ingredients in a small bowl. Use as called for in a recipe, or
store in a sealed container in the refrigerator until ready to use. (Use the
sauce within 3 to 4 days.)

What's in a Bowl? When marinating food, the last thing you want is a chemical
reaction between the material of the bowl and the acid in the marinade. Not only will the
reaction wreak havoc with the marinade, but it can damage the bowl. For best results, use
a container made of glass, ceramic, stainless steel, or plastic when marinating food. Never
use an aluminum bowl.

Easy Oyster-Flavored Marinade for Beef

Flavored with oyster sauce, this marinade is a great way to add flavor to a simple beef and vegetable stir-fry that doesn't include a finishing sauce, as in the recipe for Easy Beef Stir-Fry with Vegetables (page 66).

Cut the beef according to recipe instructions. Place the beef in a bowl and add the marinade ingredients to the beef one at a time, adding the cornstarch last. Marinate the beef for 15 to 25 minutes.

Serves 3 to 4

1½ tablespoons oyster sauce
1 tablespoon dark soy sauce
½ teaspoon sugar
1 teaspoon Asian sesame oil
¼ teaspoon salt
2 teaspoons cornstarch

Orange Sauce

This sauce adds a powerful orange flavor to Orange Pork Chops (page 145). If you want a thicker sauce, leave the water out of the sauce and combine the water with 1½ teaspoons cornstarch in a separate small bowl. Add the sauce as called for in the recipe, bring to a boil, and then add in the cornstarch and water mixture, stirring to thicken.

Combine the orange juice, water, rice vinegar, dark soy sauce, light soy sauce, and brown sugar in a bowl. Either use immediately in a stir-fry recipe or store in a sealed container in the refrigerator until ready to use. (Use the sauce within 3 to 4 days.)

Yields ⅔ cup

6 tablespoons orange juice
2 tablespoons water
1 tablespoon rice vinegar
1 tablespoon dark soy sauce
2 teaspoons light soy sauce
2 teaspoons brown sugar

2½ tablespoons beef broth

2 teaspoons soy sauce

1½ teaspoons Asian sesame oil

1 teaspoon rice wine or sherry

1 teaspoon granulated sugar

2 teaspoons cornstarch

Korean-Inspired Marinade

Marinade's role as flavor enhancer is particularly important in stir-frying, which is all about quick cooking as opposed to slow simmering. Use this flavorful marinade to marinate between 1 and 1½ pounds of beef before stir-frying.

Prepare the beef for stir-frying, cutting according to the recipe directions. Place the beef in a bowl and add the marinade ingredients one at a time, adding the cornstarch last. Marinate the beef in the refrigerator for 20 minutes.

The Purpose of Marinating Marinades tenderize and add flavor to food. While many stir-fries contain a finishing sauce, loading the sauce with too many seasonings causes flavors to run together. Using some of the seasonings in the marinade instead of the sauce helps the individual flavors to remain distinct.

Sesame Sauce

Sesame sauce makes a great dipping sauce to go with Spring Rolls (page 192), or it can be added to a stir-fry dish at the end of cooking, as in Sesame Tofu (page 286). If chile paste is already included in the recipe (as in Sesame Tofu with Vegetables (page 291), do not add it to the sauce.

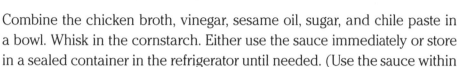

Yields ½ cup

4 tablespoons chicken broth

2 tablespoons red wine vinegar or Chinese red rice vinegar

2 tablespoons sesame oil

2 teaspoons granulated sugar

¼ teaspoon chile paste, optional

2 teaspoons cornstarch

Combine the chicken broth, vinegar, sesame oil, sugar, and chile paste in a bowl. Whisk in the cornstarch. Either use the sauce immediately or store in a sealed container in the refrigerator until needed. (Use the sauce within 3 to 4 days.) Stir the sauce before adding to the stir-fry to bring up any cornstarch that has settled on the bottom.

Where to Marinate Bacteria can form in meat that is allowed to marinate at room temperature. Food that is going to be marinated for 30 minutes or longer should always be refrigerated. With the exception of recipes that call for velveting the food, the marinating time for stir-fries is normally under 30 minutes. Experts offer conflicting advice as to whether these need to be refrigerated as well, but definitely do so if you're concerned about food safety.

Yields about ¾ cup

½ cup chicken broth

3 tablespoons curry powder

2 teaspoons brown sugar

1 tablespoon dark soy sauce

½ teaspoon chile paste,
  optional

Curry Sauce

For best results, use an Indian Madras curry powder in this recipe.

In a small bowl, combine the chicken broth, curry powder, brown sugar, dark soy sauce, and chile paste. Either use immediately in a stir-fry recipe or keep covered in a sealed container in the refrigerator until ready to use. (Use the sauce within 3 to 4 days.)

Curry While many people believe that curry is a single dry spice, curry powder is a compilation of spices that may or may not include curry leaves. Furthermore, the word *curry* actually comes from the Tamil word *kahri*, meaning "sauce."

Yields 2/3 cup

½ cup beef broth

1 tablespoon light soy sauce

4 teaspoons dark soy sauce

1 tablespoon Chinese rice
  wine or dry sherry

1 teaspoon granulated sugar

1 teaspoon Asian sesame oil,
  optional

2 teaspoons cornstarch

Basic Brown Sauce

*Either store-bought beef broth or beef bouillon cubes
dissolved in boiling water can be used in this recipe.*

Combine the beef broth, light soy sauce, dark soy sauce, rice wine or dry sherry, sugar, and sesame oil (if using) in a bowl. Whisk in the cornstarch. Either use the sauce immediately or store in a sealed container in the refrigerator until ready to use. (Use the sauce within 3 to 4 days.) Stir the sauce before adding it to the stir-fry to bring up any cornstarch that has settled on the bottom.

Orange Marinade

The orange flavor in this marinade goes very nicely with pork, as in Spicy Orange Pork Chops (page 145). Use the marinade with ¾ to 1 pound of lean pork, adding 2 teaspoons cornstarch to seal in the other ingredients, if desired.

Cut the pork according to the recipe directions. Place the pork in a bowl and add the marinade ingredients. Discard any unused marinade.

Reusing Marinade If you want to use a marinade as a sauce, add it to the stir-fry in the final stages of cooking. If the marinade was used to marinate meat or poultry, there is a danger that the marinade picked up bacteria from the uncooked meat. You can boil the marinade for 5 minutes to kill bacteria, or you can make a second batch of the marinade, reserving it for the sauce.

Yields ¼ cup

2 tablespoons orange juice
1 tablespoon water
1 tablespoon soy sauce
1 teaspoon brown sugar
½ green onion, finely chopped

Oyster-Flavored Brown Sauce

The amount of sugar needed for the sauce will depend partly on the other ingredients in this stir-fry recipe. If no other sugar is being added, you may want to increase the amount of sugar to 2½ or 3 teaspoons.

Combine the beef broth, oyster sauce, light soy sauce, dark soy sauce, black pepper, and sugar in a bowl. Whisk in the cornstarch. Either use the sauce immediately as called for in the stir-fry recipe or place the brown sauce in a sealed container and refrigerate until needed. (Use the sauce within 3 to 4 days.) Stir the sauce before adding it to the stir-fry to bring up any cornstarch that has settled on the bottom.

Versatile Brown Sauce A savory combination of beef broth and soy sauce, sometimes flavored with oyster sauce, brown sauce is used in several Chinese dishes. Besides making an excellent gravy to pour over Egg Foo Yung, restaurants frequently use it to lend flavor to beef-and-broccoli dishes.

Yields ¾ cup

½ cup beef broth
2 tablespoons oyster sauce
2 tablespoons light soy sauce
4 teaspoons dark soy sauce
Black pepper to taste
2 teaspoons granulated sugar
2 teaspoons cornstarch

Peking Sauce

Yields ¼ cup

2 tablespoons water

1½ tablespoons hoisin sauce

1 tablespoon Asian sesame oil

¼ teaspoon chile paste with garlic, or to taste

1 teaspoon minced garlic

½ green onion, finely chopped

½ teaspoon cornstarch dissolved in 1 teaspoon water (optional)

Peking sauce is another name for hoisin sauce. In this recipe,
the hoisin sauce is combined with chile paste, garlic,
green onion, and Asian sesame oil for extra flavor.

Combine the water, hoisin sauce, sesame oil, chile paste, minced garlic, and chopped green onion in a bowl. If using in a stir-fry recipe, store in a sealed container in the refrigerator until ready to use. (Use the sauce within 3 to 4 days.) If desired, thicken the sauce by adding the cornstarch and water: After the Peking Sauce has been added to the stir-fry, bring the sauce to a boil and then add the cornstarch and water mixture, stirring quickly to thicken.

Peking Dipping Sauce If using Peking Sauce as a dipping sauce, heat the water, hoisin sauce, sesame oil, chile paste, garlic, and green onion in a small saucepan. Add the cornstarch and water mixture, stirring quickly to thicken. Use immediately or store in a sealed container in the refrigerator until ready to use. (Use the sauce within 3 to 4 days.)

Italian Pesto Sauce

The name pesto refers to the fact that this famous Italian sauce is traditionally made with a mortar and pestle. However, modern cooks find that a food processor or a blender works just as well.

Yields 2 cups

2 cloves garlic

½ cup walnuts

2 cups fresh basil leaves

½ cup grated Parmesan cheese

2/3 cup olive oil

Peel and mince the garlic. Process the garlic and walnuts in the food processor or blender. Add the basil leaves and process again. Add the cheese and process again. Slowly add the olive oil, and process until the pesto is creamy. Either use the pesto immediately or store in a sealed container in the refrigerator until ready to use. (Use the pesto within 1 week.)

Pesto Variations While pesto sauce is an Italian creation, many cuisines have developed their own versions. Thai pesto recipes usually have either licorice-flavored sweet basil or peppery Thai holy basil and may include toasted coconut. Greek variations on pesto sauce frequently replace the basil with parsley and add lemon juice and bread crumbs. French pistou is really just another version of pesto, minus the nuts.

Feisty Fajita Marinade

Both sea salt and kosher salt contain fewer additives and have a richer flavor than ordinary table salt. Use one of these in this marinade to bring out the other flavors in the recipe.

Yields ¼ cup

2 tablespoons lime juice

1 teaspoon chile powder

1 teaspoon kosher or sea salt

¼ teaspoon ground cumin

¾ teaspoon freshly ground black pepper

⅛ teaspoon garlic salt

1 tablespoon extra-virgin olive oil

In a small bowl, combine the lime juice, chile powder, kosher or sea salt, ground cumin, black pepper, and garlic salt. Whisk in the olive oil. Either use the marinade immediately or store in a sealed container in the refrigerator. Use within 1 week, stirring the marinade before adding to the meat, poultry, or tofu.

Citrusy Mediterranean Marinade

Be sure to use extra-virgin olive oil in this recipe. While pure olive oil (also simply called olive oil) has the high smoke point needed for stir-frying, extra-virgin olive oil is the best choice for marinades and salad dressings.

Yields 1 cup

5 tablespoons orange juice

3 tablespoons lemon juice

¼ cup red wine vinegar

2 cloves garlic, chopped

2 tablespoons freshly chopped basil

1/8 teaspoon black pepper, or to taste

¼ cup olive oil

Combine the orange juice, lemon juice, red wine vinegar, garlic, basil, and black pepper in a bowl. Whisk in the olive oil. Refrigerate in a sealed container until needed. (Use the marinade within 1 week.)

How to Peel Garlic   To peel garlic, lay an unpeeled clove on the cutting board. Take a knife with a wide blade and lay the blade flat over the garlic clove. Press down hard with the palm of your hand. The garlic peel should slide off easily.

Pineapple Sweet and Sour Sauce

A 14-ounce can of pineapple chunks will give you the right amount needed for this sauce. The brown sugar complements the sweetness of the pineapple, while the vinegar and salt give the sauce a multifaceted flavor.

In a small bowl, combine the pineapple juice, salt, vinegar, and brown sugar. Whisk in the cornstarch. Use the sauce as called for in a recipe. Reserve the pineapple chunks to add directly to the stir-fry, as called for in the recipe. If not using immediately, store the sauce in a sealed container in the refrigerator. (Use within 3 to 4 days.) Stir the sauce before adding it to the stir-fry to bring up any cornstarch that has settled on the bottom.

Yields 1 cup

¾ cup pineapple juice

½ teaspoon salt

3 tablespoons vinegar

¼ cup brown sugar

1 tablespoon cornstarch

1 cup pineapple chunks

Pineapple Sweet and Sour Dipping Sauce

*This sauce can be used as a dipping sauce with
Pork Egg Rolls (page 170) or Spring Rolls (page 192).*

1. In a small bowl, dissolve the cornstarch in 2 tablespoons water. Set aside.

2. In a saucepan, bring the brown sugar, pineapple juice, and salt to a boil on medium heat. Stir in the vinegar. Add the cornstarch and water mixture, stirring to thicken.

3. Add the bell pepper and pineapple chunks. Stir briefly to heat through. If not using immediately, store the sauce in a sealed container in the refrigerator. (Use within 3 to 4 days.)

Yields 1¼ cups

2 tablespoons cornstarch

2 tablespoons water

5 tablespoons brown sugar

¾ cup pineapple juice

½ teaspoon salt

¼ cup vinegar

½ green bell pepper, diced

½ red bell pepper, diced

2 tablespoons pineapple chunks

Korean-Inspired Sesame Sauce

*This simple sauce makes a flavorful marinade for pork or lends a nice finishing
touch to a pork and vegetable stir-fry. The proportions are easy to adjust.*

Combine all the ingredients in a small bowl. If not using immediately, store
the sauce in a sealed container in the refrigerator. (Use the sauce within
3 to 4 days.)

Strange Flavor Sauce

*This is the sauce that is served with Strange Flavor Chicken Salad (page 42), a popular
Szechuan restaurant dish. Traditionally, the sauce includes freshly ground roasted Szechuan
peppercorns—feel free to add ½ teaspoon if desired. If Szechuan peppercorns are
unavailable, you could substitute a small amount of freshly ground white pepper.*

1. Whisk all the ingredients together. The mixture will be quite thick at first
   but will become runny—add a small amount of water if needed. If not using
   immediately, store in a sealed container in the refrigerator. (Use the sauce
   within 3 to 4 days.) Stir the sauce before using.

   Chicken with a Strange Flavor The Chinese take on chicken salad, Strange Flavor Chicken, gets it name from the intriguing combination of sweet, sour, salty, nutty, and
   spicy flavors in the sauce. Strange Flavor Chicken is also called Bang Bang Chicken, due to
   the fact that the chicken was traditionally pounded to make it more tender and the meat
   easier to shred by hand.

Easy Teriyaki Marinade

This is a "quick and dirty" version of teriyaki marinade you can use whenever the real thing isn't available. For best results use a Japanese soy sauce, such as Kikkoman. Chinese light soy sauce will impart a salty flavor to the marinade.

Yields ¼ cup

¼ cup Japanese soy sauce

4 teaspoons liquid honey

1 teaspoon chopped ginger

Combine the soy sauce, honey, and chopped ginger in a small bowl. Use as called for in the recipe, with 1 pound of chicken, pork, or beef.

Teriyaki Secrets Flavorful teriyaki marinade is what gives Japanese dishes such as grilled teriyaki chicken their sweet flavor. (The word *teriyaki* comes from the Japanese words *teri,* meaning "luster," and *yaki,* meaning "roast.") Authentic teriyaki marinades use a combination of Japanese mirin rice wine, granulated sugar, and fresh ginger. Liquid honey makes a convenient substitute for the mirin in Easy Teriyaki Marinade (page 27).

Hot and Sour Sauce

Rice vermicelli noodles soak up this spicy sauce in Spicy Shredded Beef with Rice Noodles (page 216).

Yields ½ cup

¼ cup chicken broth

2 tablespoons red wine vinegar

1 tablespoon dark soy sauce

2 teaspoons granulated sugar

½ teaspoon chile paste

In a medium bowl, whisk together all the ingredients. Use as called for in the recipe. If not using immediately, store in a sealed container in the refrigerator. (Use the sauce within 3 to 4 days.)

Yields 1 cup

¼ cup granulated sugar

¼ cup vinegar

2 tablespoons ketchup

¾ cup water

1 tablespoon cornstarch

Simple Sweet and Sour Sauce

To turn this into a dipping sauce, simply bring the ingredients to boil in a medium saucepan over low heat, stirring constantly. Use the dipping sauce immediately or store in a sealed container in the refrigerator until ready to serve.

Combine the sugar, vinegar, ketchup, and water in a medium bowl. Whisk in the cornstarch. Use as called for in the stir-fry recipe. Stir the sauce before adding to the stir-fry to bring up any cornstarch that has settled on the bottom. If not using immediately, store the sauce in a sealed container in the refrigerator. (Use the sauce within 3 to 4 days.)

Sweet and Sour Sauce Substitutions Adapt this basic recipe for Simple Sweet and Sour Sauce by using different combinations of flavorings. For example, try replacing the vinegar with rice vinegar or cider vinegar, or using brown or palm sugar instead of granulated white sugar. It's best to stick with ketchup though, as the seasonings from this popular condiment—including vinegar, sugar, allspice, and cinnamon—lend extra flavor to the sauce.

Chapter 3

Chicken and Other Poultry Dishes

1 pound boneless, skinless
chicken breasts

1 tablespoon soy sauce

1 tablespoon Chinese rice
wine or dry sherry

2 teaspoons cornstarch

3 tablespoons vegetable or
peanut oil, divided

1 clove garlic, minced

1 slice ginger, minced

3 cups packaged fresh stir-fry
vegetable mix

Salt to taste

Sugar to taste

1–2 tablespoons additional
rice wine, chicken broth,
or water, optional

½ cup store-bought stir-fry
sauce (such as Kikkoman)

Quick and Easy Chicken Stir-Fry

*Stir-fry sauce and a prepackaged stir-fry vegetable mix make
this recipe a great choice for busy weeknights. Cooking wine
can be used in place of the rice wine or dry sherry.*

1. Cut the chicken into bite-sized cubes. Place the chicken in a bowl and add the soy sauce, rice wine or sherry, and cornstarch. Marinate the chicken in the refrigerator for 30 minutes.

2. Heat a wok or skillet over medium-high heat until it is nearly smoking. Add 2 tablespoons oil. When the oil is hot, add the garlic. Stir-fry until it is aromatic, then add the chicken. Let brown briefly, then stir-fry, stirring and tossing the chicken for 3 to 4 minutes, until it turns white and is nearly cooked. Remove the chicken from the pan. Drain in a colander or on paper towels.

3. Add 1 tablespoon oil to the wok or skillet. When the oil is hot, add the ginger. Stir-fry until aromatic, then add the vegetables. Stir-fry for 1 to 2 minutes, until the vegetables are tender but still crisp. Stir in salt and sugar while stir-frying the vegetables, if desired. Add 1 to 2 tablespoons of rice wine, water, or chicken broth if the vegetables are drying out during stir-frying.

4. Add the stir-fry sauce and bring to a boil. Add the chicken back into the pan. Stir-fry for 2 more minutes to heat through and thoroughly cook the chicken. Serve hot.

Stir-Fry Sauce Stir-fry sauce is a great choice for those nights when you don't have ingredients on hand to prepare a sauce. Stir-fry sauce can be found in the international or ethnic cuisine section of most supermarkets. Kikkoman stir-fry sauce, flavored with wine, oyster sauce extract, sugar, and other seasonings, is a good brand.

Easy Chicken with Almonds

*To make this stir-fry even easier, you can replace the vegetables
with 3 cups of a packaged stir-fry vegetable mix.*

1. Cut the chicken breasts into 1-inch cubes (it's easiest to do this if the chicken is partially frozen). Place the chicken in a bowl and add the Easy Chicken Marinade (page 16). Marinate the chicken for 20 minutes.

2. Heat a wok or skillet over medium-high heat until it is almost smoking. Add 2 tablespoons oil. When the oil is hot, add the garlic. Stir-fry for 10 seconds, then add the chicken cubes. Stir-fry the chicken until it turns white and is nearly cooked. Remove the chicken and drain in a colander or on paper towels.

3. Heat 1 tablespoon oil in the wok or skillet. Add the ginger and stir-fry for 10 seconds. Add the zucchini and stir-fry for 1 minute, stirring in the soy sauce. Add the mushrooms. Stir-fry for 1 minute, then add the red bell pepper. Add 1 to 2 tablespoons of water if the vegetables begin to dry out during stir-frying.

4. Add the stir-fry sauce and bring to a boil. Stir in the almonds. Stir-fry for 2 more minutes to mix the ingredients together and make sure the chicken is cooked through. Taste and adjust seasonings if desired.

Serves 4

1 pound boneless, skinless chicken breasts

Easy Chicken Marinade (page 16)

3 tablespoons vegetable or peanut oil, divided

2 cloves garlic, chopped

2 slices ginger, chopped

½ zucchini, cut on the diagonal into ½-inch slices

1 tablespoon soy sauce

¼ pound fresh mushrooms, thinly sliced

1 red bell pepper, seeded and cut into chunks

1–2 tablespoons water, if needed

½ cup homemade Simple Stir-Fry Sauce (page 16)

½ cup almonds

Serves 3 to 4

¾ pound boneless, skinless
chicken breasts

1½ tablespoons oyster sauce

2 teaspoons Chinese rice
wine or dry white sherry

1½ teaspoons Asian sesame
oil

¼ teaspoon salt

Pepper to taste

1½ teaspoons cornstarch

½ cup raw, unsalted cashews

3 tablespoons vegetable or
peanut oil, divided

1 thin slice fresh ginger

1 tablespoon chopped garlic

2½ tablespoons hoisin sauce

Hoisin Glazed Chicken with Cashews

Cashews are a good source of healthy, monounsaturated fats.
This dish would go nicely with Stir-Fried Baby Corn (page 266).

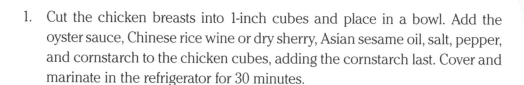

1. Cut the chicken breasts into 1-inch cubes and place in a bowl. Add the oyster sauce, Chinese rice wine or dry sherry, Asian sesame oil, salt, pepper, and cornstarch to the chicken cubes, adding the cornstarch last. Cover and marinate in the refrigerator for 30 minutes.

2. While the chicken is marinating, roast the cashews in a wok or skillet over medium heat, shaking the pan continuously so that the nuts do not burn. Roast until the cashews are browned (about 5 minutes). Remove the cashews from the pan to cool.

3. Turn the heat up to medium-high and add 2 tablespoons oil to the wok or skillet. When the oil is almost smoking, add the slice of ginger. Let it cook for 2 to 3 minutes, until browned, then remove it with a spatula. (This is to flavor the oil.)

4. Add the marinated chicken cubes to the wok or skillet. Let brown briefly, then stir-fry, stirring and tossing the chicken for 3 to 4 minutes, until it turns white and is nearly cooked. Remove the chicken from the pan. Drain in a colander or on paper towels.

5. Heat 1 tablespoon oil in the pan. When the oil is hot, add the chopped garlic. Stir in the hoisin sauce. Add the chicken. Stir-fry for 1 minute or until the chicken is nicely glazed with the hoisin sauce. Stir in the cashews. Remove and serve immediately.

Handling Raw Poultry Raw poultry can carry salmonella bacteria. To prevent cross-contamination between raw meat and food that isn't going to be cooked, always thoroughly wash the cutting board, knife, and other utensils in hot, soapy water after handling raw poultry. If possible, use a separate cutting board and knife for raw poultry.

Easy Kung Pao Chicken

While white rice vinegar works best in the marinade for this recipe, feel free to experiment with using other types of rice vinegar when preparing the sauce.

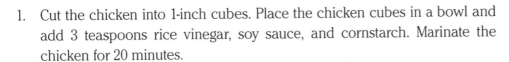

1. Cut the chicken into 1-inch cubes. Place the chicken cubes in a bowl and add 3 teaspoons rice vinegar, soy sauce, and cornstarch. Marinate the chicken for 20 minutes.

2. Combine the dark soy sauce, water, sugar, 2 teaspoons rice vinegar, and chile paste in a bowl. Set aside.

3. Heat a wok or skillet on medium-high heat until it is almost smoking. Add the oil. When the oil is hot, add the ginger slices. Let brown for 2 to 3 minutes, then remove. Add the chicken. Let brown briefly, then stir-fry, stirring and tossing the chicken until it turns white and is nearly cooked. Remove the chicken from the pan.

4. Add the garlic to the wok or skillet. Stir-fry until aromatic, then add the sauce. Bring to a boil, then add the chicken back into the pan. Stir-fry, stirring to mix the chicken with the sauce. Stir in the peanuts. Serve hot.

Serves 4

¾ pound boneless, skinless chicken breasts

5 teaspoons rice vinegar, divided

2 teaspoons soy sauce

1½ teaspoons cornstarch

1½ tablespoons dark soy sauce

1 tablespoon water

1 teaspoon granulated sugar

½ teaspoon chile paste, or to taste

2 tablespoons vegetable or peanut oil

2 slices ginger

1 tablespoon chopped garlic

½ cup unsalted peanuts

Broccoli Chicken

*In this recipe the chicken is "velveted" in egg white and cornstarch,
giving it a velvety texture that contrasts nicely with the broccoli.*

1 pound boneless, skinless chicken breast

1 tablespoon cornstarch

1 egg white

1 teaspoon salt, divided

1 tablespoon Chinese rice wine or dry sherry

1 pound broccoli

2 tablespoons oyster sauce

3 tablespoons water

1 teaspoon brown sugar

2 cups vegetable or peanut oil

1 tablespoon minced ginger

1. Cut the chicken into bite-sized cubes. In a bowl, stir together the cornstarch, egg white, ½ teaspoon salt, and rice wine or sherry. Add the chicken and marinate in the refrigerator for 30 minutes.

2. Chop the broccoli into bite-sized pieces. Blanch in boiling water for 2 to 3 minutes, until the broccoli turns bright green. Plunge the broccoli into cold water to stop the cooking process. Drain thoroughly.

3. In a small bowl, combine the oyster sauce, water, and brown sugar. Set aside.

4. Heat a wok or skillet over medium-high heat. Add 2 cups oil. When the oil is hot, add the chicken. Stir-fry the chicken cubes until they turn white (about 30 seconds), using a spatula to separate the cubes. Remove from the wok and drain in a colander or on paper towels.

5. Remove all but 1½ tablespoons oil from the wok or skillet. When the oil is hot, add the minced ginger. Stir-fry for 10 seconds, then add the broccoli and ½ teaspoon salt. Stir-fry for 1 minute, then add the chicken. Stir-fry the chicken for 1 minute, then add the sauce. Cook for another minute, mixing everything together. Taste and adjust seasonings if desired. Serve hot.

Chicken Breasts Chicken breasts play a prominent role in Chinese stir-fry dishes. The firm flesh of breast meat holds up well under the tossing and stirring needed for stir-frying. Breast meat can be dry though, so Chinese cooks frequently "velvet" the chicken by coating it in an unbeaten egg white and cornstarch mixture before cooking. The egg white coats the chicken, protecting it from the heat of the stir-fry pan.

Mongolian Chicken

*While the breast is the most popular part of the chicken for
stir-frying, thighs can be used as well. This is a good recipe
for people who enjoy the dark meat of the chicken.*

1. Cut the chicken into thin strips, about 1½ to 2 inches long. Place the chicken in a bowl and add the soy sauce, dry sherry, and 2 teaspoons cornstarch. Marinate the chicken for 20 minutes.

2. Combine 2 tablespoons water, hoisin sauce, and red wine vinegar in a small bowl.

3. In a separate small bowl, dissolve 1 teaspoon cornstarch in 2 teaspoons water.

4. Heat a wok or skillet over medium-high heat until it is nearly smoking. Add 2 tablespoons oil. When the oil is hot, add the garlic. Stir-fry for 10 seconds, then add the chicken. Let sit briefly, then stir-fry, stirring and moving the chicken around the pan until it turns white and is nearly cooked through. Remove from the pan and drain in a colander or on paper towels.

5. Heat 1½ tablespoons oil in the wok or skillet. When the oil is hot, add the ginger, green onions, and chile paste. Stir-fry for 30 seconds, then add the mushrooms. Stir-fry the mushrooms for 1 minute, then add the bamboo shoots. Stir-fry for another minute, or until the mushrooms have darkened.

6. Push the vegetables to the side and add the sauce in the middle. Stir the cornstarch and water mixture and then add to the sauce, stirring quickly to thicken. When the sauce has thickened, add the chicken back into the pan. Stir-fry for 2 more minutes to mix everything together, and make sure the chicken is cooked through. Serve hot.

Serves 3 to 4

- 1 pound boneless, skinless chicken thighs
- 1 tablespoon soy sauce
- 1 tablespoon dry sherry
- 3 teaspoons cornstarch, divided
- 2 tablespoons plus 2 teaspoons water, divided
- 1½ tablespoons hoisin sauce
- 1 tablespoon red wine vinegar
- 3½ tablespoons vegetable or peanut oil, divided
- 1 teaspoon minced garlic
- 1 teaspoon minced ginger
- 2 green onions, cut on the diagonal into quarters
- ½ teaspoon chile paste, or to taste
- ¼ pound fresh mushrooms, thinly sliced
- 1 cup canned bamboo shoots, drained

Easy Chicken with Snow Peas

Snow peas turn a beautiful dark green when stir-fried.
Their crunchy texture pairs nicely with the chicken in this dish.

1. Cut the chicken breasts into thin strips 1½ to 2 inches long. (It's easier to do this if the chicken breasts are partially frozen.) Place the chicken strips in a bowl and add the soy sauce, oyster sauce, and cornstarch. Marinate the chicken for 20 minutes.

2. Heat a wok or frying pan on medium-high heat until it is almost smoking. Add 2 tablespoons oil. When the oil is hot, add the ginger slices. Let brown for 2 to 3 minutes, then remove. (This is to flavor the oil.) Add the chicken strips. Let them brown briefly, then stir-fry, stirring and tossing the chicken until it turns white and is nearly cooked. Remove the chicken from the pan.

3. Heat 1½ tablespoons oil in the wok or skillet. When the oil is hot, add the snow peas and the salt. Stir-fry the snow peas for 2 minutes or until they turn bright green.

4. Add the chicken back into the pan. Add a bit of water if the stir-fry is too dry. Taste and add black pepper if desired. Stir to mix everything together and serve hot.

Nutritional Benefits of Chicken Chicken is a dieter's dream. Besides being high in protein and low in fat, it is a good source of the B vitamin niacin and important minerals such as selenium. Stir-frying is one of the most nutritious ways to prepare chicken, especially when it is paired with a healthy food such as mushrooms.

Chicken Fajitas

*Shredded Monterey jack cheese makes a nice topping
for these chicken fajitas. The lime juice in the Feisty Fajita
Marinade provides additional depth to the flavor of this dish.*

Yields 8 to 10

8–10 flour tortillas, as needed

1 pound boneless, skinless chicken breast halves

Feisty Fajita Marinade (page 24)

¼ cup water

1 tablespoon oyster sauce

1 tablespoon soy sauce

3 tablespoons vegetable oil, divided

2 slices ginger

1 medium white onion, chopped

2 green onions, white parts only, finely chopped

1 green bell pepper, seeded and cut into bite-sized chunks

1 red bell pepper, seeded and cut into bite-sized chunks

6 ounces fresh mushrooms, thinly sliced

1. Heat the flour tortillas according to the package directions. Keep warm in a preheated 250°F oven while preparing the chicken.

2. Cut the chicken breasts into thin strips 1½ to 2 inches long. Place the chicken strips in a bowl and add the Feisty Fajita Marinade. Marinate the chicken in the refrigerator for 30 minutes. In a small bowl, combine the water, oyster sauce, and soy sauce. Set aside.

3. Heat a wok or frying pan on medium-high heat until it is almost smoking. Add 2 tablespoons oil. When the oil is hot, add the ginger slices. Let brown for 2 to 3 minutes, then remove. (This is to flavor the oil.) Add the chicken strips. Let them brown briefly, then stir-fry, stirring and tossing the chicken until it is nearly cooked. Remove the chicken from the pan.

4. Add 1 tablespoon oil. When the oil is hot, add the onion and the green onions. Stir-fry until the onion begins to soften (about 2 minutes), then add the green and red bell peppers. Add the mushrooms. Stir-fry for another minute, then add the sauce. Heat to boiling, then add the chicken back into the pan. Stir to mix everything together.

5. Lay a tortilla out flat on a plate. Spoon a portion of the stir-fried chicken and vegetable mixture onto the tortilla, making sure the filling isn't too close to the edges. Fold in the left and right sides of the tortilla and tuck in the edges. Repeat with the remainder of the tortillas until the filling is used up.

Faux Fajitas Technically speaking, a chicken fajita is not really a fajita at all, since the word *fajita* refers to a specific cut of beef called skirt steak. However, the spicy lime-based marinade used to season traditional beef fajitas works equally well with chicken.

1 pound boneless, skinless
  chicken breast

1 tablespoon white rice
  vinegar

1 tablespoon soy sauce

2 teaspoons cornstarch

2 tablespoons dark soy sauce

2 tablespoons water

1 teaspoon sugar

3 tablespoons vegetable oil,
  divided

2 slices ginger

¼ teaspoon salt

2½ cups mung bean sprouts

Chicken with Bean Sprouts

*To give this dish a neater, more elegant appearance, trim the
tops and bottoms of the mung bean sprouts before stir-frying.*

1. Cut the chicken breasts into thin strips approximately 1½ to 2 inches long.
    Place the chicken strips in a bowl and add the white rice vinegar, soy sauce,
    and cornstarch. Marinate the chicken for 20 minutes.

2. Combine the dark soy sauce, water, and sugar in a bowl. Set aside.

3. Heat a wok or skillet on medium-high heat until it is almost smoking. Add 2
    tablespoons oil. When the oil is hot, add the ginger slices. Let brown for 2
    to 3 minutes, then remove. (This is to flavor the oil.) Add the chicken strips.
    Let them brown briefly, then stir-fry, stirring and tossing the chicken for 3
    to 4 minutes, until it turns white and is nearly cooked. Remove the chicken
    from the pan.

4. Heat 1 tablespoon oil in the wok or skillet. When the oil is hot, add the salt
    and the mung bean sprouts. Stir-fry for 1 minute, then add the sauce. Add
    the chicken back into the pan. Stir-fry for 2 more minutes to heat everything
    through. Serve hot.

Chicken with Peaches

This is another stir-fry dish that is meant to have lots of sauce to mix in with cooked rice. In addition to the rice, it would go very nicely with a stir-fried green vegetable. Be sure to use firm peaches that are not too ripe so they do not fall apart during stir-frying.

Serves 4 to 6

1 pound boneless, skinless chicken breasts

1 tablespoon lemon juice

1½ tablespoons soy sauce

4 teaspoons cornstarch, divided

½ cup orange juice

1½ tablespoons brown sugar

2 or 4 teaspoons water, as desired

3 tablespoons vegetable or peanut oil, divided

1 teaspoon minced garlic

1 tablespoon minced ginger

2 large peaches, cut into thin slices

1. Cut the chicken into thin strips 1½ to 2 inches long. Place the chicken in a bowl and add the lemon juice, soy sauce, and 3 teaspoons cornstarch. Marinate the chicken for 20 minutes.

2. In a small bowl, combine the orange juice with the brown sugar.

3. In a separate small bowl, dissolve 1 teaspoon cornstarch with either 2 or 4 teaspoons water, depending on whether you want a thick or thinner sauce. Set aside.

4. Heat a wok or skillet over medium-high heat until it is nearly smoking and add 2 tablespoons oil. When the oil is hot, add the garlic. Stir-fry for 10 seconds, then add the chicken strips. Let them brown briefly, then stir-fry, stirring and tossing the chicken for 3 to 4 minutes, until the chicken turns white and is nearly cooked through. Remove the chicken from the pan. Drain in a colander or on paper towels.

5. Add 1 tablespoon oil to the wok or skillet. When the oil is hot, add the ginger. Stir-fry for 10 seconds, then add the peaches. Stir-fry for 1 minute, then add the orange juice, stirring to dissolve the sugar.

6. Stir the cornstarch and water mixture and add it to the juice, stirring continually to thicken. When the sauce has thickened, add the chicken back into the pan. Stir-fry for 1 to 2 more minutes to mix everything together. Serve hot.

Stir-Frying Fruit Stir-frying fruit allows you to cook the fruit quickly, which causes the fruit to retain most of its nutrients. When choosing fruit for stir-fries, make sure the fruit is fairly firm so that it doesn't become mushy during stir-frying. Keep the stir-frying time short, cooking it just until the fruit releases its juices.

1 pound boneless, skinless chicken breasts

¾ cup unsalted cashews

2 tablespoons vegetable or peanut oil

6–10 small hot red chili peppers

1½ tablespoons oyster sauce

1 medium white onion, chopped

2 green onions, finely chopped

¼ cup chicken broth

1½ tablespoons fish sauce

1 tablespoon palm sugar or brown sugar

Thai pepper powder to taste

Thai-Style Cashew Chicken

Thai pepper powder is a fragrant mixture that includes white pepper. Feel free to substitute freshly ground white pepper if Thai pepper powder is unavailable.

1. Cut the chicken into bite-sized cubes.

2. Roast the cashews in a heavy skillet over medium heat, shaking the pan continuously so that the nuts do not burn. Roast until the cashews are browned (about 5 minutes). Remove the cashews from the pan to cool.

3. Turn up the heat to medium-high and add the oil. When the oil is hot, add the red chili peppers. Cook until they begin to darken. Use a slotted spoon to remove the chilies.

4. Add the chicken and stir-fry until it is nearly cooked through. Stir in the oyster sauce while the chicken is stir-frying. Add the onion and the green onions. Stir-fry for 2 minutes, until the onion begins to soften. Add the chicken broth. Stir in the fish sauce.

5. Add the chilies back into the pan. Stir in the roasted cashews. Sprinkle the palm sugar and Thai pepper powder over the mixture. Stir to mix everything together and serve hot.

Chicken with Leeks

*Leeks are a popular vegetable in northern China, where
a short growing season forces cooks to rely extensively
on root vegetables such as leeks, onion, and garlic.*

Serves 2 to 4

¾ pound boneless, skinless
chicken breasts

1 tablespoon dark soy sauce

1 tablespoon Chinese rice
wine or dry sherry

Freshly ground white pepper
to taste

2 teaspoons cornstarch

3 tablespoons vegetable or
peanut oil, divided

1 teaspoon minced ginger

½ teaspoon chile paste with
garlic, or to taste

½ teaspoon salt

½ pound leeks, cut
diagonally into ½-inch
pieces

Peking Sauce (page 22)

1. Cut the chicken into thin strips 1½ to 2 inches in length. Place the chicken in a bowl and add the dark soy sauce, rice wine or sherry, white pepper, and cornstarch. Marinate the chicken for 20 minutes.

2. Heat a wok or skillet over medium-high heat until it is nearly smoking. Add 2 tablespoons oil. When the oil is hot, add the ginger. Stir-fry for 10 seconds, then add the chicken. Let brown briefly, then stir-fry for 3 to 4 minutes, until the chicken turns white and is nearly cooked through. Remove the chicken from the pan and drain in a colander or on paper towels.

3. Heat 1 tablespoon oil in the wok or skillet. When the oil is hot, add the chile paste. Stir-fry for 20 seconds, then add the salt and the leeks. Stir-fry for 1 minute, then add the Peking Sauce. Bring to a boil, then add the chicken back into the pan. Stir-fry for 1 to 2 more minutes to combine all the flavors and make sure the chicken is cooked through. Serve hot.

Coconut Milk Coconut milk is not really milk at all, but a mixture of shredded coconut and water. Coconut milk can be made with fresh or desiccated (dried) shredded coconut. Its nondairy status makes coconut milk the perfect alternative to cow's milk for people on a lactose-free diet.

Strange Flavor Chicken Salad

*This popular Chinese version of chicken salad originated in
Szechuan Province. The secret lies in the dressing, which is
an intriguing mix of salty, sweet, sour, and spicy flavors.*

1. Cut the chicken into thin strips about 1½ to 2 inches long. Peel the cucumber and cut into thin strips the same width and length as the chicken.

2. Arrange the cucumber on a plate. Add the chicken strips. Pour the dressing over the cucumber and chicken. Garnish with the toasted sesame seeds.

Indian Curried Chicken

*Feel free to alter the spiciness of this dish by
using hotter or milder curry paste as desired.*

1. Cut the chicken breasts into 1-inch cubes.

2. Heat a wok or skillet on medium-high heat until it is almost smoking. Add the oil. When the oil is hot, add the shallots. Stir-fry until the shallots begin to soften, then stir in the curry paste. Stir-fry for about 30 seconds, then add the tomatoes. Stir-fry for 1 minute, then add the chicken. Toss the chicken to mix it with the other ingredients, until it turns white and is nearly cooked.

3. Add the coconut milk and bring to a boil. Add the potatoes. Turn down the heat to medium, cover, and simmer for 10 minutes. Taste and adjust seasoning, adding salt, black pepper, and more curry paste if desired. Cook for another minute and serve hot.

Sweet and Sour Chicken Wings

To tell if these chicken wings are cooked, pierce one with a knife—
the juice from the wings should run clear when the meat is cooked through.

2 tablespoons vegetable or peanut oil

1 clove garlic, minced

2 slices ginger, minced

2 green onions, finely chopped

12 chicken wings

Simple Sweet and Sour Sauce (page 28)

1 tablespoon cornstarch

2 tablespoons water

1. Heat a wok or skillet on medium-high heat until it is almost smoking. Add the oil. When the oil is hot, add the garlic, ginger, and green onions. Stir-fry for 15 seconds, then add the chicken wings. Let sit for a minute, then stir-fry, moving the wings around the pan. Continue stir-frying for 5 minutes or until the wings are browned.

2. Pour the sweet and sour sauce over the chicken wings. Reduce the heat, cover, and simmer for 10 minutes or until the wings are cooked.

3. In a small bowl, stir the cornstarch into the water to make a slurry. Add the slurry to the sauce, turn up the heat to medium-high, and stir quickly to thicken. Serve hot.

Thick Sauce Versus Thin Sauce When preparing a cornstarch slurry, the ratio of cornstarch to water will depend on whether you prefer a thicker or thinner sauce. Chinese cooks normally use a 1:2 ratio of cornstarch to water to make a thick sauce, and a 1:4 ratio of cornstarch to water for a thinner sauce.

Teriyaki "Wings"

*For an interesting contrast in flavors, serve these boneless wings
with Stir-Fried Cauliflower (page 260) and plain cooked rice.*

1. Cut the chicken breasts into thin strips approximately 1½ to 2 inches long. Combine the teriyaki sauce, green onions, sugar, and ginger in a bowl. Store half the teriyaki-sauce mixture in a sealed container in the refrigerator. Combine the chicken in the bowl with the remainder of the teriyaki sauce mixture, and marinate in the refrigerator for 30 minutes.

2. Heat a wok or skillet on medium-high heat until it is almost smoking. Add the oil. When the oil is hot, add the crushed garlic and the red pepper flakes. Stir-fry for 30 seconds, then add the chicken. Let brown briefly, then stir-fry, moving the chicken around the pan until it turns white and is nearly cooked.

3. Add the reserved marinade into the pan. Reduce the heat and cook, stirring occasionally, until the chicken is fully cooked and nicely glazed with the sauce. Serve hot.

Chicken Cacciatore

*In this dish, use fresh herbs if possible. Dried herbs work
best in marinades or dishes with longer cooking times.*

Serves 2 to 4

1 pound boneless, skinless
    chicken breasts

5 tablespoons dry white
    wine, divided

½ teaspoon salt

Freshly ground black pepper
    to taste

2 teaspoons cornstarch

3 tablespoons chicken broth

3½ tablespoons olive oil,
    divided

2 shallots, chopped

¼ pound thinly sliced fresh
    mushrooms

2 tablespoons tomato sauce

2 teaspoons chopped fresh
    basil leaves

1 teaspoon chopped fresh
    thyme

1. Cut the chicken breasts into thin strips approximately 1½ to 2 inches long.
    Place the chicken in a bowl and add 2 tablespoons dry white wine, salt,
    black pepper, and cornstarch. Marinate the chicken for 20 minutes.

2. Combine the chicken broth and 3 tablespoons white wine in a bowl. Set
    aside.

3. Heat a wok or skillet on medium-high heat until it is almost smoking. Add
    2 tablespoons oil. When the oil is hot, add the chicken strips. Let them brown
    briefly, then stir-fry, stirring and tossing the chicken for 4 to 5 minutes, until it
    turns white and is nearly cooked. Remove the chicken from the pan.

4. Heat 1½ tablespoons oil in the pan. When the oil is hot, add the shallots.
    Stir-fry until they begin to soften, then add the sliced mushrooms. Stir-fry for
    about 10 seconds, then add the chicken broth and white wine mixture. Stir
    in the tomato sauce. Bring to a boil, then add the chicken back into the pan.
    Stir in the chopped basil and thyme. Stir-fry for 2 more minutes to blend all
    the ingredients and make sure the chicken is cooked. Serve hot.

Hunter's Chicken   Commonly called chicken cacciatore, the full name of this popular
Italian dish is *pollo alla cacciatore*, or "hunter's chicken." It is reputed to have been created in
Italy in the seventeenth century by hunters looking for the perfect recipe to bring out the
flavor of freshly caught game.

Serves 3 to 4

1–1½ pounds chicken
breasts

1 tablespoon soy sauce

1 tablespoon oyster sauce

2 teaspoons cornstarch

¼ cup pineapple juice

2 tablespoons vinegar

2 tablespoons brown sugar

2 tablespoons olive oil

3 slices fresh ginger

3 green onions, cut into
thirds

Simple Sweet and Sour Chicken

*Serve this quick and easy stir-fry dish with cooked rice
and a green vegetable for a complete meal.*

1. Cut the chicken into bite-sized cubes. Place the chicken cubes in a bowl and add the soy sauce, oyster sauce, and cornstarch. Marinate the chicken for 20 minutes.

2. Combine the pineapple juice, vinegar, and brown sugar in a bowl. Set aside.

3. Heat a wok or skillet on medium-high heat until it is nearly smoking. Add the oil. When the oil is hot, add the ginger slices. Let the ginger slices cook for 2 to 3 minutes, until they are browned. Remove the ginger.

4. Add the chicken cubes. Stir-fry, stirring and tossing the chicken for 3 to 4 minutes, until it changes color and is nearly cooked through.

5. Add the sauce into the pan, and bring to boil. Stir in the green onions. Stir-fry for 1 to 2 more minutes, until the chicken is thoroughly coated with the sauce and cooked through. Serve hot.

Asparagus Chicken

Look for oyster sauce, soy sauce, and chile paste in the
international or ethnic cuisine section of the supermarket.

———/———

1. Cut the chicken breasts into thin strips approximately 1½ to 2 inches long. Place the chicken strips in a bowl and add the lemon juice, soy sauce, granulated sugar, and cornstarch. Marinate the chicken for 20 minutes.

2. Combine the chicken broth, oyster sauce, and chile paste in a bowl. Set aside.

3. Heat a wok or frying pan on medium-high heat until it is almost smoking. Add 2 tablespoons oil. When the oil is hot, add the garlic. Stir-fry for 15 seconds or until the garlic is aromatic, then add the chicken strips. Let them brown briefly, then stir-fry, stirring and tossing the chicken for 3 to 4 minutes, until it turns white and is nearly cooked. Remove the chicken from the pan.

4. Heat 1 tablespoon oil in the wok or skillet. When the oil is hot, add the salt. Add the asparagus. Stir-fry the asparagus, stirring and moving it around the pan for 1 minute, then add the red bell pepper. Stir-fry for another minute, then add the sauce. Add the chicken back into the pan. Stir-fry for another 1 to 2 minutes to heat everything through. Serve hot.

How to Crush Garlic Crushing a clove of garlic makes it easier to peel the skin and prepare it for cooking. To crush garlic, lay a garlic clove flat on a cutting board. Take a knife with a wide blade (such as a chef's knife or a cleaver) and hit down hard. Remove the peel and hit down once again. It will now be easy to chop the garlic.

Serves 3 to 4

1 pound boneless, skinless chicken breasts

1 tablespoon lemon juice

1½ tablespoons soy sauce

½ teaspoon granulated sugar

2 teaspoons cornstarch

3 tablespoons chicken broth

1 tablespoon oyster sauce

½ teaspoon chile paste

3 tablespoons vegetable or peanut oil, divided

2 cloves garlic, chopped

¼ teaspoon salt

½ pound fresh asparagus, trimmed and cut into 1-inch pieces

1 red bell pepper, seeded and cut into thin strips

1 pound boneless, skinless
   chicken thighs

1 egg white

¼ teaspoon salt

1 tablespoon Chinese rice
   wine or dry sherry

1½ teaspoons cornstarch

2 tablespoons plum sauce

3 tablespoons water

2 cups olive oil

1 tablespoon minced ginger

2 green onions, finely
   chopped

2 teaspoons chile paste with
   garlic

Plum Chicken Thighs

*Plum sauce can be found in the international or ethnic section of
most supermarkets. For extra flavor, stir 1 tablespoon Chinese dark soy
sauce into the plum sauce and water mixture before adding it to the stir-fry.*

1. Cut the chicken into 1-inch cubes. Combine the egg white, salt, rice wine or sherry, and cornstarch in a bowl and mix in the chicken cubes. Marinate the chicken in the refrigerator for 30 minutes.

2. Combine the plum sauce and water in a bowl. Set aside.

3. Heat a wok or skillet over medium-high heat. Add 2 cups oil. When the oil is hot, add the chicken. Cook the chicken cubes until they turn white (about 30 seconds), using a spatula to separate the cubes. Remove the chicken from the wok and drain in a colander or on paper towels. Clean out the pan.

4. Drain all but 1 tablespoon oil in the wok or skillet. Add the minced ginger, green onions, and chile paste with garlic. Stir-fry for about 30 seconds, then add the chicken. Stir-fry for 1 minute, then add the plum sauce. Heat the sauce to boiling. Stir-fry for 2 minutes to mix the chicken with the sauce and make sure the chicken is thoroughly cooked. Serve hot.

Thai-Spiced Hot and Sour Wings

Arrowroot powder is frequently used as a thickener in Thai recipes.
You can substitute cornstarch if arrowroot powder is unavailable.
Liquid tamarind concentrate is available in Asian markets.

Yields 10 chicken wings

10 chicken wings

1 teaspoon salt

1 teaspoon black pepper

2 tablespoons fish sauce

1 tablespoon soy sauce

3 tablespoons tamarind liquid

6 tablespoons water, divided

2 tablespoons vegetable or peanut oil

2 tablespoons minced ginger

6 Thai red chilies, cut in half, seeded, and finely chopped

1 tablespoon arrowroot powder

1. Place the chicken wings in a bowl. Rub the salt and pepper over the wings and let stand for 10 minutes.

2. Combine the fish sauce, soy sauce, tamarind liquid, and 4 tablespoons water in a bowl. Set aside.

3. Heat a wok or skillet on medium-high heat until it is almost smoking. Add the oil. When the oil is hot, add the ginger and the chilies. Stir-fry for 30 seconds, then add the chicken wings. Let sit for a minute, then stir-fry, moving the wings around the pan. Continue stir-frying for 5 minutes, or until the wings are browned.

4. Pour the sauce over the chicken wings. Reduce the heat, cover, and simmer for 10 minutes or until the wings are cooked.

5. Remove the wings from the pan. In a small bowl, stir the arrowroot powder into 2 tablespoons water. Add the arrowroot powder/water mixture to the sauce, turning up the heat so that the sauce comes to a boil, and stirring quickly to thicken. When the sauce has thickened, pour it over the chicken wings. Serve hot.

Tangy Tamarind Tamarind is the sticky pulp contained in the pods of the tamarind tree. Juice from the pulp is used to give a distinctive sweet-and-sour flavor to Thai sauces. "Son-in-law eggs," made by coating hard-boiled eggs with a spicy tamarind-flavored sauce, is a signature Thai dish.

¾ pound boneless, skinless chicken breast

1 head lettuce leaves, shredded

1 red bell pepper, seeded and cut into thin strips

1 orange bell pepper, seeded and cut into thin strips

3 ribs celery, strung and cut on the diagonal into ¼–½-inch slices

3 green onions, cut on the diagonal into thin slices

1 cup pineapple slices, drained

2 tablespoons pineapple juice

1 tablespoon soy sauce

½ teaspoon sugar

1 tablespoon Asian sesame oil

3 tablespoons olive oil, divided

1 tablespoon minced garlic

1 tablespoon minced ginger

Salt and pepper to taste

Hot Chicken Salad

On nights when you don't feel like stir-frying, another option is to bake the chicken for this dish. Bake the whole breast at 350°F for 45 minutes, cool, and cut into thin strips. Whisk together the dressing ingredients and pour over the chicken and vegetables.

1. Cut the chicken into thin strips about 2 inches long. Arrange the lettuce leaves in a salad bowl, placing the other vegetables and the pineapple slices on top.

2. Whisk together the pineapple juice, soy sauce, sugar, Asian sesame oil, and 1 tablespoon olive oil in a small bowl. Set aside.

3. Heat a wok or skillet over medium-high heat until it is nearly smoking. Add 2 tablespoons oil. When the oil is hot, add the garlic and ginger. Stir-fry for 10 seconds, then add the chicken strips. Let them brown briefly, then stir-fry, stirring and tossing the chicken for 3 to 4 minutes, until it turns white and is nearly cooked.

4. Pour the dressing over the chicken. Stir-fry for 1 to 2 more minutes, until heated through. Stir in salt and/or pepper if desired. Pour the chicken and dressing into the salad and toss.

Coq au Vin

*For best results, use a good, dry French red wine such as
a Burgundy, Merlot, or Côtes du Rhône in this recipe.*

1. Cut the chicken thigh meat into thin strips approximately 1½ to 2 inches long. Place the chicken in a bowl and add 2 tablespoons red wine, dried thyme, dried parsley, salt, pepper, and cornstarch. Marinate the chicken in the refrigerator for 30 minutes.

2. Heat a wok or frying pan on medium-high heat until it is almost smoking. Add the oil. When the oil is hot, add the garlic. Stir-fry until it is aromatic, then add the chicken strips. Let them brown briefly, then stir-fry, stirring and tossing the chicken for 3 to 4 minutes, until it changes color and is nearly cooked through. Remove the chicken from the pan.

3. Heat a wok or frying pan on medium heat. Add the chopped bacon and cook until it is crisp. Push the bacon up the sides of the pan. Turn up the heat to medium-high. Add the onion. Stir-fry for about 2 minutes, until it begins to soften. Add the mushrooms. Stir-fry for 1 minute.

4. Add 1 cup red wine and the chicken broth. Stir in the tomato paste and the brown sugar. Bring to a boil. Stir in the cooked chicken. Stir in the green onions. Turn down the heat, cover, and simmer for 5 minutes or until heated through. Taste and adjust seasoning if desired. Serve hot.

Origins of Coq au Vin The French version of chicken stew, coq au vin is reputed to have been created by Julius Caesar's chef in honor of the Roman emperor's conquest of Gaul. In reality, the recipe for chicken and vegetables stewed in red wine was probably invented by a local French cook whose name is lost to history.

Serves 4

1 pound chicken thigh meat

1 cup plus 2 tablespoons red wine, divided

¼ teaspoon dried thyme

¼ teaspoon dried parsley

Salt and black pepper to taste

2 teaspoons cornstarch

2 tablespoons peanut or vegetable oil

2 cloves garlic, chopped

2 slices bacon, chopped

1 medium onion, chopped

¼ pound fresh mushrooms, thinly sliced

1 cup chicken broth

2 tablespoons tomato paste

1 teaspoon brown sugar

2 green onions, finely chopped

1 pound chicken thigh meat

2 tablespoons dry white wine

1 teaspoon dried rosemary

Salt and pepper to taste

2 teaspoons cornstarch

2 tablespoons olive oil

4 garlic cloves, finely chopped

¼ teaspoon crushed red pepper flakes

1½ tablespoons chicken broth

1½ tablespoons red wine vinegar

½ teaspoon granulated sugar

Italian-Inspired Garlic Chicken

Though Italian dishes aren't known for their spiciness, hot pepper is used in this dish to give the final product a little heat.

1. Cut the chicken into thin strips 1½ to 2 inches long. Place the chicken in a bowl and add the white wine, dried rosemary, salt, pepper, and cornstarch. Marinate the chicken for 15 minutes.

2. Heat a wok or skillet over medium-high heat until it is nearly smoking. Add the oil. When the oil is hot, add the chicken. Stir-fry for a minute, then add the garlic and the crushed red pepper. Stir-fry the chicken until it turns white and is nearly cooked.

3. Stir in the chicken broth, red wine vinegar, and sugar. Continue stir-frying until the chicken is cooked through. Serve hot.

Marengo-Style Chicken

Traditionally, this dish is served with fried eggs, which pair nicely with tomatoes. For an extra touch of authenticity, use oblong Italian-style tomatoes called plum tomatoes in this recipe.

Serves 4

¾ pound boneless, skinless chicken breasts

1 teaspoon salt

1 teaspoon dried thyme

1 teaspoon dried parsley

Black pepper to taste

6 tablespoons dry white wine, divided

1½ teaspoons cornstarch

¼ cup chicken broth

3 tablespoons olive oil, divided

2 cloves garlic, peeled and chopped

1 white onion, thinly sliced

2 ribs celery, cut on the diagonal into ½-inch pieces

2 tomatoes, halved and thinly sliced

1. Cut the chicken into bite-sized pieces. Place the chicken in a bowl and add the salt, thyme, parsley, black pepper, 2 tablespoons dry white wine, and cornstarch. Marinate the chicken for 20 minutes.

2. Combine 4 tablespoons white wine with the chicken broth. Set aside.

3. Heat a wok or skillet on medium-high heat until it is nearly smoking. Add 2 tablespoons oil. When the oil is hot, add the chicken. Let it brown briefly, then stir-fry for 3 to 4 minutes, until the chicken has changed color and is nearly cooked. Push the chicken to the sides of the wok.

4. Add 1 tablespoon oil to the middle of the wok or skillet. Add the garlic, onion, and celery. Stir-fry for about 1 minute, then add the tomatoes. Add the white wine and chicken broth mixture. Stir to mix everything together, then reduce the heat, cover, and simmer for 10 minutes. Taste and adjust seasoning if desired. Serve hot.

Chicken Fit for an Emperor Chicken Marengo was created in honor of Napoleon's victory over the Austrians at Marengo, in Italy. While some versions of the story claim the emperor created the dish himself, most agree the real credit should go to his chef. The dish originally included crayfish, but modern cooks rarely include it.

Serves 4

1 pound chicken thigh meat

1 teaspoon salt

1 egg white

1 tablespoon cornstarch

1 cup plus 1½ tablespoons vegetable or peanut oil, divided

1 teaspoon minced ginger

1 cup canned artichoke hearts, drained, halved

1 cup mung bean sprouts

1 tablespoon water or soy sauce

2 tablespoons tomato sauce

1 tablespoon dry white wine

Black pepper to taste

Chicken with Artichokes

The pleasant flavor of artichoke hearts goes nicely with chicken and bean sprouts in this dish. Serve over cooked white rice for a complete meal.

1. Cut the chicken into bite-sized cubes. Place the chicken in a bowl and add 1 teaspoon salt, the egg white, and the cornstarch. Marinate the chicken in the refrigerator for 30 minutes.

2. Heat a wok or skillet over medium-high heat until it is nearly smoking. Add 1 cup oil. When the oil is hot, add the chicken. Stir-fry the chicken cubes until they turn white (about 30 seconds), using a spatula to separate the cubes. Remove from the wok and drain in a colander or on paper towels.

3. Remove all but 1½ tablespoons oil from the wok or skillet. When the oil is hot, add the minced ginger. Stir-fry for 15 seconds, then add the artichoke hearts. Stir-fry for a minute, then add the bean sprouts. Stir-fry for 30 seconds, seasoning the bean sprouts with salt if desired, and adding 1 tablespoon water or soy sauce if they are drying out.

4. Add the chicken back into the pan. Stir in the tomato sauce and white wine. Add black pepper to taste. Stir-fry for another minute to mix all the ingredients together and serve hot.

Chicken with Ground Peanuts for Guests

Like Kung Pao Chicken, this stir-fry dish comes from Szechuan Province
in western China. Feel free to replace the chile paste with dried red chili peppers.

Serves 2 to 4

1 pound boneless, skinless
   chicken breast

1 tablespoon cornstarch

½ teaspoon salt

¼ teaspoon freshly ground
   white pepper, or to taste

1 large egg white

2 tablespoons chicken broth

2 tablespoons dark soy sauce

1 tablespoon red wine
   vinegar

1 teaspoon granulated sugar

½ cup unsalted peanuts

2 cups oil

2 cloves garlic, chopped

2 green onions, quartered

1 tablespoon chile paste, or
   to taste

1. Cut the chicken into 1-inch cubes. Combine the cornstarch, salt, white pepper, and egg white in a bowl. Stir in the chicken cubes. Cover and marinate the chicken in the refrigerator for 30 minutes.

2. Combine the chicken broth, dark soy sauce, red wine vinegar, and sugar in a bowl. Set aside.

3. Roast the peanuts in a heavy frying pan over medium heat, shaking the pan continuously so that the nuts do not burn. Roast until the peanuts are browned (about 5 minutes). Remove the peanuts from the pan to cool. Grind in a food processor or using a mortar and pestle.

4. Heat a wok or a heavy, deep-sided skillet over medium-high heat. Add the oil. When the oil is hot, add half the chicken. Stir-fry the chicken cubes until they turn white (about 30 seconds) using a spatula to separate the cubes. Remove from the wok and drain in a colander or on paper towels. Repeat with the remainder of the chicken.

5. Remove all but 2 tablespoons oil from the wok or skillet. Add the garlic, green onions, and chile paste. Stir-fry for 10 seconds, then add the ground peanuts. Stir-fry briefly, then add the chicken. Stir-fry, mixing the chicken in with the ground peanuts.

6. Add the sauce and bring to a boil. Stir-fry for 1 to 2 minutes to mix everything together. Serve hot.

Heart-Healthy Peanuts Researchers believe that including peanuts in your diet can result in long-term cardiovascular benefits. Peanuts are a rich source of monounsaturated fats, the "healthy" fat that is believed to help reduce the risk factors associated with heart disease. Peanuts are also a good source of magnesium, folic acid, copper, and vitamin E.

1 whole boneless, skinless
  chicken breast

2 tablespoons oyster sauce

Black pepper to taste

1 teaspoon cornstarch

½ pound linguini

2 tablespoons olive oil

2 cloves garlic, peeled and
  chopped

1 red bell pepper, seeded and
  cut into thin strips

3–4 ounces snow peas,
  trimmed

1 cup mung bean sprouts

¼ teaspoon salt, optional

2 tablespoons red wine
  vinegar

2 tablespoons water

1 teaspoon granulated sugar

Easy Chicken and Pasta Lunch

*If you're planning to entertain and want time to spend with your guests,
prepare the vegetables in the morning and refrigerate until needed.*

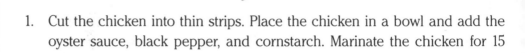

1. Cut the chicken into thin strips. Place the chicken in a bowl and add the oyster sauce, black pepper, and cornstarch. Marinate the chicken for 15 minutes.

2. Prepare the linguine according to the package directions. Drain thoroughly.

3. Heat a wok or skillet on medium-high heat until it is nearly smoking. Add the olive oil. When the oil is hot, add the garlic. Stir-fry until it is aromatic, then add the chicken. Let the chicken brown briefly, then stir-fry for 3 to 4 minutes, until it turns white and is nearly cooked.

4. Push the chicken to the sides of the pan and add the bell pepper and snow peas in the middle. Stir-fry for 1 minute, then add the mung bean sprouts. Stir-fry for 30 seconds, stirring in salt if desired. Stir in the noodles. Stir in the red wine vinegar, water, and sugar. Stir-fry to heat everything through, and serve hot.

Speedy Sesame Chicken

Feel free to use Chinese rice vinegar, cider vinegar,
or regular white vinegar in this recipe as desired.

Serves 3 to 4

½ pound boneless, skinless chicken breast

1 tablespoon soy sauce

1 egg white

3 teaspoons cornstarch, divided

1/3 cup plus 4 teaspoons water, divided

1 tablespoon vinegar

1 tablespoon granulated sugar

½ teaspoon chile paste

2 tablespoons vegetable or peanut oil, divided

1 thin slice ginger

2 cloves garlic, chopped

1 green onion, finely chopped

1 tablespoon toasted sesame seeds

1. Cut the chicken into bite-sized cubes and place in a bowl. Combine with the soy sauce, egg white, and 1 teaspoon cornstarch. Marinate the chicken in the refrigerator for 30 minutes.

2. In a bowl, combine ⅓ cup water, vinegar, sugar, and the chile paste. In a separate bowl, dissolve 2 teaspoons cornstarch in 4 teaspoons water. Set aside.

3. Heat a wok or skillet over medium-high heat until it is nearly smoking. Add 1½ tablespoons oil. When the oil is hot, add the ginger. Let brown for 2 to 3 minutes, then remove from the pan. Add the chicken. Cook the chicken cubes until they turn white and are nearly cooked through. Remove the chicken from the pan and drain in a colander or on paper towels.

4. Heat ½ tablespoon oil in the same wok or skillet. When the oil is hot, add the garlic and green onion. Stir-fry for 10 seconds, then add the sauce. Bring to a boil. Add the cornstarch and water mixture, stirring to thicken.

5. When the sauce has thickened, add the chicken back into the pan. Stir-fry until it is browned and cooked through. Garnish with the toasted sesame seeds.

How Much Is Half a Tablespoon? Don't have a measuring spoon set that includes ½ tablespoon? It helps to know that 1 tablespoon is equivalent to 3 teaspoons. So when a recipe calls for ½ tablespoon, just measure out 1½ teaspoons.

Serves 4

1 pound boneless, skinless
chicken breasts

1 egg white

1 teaspoon Asian sesame oil

½ teaspoon salt

1 tablespoon cornstarch

¼ cup chicken broth

1 tablespoon dark soy sauce

2 teaspoons brown sugar

1 teaspoon cornstarch

4 teaspoons water

2 cups vegetable or peanut
oil

4 garlic cloves, crushed

1 green onion, chopped

¼ teaspoon chile paste

Asian Garlic Chicken

*A bit of chile paste gives this dish extra bite. If you enjoy spicy
food, you can increase the heat by adding more if desired.*

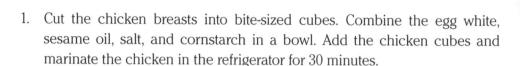

1. Cut the chicken breasts into bite-sized cubes. Combine the egg white,
    sesame oil, salt, and cornstarch in a bowl. Add the chicken cubes and
    marinate the chicken in the refrigerator for 30 minutes.

2. Combine the chicken broth, dark soy sauce, and brown sugar. Set aside. In
    a small bowl, dissolve the cornstarch into the water and set aside.

3. Heat a wok or skillet over medium-high heat and add the oil. When the oil is
    hot, add the chicken. Stir-fry the chicken cubes until they turn white (about
    30 seconds), using a spatula to separate the cubes. Remove from the wok
    and drain in a colander or on paper towels.

4. Remove all but 1 tablespoon oil from the wok or skillet. Heat the oil over
    medium-high heat. When the oil is hot, add the garlic, green onion, and the
    chile paste. Add the sauce and bring to a boil. Stir in the cornstarch and
    water mixture. Add the chicken. Stir-fry until the chicken is cooked through.
    Serve hot.

Chicken with Marsala Wine

You can experiment with different combinations of fresh mushrooms in this recipe—oyster, porcini, and fresh shiitake mushrooms all add subtle variations in flavor and texture.

1. Cut the chicken breasts into thin strips approximately 1½ to 2 inches long. Place the chicken strips in a bowl, and add 2 tablespoons dry Marsala wine, salt, black pepper, and cornstarch. Marinate the chicken for 20 minutes.

2. Combine the chicken broth and 4 tablespoons Marsala wine in a bowl. Set aside.

3. Heat a wok or skillet on medium-high heat until it is almost smoking. Add 2 tablespoons oil. When the oil is hot, add the chicken strips. Let them sit briefly, then stir-fry, stirring and tossing the strips for 4 to 5 minutes, until they turn white and are nearly cooked. Remove the chicken from the pan.

4. Heat 1½ tablespoons oil in the pan. When the oil is hot, add the ginger and garlic. Stir-fry for 10 seconds, then add the shallots. Stir-fry until they begin to soften, then add the sliced mushrooms. Stir-fry for about 2 minutes, then add the broth and wine mixture. Bring to a boil, then add the chicken back into the pan. Stir in the chopped basil. Stir-fry for 2 more minutes to blend all the ingredients and make sure the chicken is cooked through. Garnish with the fresh parsley.

Marvelous Marsala Wine Originating in Sicily, Marsala wine is fortified with ethyl alcohol, giving it an alcohol level of over 15 percent. One of Italy's best kept secrets, Marsala wine was introduced to the rest of the world in the eighteenth century by Englishman John Woodhouse, who realized that the fortification process meant that the wine would survive the voyage to England without going bad.

Serves 3 to 4

- 1 pound boneless, skinless chicken breasts
- 6 tablespoons dry Marsala wine, divided
- ½ teaspoon salt
- Freshly ground black pepper to taste
- 2 teaspoons cornstarch
- ¼ cup chicken broth
- 3½ tablespoons olive oil, divided
- 2 thin slices ginger, chopped
- 2 cloves garlic, chopped
- 2 shallots, chopped
- ¼ pound fresh mushrooms, thinly sliced
- 1 tablespoon chopped fresh basil leaves
- Fresh parsley, to garnish

1 pound boneless, skinless chicken breasts

1 large egg white

½ teaspoon salt

1 teaspoon five-spice powder

4 teaspoons cornstarch, divided

½ cup chicken broth

1½ tablespoons dark soy sauce

2 teaspoons brown sugar

½ teaspoon chile paste, or to taste

4 teaspoons water

2 cups vegetable or peanut oil

2 cloves garlic, chopped

1 zucchini, sliced into ¼-inch pieces

¼ teaspoon salt

¼ teaspoon black pepper, or to taste

Five-Spiced Chicken

Be careful to gently slide the chicken cubes into the hot oil to prevent the hot oil from splashing back up at you. Use a slotted spoon to remove the chicken pieces from the oil.

1. Cut the chicken into bite-sized cubes. In a bowl, stir together the egg white, salt, five-spice powder, and 3 teaspoons cornstarch. Add the chicken cubes, cover, and marinate in the refrigerator for 30 minutes.

2. Combine the chicken broth, dark soy sauce, brown sugar, and chile paste in a bowl. Set aside. In a separate small bowl, dissolve 1 teaspoon cornstarch into the water.

3. Heat 2 cups oil on medium-high heat in a wok or heavy, deep-sided skillet. When the oil is hot, add the chicken. Cook the chicken for 30 seconds or until the cubes turn white, stirring gently to separate the pieces. Remove the chicken with a slotted spoon and drain in a colander or on paper towels.

4. Drain all but 2 tablespoons oil from the wok or skillet. Add the garlic. Stir-fry the garlic for 10 seconds, then add the zucchini. Stir-fry the zucchini, sprinkling the salt over it, until the zucchini turns a darker green and is tender but still crisp. Remove from the pan and drain.

5. Add the chicken cubes back into the pan. Stir-fry for a minute, then add the sauce and bring to a boil. Add the cornstarch and water mixture to the sauce, stirring quickly to thicken.

6. When the sauce has thickened, add the zucchini back into the pan. Stir in the black pepper. Stir-fry for 1 to 2 more minutes to heat everything through. Serve hot.

Thai-Style Chicken with Basil

The secret ingredient in this dish is Thai holy basil, which has a peppery flavor. You'll recognize Thai basil by its distinctive purple-tinged leaves, but if it's not available, you may substitute sweet basil, which has a licorice-like flavor.

Serves 4

1 pound boneless, skinless chicken thighs

½ teaspoon salt

½ teaspoon freshly ground white pepper, or to taste

2 teaspoons cornstarch

2 tablespoons vegetable or peanut oil

2–4 dried red chilies, or to taste

2 cloves garlic, minced

2 shallots, chopped

1 red bell pepper, diced

¼ cup chicken broth

2 tablespoons fish sauce

1 tablespoon dark soy sauce

1 tablespoon granulated sugar

1 cup Thai basil leaves, chopped

1. Cut the chicken into thin strips. Place the chicken strips in a bowl, and add the salt, freshly ground white pepper, and cornstarch.

2. Heat a wok or skillet over medium-high heat until it is nearly smoking, and add the oil. When the oil is hot, add the dried chilies. Stir-fry briefly, then add the garlic. Stir-fry for 10 seconds, then add the chicken. Let sit for a minute, then stir-fry, stirring and moving the chicken around the pan, until it turns white and is nearly cooked through. (Remove the dried chilies from the pan if desired.)

3. Push the chicken to the sides of the pan and add the shallots in the middle. Stir-fry briefly, until they begin to soften, then add the diced bell pepper. Stir-fry for 1 minute, then add the chicken broth. Bring to a boil, then stir in the fish sauce, dark soy sauce, and sugar. Bring to a boil.

4. Stir in the fresh basil. Stir-fry for 30 seconds to mix with the other ingredients. Serve hot.

Beautiful Basil Ancient Greeks called basil the "King of Herbs," while the Romans considered it an aphrodisiac. One variety, holy basil, is considered to be a holy plant in India. Dishes featuring basil include Italian pesto sauce and a Thai beverage made with basil seeds. Interestingly, it is not used in Vasilopita, a Greek New Year's bread made to honor St. Basil.

1 pound boneless, skinless
  chicken breasts

2 tablespoons oyster sauce

2 teaspoons cornstarch

3 tablespoons chicken broth

1 tablespoon soy sauce

1 tablespoon rice wine or dry
  sherry

3½ tablespoons vegetable or
  peanut oil, divided

1 teaspoon minced ginger

1 teaspoon minced garlic

2 tablespoons Chinese brown
  bean sauce

1 cup walnut halves

Walnut Chicken

*Brown bean sauce is available at Asian markets. If you find
the walnut flavor in this dish a bit too strong, try blanching
the walnut halves in boiling water for a minute before stir-frying.*

1. Chop the chicken into thin strips 1½ to 2 inches long. Place the chicken in a bowl and add the oyster sauce and cornstarch. Marinate the chicken for 20 minutes.

2. Combine the chicken broth, soy sauce, and rice wine or sherry in a small bowl. Set aside.

3. Heat a wok or skillet over medium-high heat until it is nearly smoking. Add 2 tablespoons oil. When the oil is hot, add the ginger. Stir-fry for 10 seconds, then add the chicken. Let sit briefly, then stir-fry the chicken, stirring and moving it around the pan, until it turns white and is nearly cooked through. Remove the chicken and drain in a colander or on paper towels.

4. Heat 1½ tablespoons oil in the wok or skillet. When the oil is hot, add the garlic and the brown bean sauce. Stir-fry for 10 seconds, then add the walnut halves. Stir-fry for a minute, mixing them in with the bean sauce. Add the chicken broth mixture and bring to a boil.

5. Add the chicken back into the pan. Taste and adjust seasoning, adding salt or pepper if desired. Stir-fry for 2 more minutes to mix everything together and make sure the chicken is cooked through. Serve hot.

Chapter 4

Beef and Lamb Stir-Fries

¾ pound sirloin steak

1 tablespoon soy sauce

1 tablespoon cooking wine or
   dry white sherry

½ teaspoon Asian sesame oil

2 teaspoons cornstarch

2 tablespoons vegetable or
   peanut oil, divided

2 cloves garlic, chopped

¼ teaspoon salt, or to taste

8 ounces snow peas,
   trimmed

Stir-Fried Beef with Snow Peas

Snow peas are a wonderful addition to stir-fries, and they pair nicely with beef.
They have a crunchy texture and sweet flavor that makes them perfect for stir-frying.

1. Cut the beef across the grain into thin slices approximately 1½ inches long. Place the beef in a bowl and add the soy sauce, cooking wine or sherry, sesame oil, and cornstarch. Marinate the beef for 15 minutes.

2. Heat a wok or skillet over medium-high heat until it is nearly smoking. Add 1 tablespoon oil. When the oil is hot, add the garlic. Stir-fry for 10 seconds, then add the beef. Let it sear for a minute, then begin stir-frying, stirring and tossing the meat. Remove the beef from the wok when it is no longer pink and is nearly cooked through. Drain the meat in a colander or on paper towels.

3. Heat 1 tablespoon oil in the wok or skillet on medium-high heat. When the oil is just starting to smoke, add the salt and the snow peas. Stir-fry the snow peas, moving them around the pan, until they turn dark green (about 2 minutes).

4. Add the beef back into the pan. Stir-fry, combining the beef with the snow peas. Do a taste test and add more seasonings if desired. Serve hot.

How to Cut Beef Across the Grain Pick up a cut of flank or shoulder steak and you'll notice lines or "grains" running across it. These are the muscle fibers. To cut the steak across the grain, cut perpendicular to these fibers. If you cut the meat along the fibers it will turn out very tough.

Beef with Celery

*This easy stir-fry is very adaptable. Feel free to substitute pork or tofu
(unmarinated) for the beef, and to use another green vegetable
such as snow peas, zucchini, or bok choy instead of the celery.*

Serves 2 to 4

¾ pound sirloin steak

1 tablespoon soy sauce

*1 tablespoon cooking wine or
dry white sherry*

½ teaspoon Asian sesame oil

2 teaspoons cornstarch

2 tablespoons dark soy sauce

*1 tablespoon Chinese rice
wine or dry sherry*

1 tablespoon water

*2 teaspoons granulated
sugar, or to taste*

*3 tablespoons vegetable or
peanut oil, divided*

2 cloves garlic, chopped

*4 ribs celery, cut on the
diagonal into thin slices*

½ teaspoon salt, or to taste

1. Cut the beef across the grain into thin slices approximately 1½ inches long. Place the beef in a bowl and add the soy sauce, cooking wine or sherry, sesame oil, and cornstarch. Marinate the beef for 15 minutes.

2. Combine the dark soy sauce, rice wine or sherry, water, and sugar in a small bowl. Set aside.

3. Heat a wok or skillet over medium-high heat until it is nearly smoking. Add 1½ tablespoons oil. When the oil is hot, add the garlic. Stir-fry for 10 seconds, then add the beef. Let sear briefly, then stir fry the beef until it is no longer pink. Remove and drain in a colander or on paper towels.

4. Heat 1½ tablespoons oil in the wok or skillet. When the oil is hot, add the celery and the salt. Stir-fry the celery until it begins to turn a brighter green (about 1 minute).

5. Add the sauce and bring to a boil. Add the beef back into the pan. Stir-fry for 1 to 2 more minutes to blend the flavors. Serve hot.

Snow Peas or Sugar Snap Peas? They may seem nearly identical, but subtle differences exist between snow peas and sugar snap peas. While snow pea pods are flat, sugar snap peas have plumper pods. It's easy to confuse the two, especially since snow peas are sometimes called sugar peas.

¾ pound boneless sirloin

Easy-Oyster-Flavored-
Marinade for Beef (page
17)

3 tablespoons vegetable oil
or peanut oil, divided

2 thin slices ginger

¼ teaspoon salt

½ cup canned sliced bamboo
shoots, rinsed

1 tablespoon Chinese rice
wine, dry sherry, or water

1 zucchini, cut on the
diagonal into ½-inch
slices

Black pepper to taste

Easy Beef Stir-Fry with Vegetables

*Canned vegetables such as bamboo shoots need to be only quickly reheated
because they are already cooked, which makes for a shorter stir-fry time.*

1. Cut the beef across the grain into thin strips approximately 2 inches long.
   Place the beef in a bowl and add the Easy Oyster-Flavored Marinade for
   Beef. Marinate the beef for 15 minutes.

2. Heat a wok or skillet on medium-high heat until it is nearly smoking. Add
   2 tablespoons oil, swirling the wok or skillet so that it covers the sides.
   When the oil is hot, add the ginger and let brown for 2 to 3 minutes. Remove
   the pieces of ginger.

3. Add the beef, laying it flat in the pan. Let sear for about 30 seconds, then
   stir-fry the beef, moving it around quickly with a spatula, until the beef is no
   longer pink and is nearly cooked through. Remove and drain in a colander
   or on paper towels.

4. Clean out the pan and add 1 tablespoon oil. When the oil is hot, add
   ¼ teaspoon salt and the bamboo shoots. Stir-fry briefly, splashing the
   bamboo shoots with the Chinese rice wine, dry sherry, or water if desired;
   then add the zucchini. Continue stir-frying for about 2 minutes or until the
   zucchini turns a darker color and is tender but still firm. Add the beef back
   into the skillet. Stir-fry for another minute to mix all the ingredients together.
   Do a taste test and add black pepper if desired. Serve immediately.

Beef with Asparagus

This simple stir-fry is a great way to celebrate the arrival of asparagus season each spring. You may substitute broccoli, mushrooms, or bamboo shoots throughout the remainder of the year, when asparagus is no longer in season.

1. Cut the steak across the grain into thin strips 1½ to 2 inches long. Place the beef strips in a bowl and add the light soy sauce, rice wine or sherry, sugar, black pepper, salt, 2 teaspoons oil, and cornstarch. Marinate the beef for 15 minutes.

2. In a small bowl, combine the chicken broth, oyster sauce, and dark soy sauce. Set aside.

3. Heat a wok or skillet over medium-high heat until it is nearly smoking, and add 2 tablespoons oil. When the oil is hot, add half the ginger and garlic. Stir-fry for 10 seconds, then add the beef. Sear briefly, then stir-fry the beef, stirring and moving the beef around the pan, until it is no longer pink. Remove the beef with a slotted spoon and drain in a colander or on paper towels.

4. Heat 2 tablespoons oil in the wok or skillet. When the oil is hot, add the remainder of the garlic and ginger. Stir-fry for 10 seconds, then add the asparagus. Stir-fry for 1 minute, then add the chicken broth mixture and bring to a boil. Cover and cook until the asparagus turns a bright green and is tender but still crisp (about 2 more minutes). Uncover and add the beef back into the pan. Stir-fry for 2 more minutes to mix everything together. Serve hot.

Serves 3 to 4

¾ pound flank or sirloin steak

1 tablespoon light soy sauce

1 tablespoon Chinese rice wine or dry sherry

1 teaspoon granulated sugar

Black pepper to taste

½ teaspoon salt, or to taste

4 tablespoons plus 2 teaspoons vegetable or peanut oil, divided

1½ teaspoons cornstarch

3 tablespoons chicken broth

2 tablespoons oyster sauce

1 tablespoon dark soy sauce

½ teaspoon minced ginger

½ teaspoon minced garlic

1 pound asparagus, cut on the diagonal into thin slices

1 pound flank steak

2 tablespoons soy sauce

Black or white pepper to
taste

1½ teaspoons cornstarch

3 tablespoons vegetable or
peanut oil, divided

2 garlic cloves, chopped

1 onion, sliced

1 green bell pepper, seeded
and cut into thin strips

1 red bell pepper, seeded and
cut into thin strips

1 tablespoon water, optional

Curry Sauce (page 20)

Easy Beef Curry

*Because of the strong flavor of beef, it is frequently paired with strongly
flavored vegetables such as onion and garlic in stir-fries like this one.*

1. Cut the steak across the grain into thin strips about 1½ inches long. Place the beef in a bowl and add the soy sauce, pepper, and cornstarch. Marinate the beef for 15 minutes.

2. Heat a wok or heavy skillet on medium-high heat and add 2 tablespoons oil. When the oil is hot, add half the beef, laying it flat in the pan. Let sear (brown) briefly, then stir-fry the meat, stirring and tossing until it is no longer pink. Remove and drain in a colander or on paper towels. Repeat with the remainder of the beef.

3. Heat 1 tablespoon oil in the wok or skillet. When the oil is hot, add the chopped garlic and stir-fry for a few seconds, until it is fragrant. (Leave the garlic in the pan or remove as desired.) Add the sliced onion and stir-fry for about 2 minutes, until it begins to soften. Add the green bell pepper. Stir-fry for a minute, then add the red bell pepper. Stir-fry for about 1 more minute. Add 1 tablespoon water if the vegetables begin to dry out during stir-frying.

4. Add the sauce into the pan and heat to boiling. Cook for 1 to 2 more minutes to blend the flavors, stirring continually. Serve hot.

Fat Facts   Monounsaturated and polyunsaturated fats are both known for their health-giving properties. These types of fats, liquid at room temperature, have been found to lower LDL (bad cholesterol). Monounsaturated fats are found in canola oil, peanut oil, and olive oil, while polyunsaturated fats are found in corn oil, sesame oil, and safflower oil.

Stir-Fried Spanish Rice

Serve this easy entrée with a green vegetable such as
Stir-Fried Zucchini (page 250) for a quick and easy meal.

1. Combine the ground beef in a bowl with the salt, pepper, ground cumin, and chili powder; let stand for 15 minutes.

2. Heat a wok or skillet on medium-high heat until it is nearly smoking. Add 2 tablespoons oil. When the oil is hot, add the ground beef. Stir-fry the beef, moving it around the pan until it loses its pink color and is nearly cooked through. Remove the beef and clean out the pan.

3. Heat 1 tablespoon oil in the same wok or skillet. Add the crushed garlic and stir-fry briefly until aromatic. Add the onion. Stir-fry until it begins to soften (about 2 minutes). Add the bell pepper and stir-fry for 2 more minutes. Add the diced tomatoes and juice and bring to a boil.

4. Add the beef, stirring to mix it in with the vegetables. Stir in the rice.

5. Cover, reduce the heat, and simmer for 5 minutes. Taste and adjust the seasonings as desired. Serve hot.

Serves 3 to 4

1 pound lean ground beef
½ teaspoon salt
½ teaspoon black pepper
½ teaspoon ground cumin
1 teaspoon chili powder
3 tablespoons vegetable or peanut oil, divided
2 cloves garlic, crushed
½ Spanish onion, peeled and chopped
1 green bell pepper, cut into thin strips
1½ cups diced tomatoes with juice
1½ cups cooked white rice

Stovetop Pepper Steak

In Japanese, umami *means "delicious essence." The irresistible flavor of* umami *is prevalent in this simple home-cooked dish.*

Serves 4

1¼–1½ pounds sirloin steak or sirloin tips

¾ cup beef broth

2 tablespoons soy sauce

1 teaspoon brown sugar

2 teaspoons cornstarch

2 tablespoons water

3½ tablespoons olive oil, divided

2 cloves garlic, chopped

1 medium onion, sliced

1 green bell pepper, seeded and cut into thin strips

1 red bell pepper, seeded and cut into thin strips

1 rib celery, strung and julienned

2 medium tomatoes, cut in half lengthwise and thinly sliced

2 green onions, finely chopped

¼ teaspoon freshly ground black pepper, or to taste

1 teaspoon salt, or to taste

1. Cut the steak into thin strips 1½ to 2 inches long. Combine the beef broth with the soy sauce and brown sugar in a bowl and set aside. In a separate small bowl, dissolve the cornstarch into the water and set aside.

2. Heat a wok or skillet over medium-high heat until it is nearly smoking. Add 2 tablespoons olive oil and the chopped garlic. When the oil is hot, add half the beef, laying it flat in the pan. Let sear (brown) briefly, then stir-fry the meat, stirring and tossing until it is no longer pink. Remove and drain in a colander or on paper towels. Repeat with the remainder of the beef.

3. Heat 1½ tablespoons oil in the wok or skillet. When the oil is hot, add the onion. Stir-fry for 2 minutes or until it begins to soften. Add the green and red bell peppers and the celery. Stir-fry for another minute, then add the tomatoes, gently stirring and pressing down on them with a spatula so that they release their juices.

4. Push the vegetables to the sides of the wok or skillet. Pour the broth mixture in the middle and heat to boiling. Quickly stir the cornstarch and water mixture and add into the middle of the pan, stirring to thicken. Once the sauce has thickened, mix with the rest of the ingredients. Add the beef back into the pan, stirring to mix it with the vegetables. Stir in the green onions, black pepper, and salt. Serve pepper steak hot over rice.

Ubiquitous Umami Umami is a taste that enhances the natural flavor of other foods. It was Professor Ikeda at the University of Tokyo who first isolated the chemical composition of umami in seaweed. He bottled and sold his discovery as monosodium glutamate (MSG). Umami occurs naturally in many foods, from tomatoes to cheese. The Chinese make use of umami's flavor-enhancing properties through the use of soy sauce.

Hot Hunan Beef

This would go nicely with Stir-Fried Zucchini (page 250),
providing an interesting contrast in texture and flavor.

1. Cut the steak across the grain into thin strips 1½ to 2 inches long. Place the beef in a bowl and add the soy sauce, 1 tablespoon rice wine or dry sherry, and cornstarch. Marinate the beef for 20 minutes.

2. In a small bowl, combine 1 tablespoon rice wine or sherry, dark soy sauce, rice vinegar, water, Asian sesame oil, and white pepper. Set aside.

3. Heat a wok or skillet until it is nearly smoking. Add 2 tablespoons oil. When the oil is hot, add the minced ginger. Stir-fry for 10 seconds, then add half the beef, laying it flat in the pan. Let sear (brown) briefly, then stir-fry the meat, stirring and tossing until it is no longer pink. Remove and drain in a colander or on paper towels.

4. Clean out the pan and add 1½ tablespoons oil. When the oil is hot, add the garlic and chile paste. Stir-fry for about 30 seconds, then add the beef back into the pan. Add the sauce. Heat to boiling, stirring to combine the meat with the sauce and chili paste. Stir in the sugar. Serve hot.

Serves 3 to 4

1 pound flank steak

1 tablespoon soy sauce

2 tablespoons rice wine or dry sherry, divided

2 teaspoons cornstarch

1 tablespoon dark soy sauce

1 tablespoon white rice vinegar

1 tablespoon water

1½ teaspoons Asian sesame oil

⅛ teaspoon white pepper, or to taste

3½ tablespoons vegetable or peanut oil, divided

2 teaspoons minced ginger

1 tablespoon minced garlic

1 teaspoon chile paste

1 teaspoon granulated sugar

¾ pound sirloin steak

1½ tablespoons soy sauce

1 tablespoon dry sherry

1½ teaspoons cornstarch

¼ cup beef broth

1 tablespoon Dijon mustard

1½ teaspoons soy sauce

2½ tablespoons vegetable or peanut oil, divided

2 slices ginger

1 green onion, finely chopped

½ medium onion, chopped

½ pound fresh porcini mushrooms, stems removed, thinly sliced

¼ cup sour cream

8 ounces cooked egg noodles

Saucy Beef Stroganoff

If you like, instead of the egg noodles you find in the supermarket, you may use fresh Chinese egg noodles, available at Asian markets, in this dish.

1. Cut the steak across the grain into thin strips 1½ to 2 inches long. Place the beef in a bowl and add the soy sauce, dry sherry, and cornstarch. Marinate the beef for 20 minutes.

2. In a medium bowl, combine the beef broth, Dijon mustard, and soy sauce. Set aside.

3. Heat a wok or skillet until it is nearly smoking. Add 1½ tablespoons oil. When the oil is hot, add the ginger slices and the green onion. Add the steak, laying it flat in the pan. Let sear (brown) briefly, then stir-fry the meat, stirring and tossing until it is no longer pink. Remove and drain in a colander or on paper towels.

4. Heat 1 tablespoon oil in the wok or skillet. When the oil is hot, add the onion. Stir-fry until it begins to soften, then add the porcini mushrooms. Stir-fry for 1 minute more. Add the sauce and bring to a boil.

5. Add the beef back into the pan. Stir to mix everything together. Stir in the sour cream. Heat through and serve over the noodles.

How to Chop an Onion Lay the onion on a cutting board. Cut off the stem, and then cut the onion in half lengthwise. Peel off the onion's papery skin. Lay one half of the onion cut-side down, and make a series of thin cuts, no more than ⅛ inch thick, without cutting through the root. Turn the onion 45 degrees and make another series of crosswise cuts, also about ⅛ inch thick. The chopped pieces of onion will fall off.

Easy Chinese Steak

*If you find the sauce a bit too spicy in this dish, try
reducing the Worcestershire sauce to 2 teaspoons.*

—————

1. Cut the steak across the grain into thin strips 1½ to 2 inches long, ⅛ inch wide, and ⅛ inch thick. Combine the ketchup, Worcestershire sauce, soy sauce, water, and brown sugar in a bowl. Set aside.

2. Heat a wok or skillet over medium-high heat until it is nearly smoking. Add the oil. When the oil is hot, add the garlic. Stir-fry for 10 seconds, then add the onion. Stir-fry until it begins to soften (about 2 minutes). Add the steak. Sear briefly, then stir-fry until the beef is no longer pink and is nearly cooked. Add the sauce and bring to a boil. Stir-fry for 2 to 3 more minutes, to blend the flavors. Serve hot.

Serves 2

½ pound flank steak

1 tablespoon ketchup

1 tablespoon Worcestershire sauce

2 teaspoons soy sauce

1 tablespoon water

1 teaspoon brown sugar

2 tablespoons vegetable or peanut oil

2 cloves garlic, chopped

1 onion, chopped

Serves 4

¾ pound flank steak

3 tablespoons vegetable or peanut oil, divided

2 cloves garlic, chopped

2 cups broccoli, chopped

1 teaspoon salt

½ portion Basic Brown Sauce (page 20)

Black pepper to taste

Quick Broccoli Beef

This quick and easy version of the popular restaurant dish is perfect for busy weeknights. Serve over rice for a complete meal.

1. Cut the flank steak across the grain into thin strips 1½ to 2 inches long.

2. Heat a wok or skillet over medium-high heat until it is nearly smoking. Add 2 tablespoons oil. When the oil is hot, add the garlic. Press the garlic down with a spatula so that it releases its juices into the oil. Add the beef, laying it flat in the pan. Let sear (brown) briefly, then stir-fry the meat, stirring and tossing until it is no longer pink. Remove the beef from the pan and drain in a colander or on paper towels.

3. Add 1 tablespoon oil. When the oil is hot, add the broccoli and sprinkle with the salt. Stir-fry for 3 to 4 minutes, until the broccoli turns a darker green and is tender but still crisp.

4. Push the broccoli to the sides of the wok or skillet. Add the sauce in the middle and bring to a boil, stirring quickly to thicken. When the sauce has thickened, add the meat back into the pan. Cook for another minute, stirring to mix everything together. Taste and adjust the seasoning, adding more salt and pepper if desired. Serve hot.

Going Against the Grain   Beef recipes normally call for the beef to be sliced across the grain prior to stir-frying because cutting the beef perpendicular to the grain cuts the muscle fibers, making the beef less chewy. Always slice cuts of flank and sirloin steak across the grain prior to stir-frying.

Chili for Two

*Adding a small amount of cornstarch to the ground beef
marinade helps it separate more easily during stir-frying. If you
like your chili hot, increase the chili powder to 2 tablespoons.*

Serves 2

¾ pound lean ground beef

½ teaspoon salt

¼ teaspoon black pepper

1 teaspoon cornstarch

5 teaspoons olive oil, divided

1 clove garlic, chopped

¾ cup chopped onion

1 tablespoon chili powder

½ teaspoon cumin

1 cup corn, fresh or frozen

1 cup kidney beans, drained

1 cup diced tomatoes with
   juice

1 tablespoon brown sugar

1. Mix the ground beef with the salt, pepper, and cornstarch and let stand for 20 minutes.

2. Heat wok or skillet on medium-high heat until it is nearly smoking. Add 2 teaspoons olive oil. When the oil is hot, add the ground beef. Stir-fry, stirring and tossing it in the pan, until there is no trace of pink and it is nearly cooked through. Remove the ground beef and drain in a colander or on paper towels.

3. Clean out the wok or skillet and add 3 teaspoons olive oil. When the oil is hot, add the garlic. Stir-fry for 10 seconds, then add the onion. Sprinkle the chili powder and cumin over the garlic and onions, and stir-fry until the onion begins to soften (about 2 minutes). Add the corn and stir-fry for a minute, mixing the corn with the onion and seasonings.

4. Stir in the kidney beans and diced tomatoes with juice. Bring to a boil. Stir in the cooked ground beef. Stir in the brown sugar. Continue stir-frying for 2 to 3 minutes to mix all the ingredients together. Taste and adjust seasoning if desired. Serve hot.

1 pound beef rouladen

5 tablespoons light soy
sauce, divided

2 tablespoons Chinese
rice wine or dry sherry,
divided

2 teaspoons dark soy sauce

1 teaspoon Asian sesame oil

5 teaspoons cornstarch,
divided

1 teaspoon brown sugar

2 tablespoons water

3½ tablespoons oil

¼ cup sliced ginger

1 tablespoon hot sauce, or
to taste

1 carrot, julienned

¼ teaspoon salt

1 rib celery, julienned

Gingered Beef

*Adding a small amount of cornstarch to the ground beef
marinade helps it separate more easily during stir-frying. If you
like your chili hot, increase the chili powder to 2 tablespoons.*

1. Cut the beef into thin strips 2 inches long. Place the meat in a bowl and add 1 tablespoon soy sauce, 1 tablespoon Chinese rice wine or dry sherry, dark soy sauce, sesame oil, and 2 teaspoons cornstarch. Marinate the beef for 15 minutes.

2. Combine the 4 tablespoons soy sauce, 1 tablespoon rice wine or dry sherry, and brown sugar in a bowl. Dissolve 3 teaspoons cornstarch into 2 tablespoons water in another bowl. Set aside.

3. Heat a wok or skillet until it is nearly smoking. Add 2 tablespoons oil. When the oil is hot, add half the beef, laying it flat in the pan. Let sear (brown) briefly, then stir-fry the meat, stirring and tossing until it is no longer pink and is nearly cooked through. Remove the meat from the pan and drain in a colander or on paper towels. Repeat with the remainder of the beef.

4. Heat 1½ tablespoons oil in the wok or skillet. When the oil is hot, add the ginger. When it begins to sizzle, stir in the hot sauce. Add the carrot. Stir-fry for a minute, stirring in the salt, then add the celery.

5. Add the sauce into the middle of the wok. Bring to a boil. Stir in the cornstarch and water mixture, and keep stirring until the sauce thickens. Add the meat back into the pan. Stir-fry for another minute, mixing everything together, and serve hot.

Thickening the Sauce with Cornstarch   It is common to thicken stir-fry sauces with a cornstarch and water slurry in the final stages of cooking. Be sure to give the cornstarch and water a quick stir before adding it to the sauce. Stir continually as you add the slurry, until the sauce thickens. Once the sauce has thickened, combine it with the other ingredients.

Mongolian Lamb

*Lamb is an extremely popular dish in northern China,
where it is often paired with garlic and green onion.*

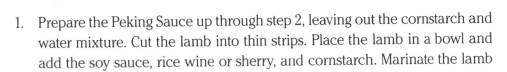

Serves 2 to 4

Peking Sauce (page 22, but
   see instructions in step 1)
¾ pound lean boneless lamb
1 tablespoon light soy sauce
1 tablespoon Chinese rice
   wine or dry sherry
1½ teaspoons cornstarch
2 tablespoons vegetable or
   peanut oil
2 cloves garlic, minced
2 green onions, shredded

1. Prepare the Peking Sauce up through step 2, leaving out the cornstarch and water mixture. Cut the lamb into thin strips. Place the lamb in a bowl and add the soy sauce, rice wine or sherry, and cornstarch. Marinate the lamb for 15 minutes.

2. Heat a wok or skillet over medium-high heat until it is nearly smoking. Add the oil. When the oil is hot, add the garlic and green onions. Stir-fry for 10 seconds, then add the lamb. Stir-fry the lamb for about 1 minute, until it is no longer red.

3. Add the Peking Sauce and bring to a boil. Stir-fry for another minute, until the lamb is cooked.

Beef with String Beans

Serve this flavorful dish over cooked noodles for a complete meal.

1. Cut the flank steak across the grain into thin strips 1½ to 2 inches long. Place the beef in a bowl and add the soy sauce, Chinese rice wine or dry sherry, five-spice powder, and cornstarch. Marinate the beef for 20 minutes.

2. Combine the chicken broth and oyster sauce in a bowl.

3. Heat a wok or skillet over medium-high heat until it is nearly smoking. Add 2 tablespoons oil. When the oil is hot, add the garlic. Stir-fry for 10 seconds, then add the beef, laying it flat in the pan. Let sear (brown) briefly, then stir-fry the meat, stirring and tossing until it is no longer pink. Remove and drain in a colander or on paper towels.

4. Push the beef to the sides and heat 1 tablespoon oil in the middle of the wok or skillet. Add the ginger. Stir-fry until aromatic, then add the string beans. Stir-fry for a minute. Add the broth and oyster sauce mixture and bring to a boil. Stir-fry for 1 more minute to mix all the ingredients together. Stir in the sesame oil. Serve hot.

One Wok or Two? When stir-frying meat, you may find it necessary to clean out the pan before adding the vegetables and other ingredients. Some people find it easier to use a second wok (or heavy skillet) instead. Use a smaller pan to stir-fry the meat, and use a larger one for the final stir-frying when all the ingredients are brought together and stir-fried with a sauce.

Beef in Black Bean Sauce

Adding oil to the marinade in this recipe helps tenderize the beef.
For extra-tough cuts of beef, you can add a small amount of baking soda.

1. Cut the flank steak across the grain into thin strips about 1½ inches long. Place the beef strips in a bowl and add the dark soy sauce, 1 tablespoon rice wine or sherry, 1½ teaspoons oil, and cornstarch. Marinate the beef for 15 minutes.

2. Heat a wok or skillet over medium-high heat until it is nearly smoking. Add 1½ tablespoons oil. When the oil is hot, add the ginger. Stir-fry for 10 seconds, then add the beef. Let sear (brown) briefly, then stir-fry the beef, stirring and moving it around the pan, until it is nearly cooked. Remove and drain in a colander or on paper towels.

3. Heat 1 tablespoon oil in the wok or skillet. When the oil is hot, add the garlic and the chopped chili. Stir-fry for 10 seconds, then add the green bell pepper. Stir-fry for a minute, then add the red bell pepper. Stir in 1 tablespoon rice wine or sherry while the peppers are stir-frying. Stir in the black bean sauce.

4. Add the beef back into the pan. Stir in the sugar. Stir-fry for 1 to 2 more minutes to blend all the flavors. Serve hot.

Serves 2 to 4

¾ pound flank steak

1 tablespoon dark soy sauce

2 tablespoons Chinese rice wine or dry sherry, divided

3 tablespoons vegetable or peanut oil, divided

1½ teaspoons cornstarch

1 teaspoon minced ginger

1 teaspoon minced garlic

1 small fresh chili pepper, seeded and finely chopped

½ green bell pepper, seeded and cut into thin strips

½ red bell pepper, seeded and cut into thin strips

1 tablespoon black bean sauce

1 teaspoon granulated sugar

¾ pound skirt or flank steak

Feisty Fajita Marinade (page 24)

8–10 flour tortillas, as needed

1 tablespoon lime juice

3½ tablespoons vegetable or peanut oil, divided

1 teaspoon minced ginger

1 teaspoon minced garlic

½ medium white onion, chopped

2 red bell peppers, seeded and cut into thin strips

Mexican Fajitas

Serve with black beans, shredded cheese, guacamole, and all the traditional fajita accompaniments.

1. Cut the skirt steak in half, and then cut crosswise into thin strips. Combine the beef in a bowl with the marinade. Marinate the beef in the refrigerator for 2 hours.

2. Heat the flour tortillas according to the package directions. Keep warm in a 250°F oven while stir-frying the beef.

3. Heat wok or skillet until it is almost smoking. Add 1½ tablespoons oil. When the oil is hot, add half the ginger and garlic. Stir-fry for 10 seconds, then add the steak, laying it flat in the pan. Let sear (brown) briefly, then stir-fry the meat, stirring and tossing until it is no longer pink. Remove and drain in a colander or on paper towels.

4. Heat 2 tablespoons oil in the wok or skillet. When the oil is hot, add the remainder of the ginger and garlic. Stir-fry for 10 seconds, then add the onion. Stir-fry for 2 minutes, or until it begins to soften. Add the red bell peppers. Stir-fry for another minute, then add the beef. Stir-fry for another minute, stirring to mix everything together.

5. Lay a tortilla out flat. Spoon a portion of the stir-fried beef and vegetables onto the tortilla, making sure the filling isn't too close to the edges. Fold in the left and right sides of the tortilla and tuck in the edges. Repeat with the remainder of the tortillas until the filling is used up.

The Origin of Fajitas The idea of marinating skirt steak in a lime-based marinade probably originated with Mexican laborers working for Texas ranchers in the Rio Grande Valley. The laborers were trying to extract more flavor from a tough, relatively cheap cut of meat. The fajita is a classic example of "Tex-Mex" cuisine, combining Mexican ingredients with the cooking style of Texas cowboys.

Meaty Egg Foo Yung

*You may replace the sausages in this recipe with Chinese sausages,
called lop cheong, which can be found at Asian supermarkets. Serve this
hearty breakfast with Basic Brown Sauce (page 20) poured over the top.*

1. Cut the sausage on the diagonal into ½-inch slices.

2. Heat a wok or skillet over medium-high heat until it is nearly smoking. Add 1 tablespoon oil. When the oil is hot, add the sausages. Stir-fry until they are cooked though. Drain in a colander or on paper towels.

3. Heat 1 tablespoon oil in the wok or skillet. When the oil is hot, add the onion. Stir-fry for about 2 minutes, or until it begins to soften. Stir in the green pepper. Stir-fry for 1 minute, then add the bean sprouts. Stir in 1 tablespoon soy sauce. Remove the vegetables from the pan.

4. In a medium bowl, lightly beat the eggs, stirring in the salt and pepper. Stir in the cooked vegetables and sausage.

5. Heat 1 tablespoon oil in the wok or skillet. When the oil is hot, add the egg mixture. Cook until golden brown on both sides, turning over once during cooking. Serve hot.

Serves 2 to 3

2 beef sausages

3 tablespoons vegetable or peanut oil, divided

½ small yellow onion, chopped

1 green bell pepper, seeded and diced

1 cup mung bean sprouts

1 tablespoon soy sauce

5 large eggs

¼ teaspoon salt

Black pepper to taste

1 pound ground beef

½ cup bread crumbs

2 green onions, finely
chopped

1 large egg

¼ teaspoon ground
cinnamon

¼ teaspoon ground allspice

¼ teaspoon ground nutmeg

1 teaspoon salt or salt
substitute

½ teaspoon black pepper

½ cup pineapple juice

½ cup water

1 tablespoon soy sauce

1 tablespoon rice vinegar

1 teaspoon granulated sugar

3 tablespoons olive oil,
divided

1 tablespoon minced fresh
ginger

1 green bell pepper, seeded
and cut into chunks

Caribbean Meatballs

*Cinnamon, allspice, and nutmeg, which Americans often use only in
sweet foods, are all spices that are commonly used in Caribbean cooking.*

1. Using your hands, in a large bowl mix together the ground beef, bread crumbs, green onions, egg, ground cinnamon, ground allspice, ground nutmeg, salt, and pepper. Mix well to combine. Form the mixture into small balls approximately the size of a golf ball.

2. Combine the pineapple juice, water, soy sauce, rice vinegar, and sugar in a bowl. Set aside.

3. Heat a wok or skillet over medium-high heat until it is nearly smoking. Add 2 tablespoons oil. When the oil is hot, add the meatballs. Stir-fry the meatballs, turning them frequently, until they are browned. Add more olive oil as needed. Remove and drain in a colander or on paper towels.

4. Heat 1 tablespoon oil in the wok or skillet. When the oil is hot, add the ginger. Stir-fry for a few seconds, then add the green pepper. Stir-fry for 2 minutes, or until the green pepper is tender but still crisp.

5. Add the sauce and bring to a boil. Turn down the heat and add the meatballs back into the pan. Cover and simmer for 15 minutes or until the meatballs are cooked through. Serve immediately.

Caribbean Cuisine—A Melting Pot   Modern Caribbean cuisine is a fascinating mix of culinary influences, from indigenous peoples and African slaves to European settlers. In the mid-1800s, Indian and Chinese laborers—many of whom were kidnapped to replace black slaves who had been freed by the British—added their own influence to the Caribbean culinary melting pot.

Gourmet Chili for Guests

Not comfortable handing hot chili peppers? Jarred chilies such as Scarpinos jalapeno peppers are available in most supermarkets. Jarred chilies tend to be a bit milder than fresh or dried chilies, so be sure to add extra if you like your chili hot!

1. Cut the sirloin across the grain into thin strips 1½ to 2 inches long. Place the beef in a bowl and add the salt, pepper, and cornstarch. Set aside.

2. Heat wok or skillet on medium-high heat until it is nearly smoking. Add 2 tablespoons oil. When the oil is hot, add half the beef, laying it flat in the pan. Let sear (brown) briefly, then stir-fry the meat, stirring and tossing until it is no longer pink. Remove and drain in a colander or on paper towels. Repeat with the remainder of the beef.

3. Heat 2 tablespoons oil in the wok or skillet. When the oil is hot, add the garlic and the chopped red chilies. Stir-fry for 20 seconds, then add the onion. Stir-fry for 2 minutes or until it begins to soften. Add the green bell pepper. Stir-fry for 2 minutes or until the green pepper is tender but still crisp.

4. Stir in the kidney beans and tomato sauce. Stir in the cumin and oregano. Bring to a boil. Stir in the cooked beef. Continue stir-frying for 2 to 3 minutes to mix all the ingredients together. Taste and adjust seasoning if desired. Serve hot.

Serves 4

- 1 pound sirloin steak
- ½ teaspoon salt
- ¼ teaspoon black pepper
- 2 teaspoons cornstarch
- 4 tablespoons olive oil, divided
- 2 cloves garlic, chopped
- 2 teaspoons chopped red chilies
- 1 medium white onion, chopped
- 1 green bell pepper, seeded, cut into thin strips
- 1 cup kidney beans
- 1 cup tomato sauce
- ¼ teaspoon cumin
- ½ teaspoon oregano

½ pound flank steak

2 teaspoons oyster sauce

2 teaspoons rice vinegar

½ teaspoon cornstarch

2 tomatoes

¼ cup chicken broth

1 tablespoon dark soy sauce

1 teaspoon sugar

2 tablespoons vegetable oil

2 slices ginger

Tomato Beef

Tomato Beef is a classic home-cooked Cantonese dish. It would go very nicely with Stir-Fried Celery (page 251) or any other stir-fried green vegetable.

1. Cut the beef across the grain into thin strips approximately 2 inches long. Place the beef in a bowl and add the oyster sauce, rice vinegar, and cornstarch. Marinate the beef for 15 minutes.

2. Peel the tomatoes if desired. Cut each tomato into 6 wedges, and then cut these in half. Combine the chicken broth, dark soy sauce, and sugar in a bowl. Set aside.

3. Heat a wok or skillet on medium-high heat until it is nearly smoking. Add the oil. When the oil is hot, add the slices of ginger. As soon as the ginger sizzles, add the beef, laying it flat in the pan. Let sear (brown) briefly, then stir-fry the meat, stirring and tossing until it is no longer pink.

4. Push the beef to the sides of the wok or skillet. Add the tomatoes in the middle. Stir-fry for a minute, then add the sauce ingredients. Bring to a boil. Serve hot.

Easy Tomato Peeling Tomatoes are difficult to peel the same way you'd peel other vegetables. To make it easier to remove the peel from tomatoes, blanch them briefly in boiling water first. Just make sure not to blanch the tomatoes too long, or they will turn mushy.

Beef and Baby Corn

Adding oil to the marinade in this dish helps tenderize the meat. Another tip is to add a bit of baking soda—try it the next time you're stir-frying an inexpensive cut of beef, which would likely be more tough when cooked than a more expensive cut.

1. Cut the flank steak across the grain across into thin strips 1½ to 2 inches long. Place the strips of beef in a bowl and add the soy sauce, rice wine or dry sherry, 1½ teaspoons oil, and the cornstarch. Marinate the beef for 20 minutes. Combine the chicken broth and oyster sauce in a bowl. Set aside.

2. Heat a wok or skillet over medium-high heat until it is nearly smoking. Add 2 tablespoons oil. When the oil is hot, add half the garlic and ginger. Stir-fry for 10 seconds, then add the beef. Let sear (brown) briefly, then stir-fry the meat, stirring and tossing until it is no longer pink. Remove and drain in a colander or on paper towels.

3. Heat 1½ tablespoons oil in the wok or skillet. Add the salt, green onion, and baby corn. Stir-fry for 1 minute, then add the chicken broth mixture. Bring to a boil.

4. Add the beef back into the pan. Stir-fry for another minute to mix the ingredients together. Taste and adjust seasoning, adding salt and pepper if desired.

Serves 2 to 4

¾ pound flank steak

1½ tablespoons soy sauce

1 tablespoon Chinese rice wine or dry sherry

4 tablespoons vegetable or peanut oil, divided

1½ teaspoons cornstarch

¼ cup chicken broth

1 tablespoon oyster sauce

1 teaspoon minced garlic

1 teaspoon minced ginger

1 teaspoon salt

2 tablespoons chopped green onion

1 cup canned baby corn, drained and cut in half

Salt and black pepper to taste

Lunch Counter Liver and Onions

*Beef liver is low in sodium and is a good source of
vitamin C and vitamin B3, more commonly called niacin.*

1. Cut the liver into thin strips 1½ to 2 inches long. Place the liver in a bowl and combine with the salt, black pepper, and cornstarch. Set aside.

2. Heat a wok or skillet on medium-high heat until it is nearly smoking. Add 2 tablespoons oil, swirling so that it covers the sides. When the oil is hot, add the minced garlic. Stir-fry for 10 seconds, then add the liver, laying it flat in the pan. Let sit for about 30 seconds, then stir-fry the meat, stirring and tossing until it is no longer pink. Remove and drain in a colander or on paper towels.

3. Heat 1 tablespoon oil in the wok or skillet. When the oil is nearly hot, add the ginger. Add the onion. Stir-fry for 2 minutes or until it begins to soften. Add the tomatoes and stir-fry for another minute. Stir in the soy sauce.

4. Add the liver back into the pan. Stir in the green onions. Remove from the heat and stir in the sesame oil. Serve hot.

Beef Liver Versus Calf's Liver   Calf's liver has a more delicate flavor and is more tender than liver from an older cow. Many people consider it safer because liver from a young cow is less likely to have picked up toxins from the animal's food and environment. To make sure you are purchasing calf's liver, look for lighter-colored beef liver that is pinkish brown, instead of reddish brown, in color.

Cashew Beef

*Feel free to replace the water chestnuts and bamboo shoots in this recipe
with other canned Chinese vegetables such as baby corn or straw mushrooms.*

1. Cut the steak across the grain into thin strips. Place the beef in a bowl and add the oyster sauce, soy sauce, black pepper, and cornstarch. Marinate the beef for 20 minutes.

2. Roast the cashews in a heavy frying pan over medium heat, shaking the pan continuously so that the nuts do not burn. Roast until the cashews are browned (about 5 minutes). Remove the cashews from the pan to cool.

3. Heat a wok or skillet over medium-high heat until it is nearly smoking. Add 2 tablespoons oil. When the oil is hot, add the beef, laying it flat in the pan. Let sear (brown) briefly, then stir-fry the meat, stirring and tossing until it is no longer pink. Remove and drain in a colander or on paper towels.

4. Heat 1 tablespoon oil in the wok or skillet. When the oil is hot, add the garlic. Stir-fry for 10 seconds, then add the water chestnuts, bamboo shoots, and the salt. Stir-fry for a minute, then add the beef. Add the cashews. Stir-fry for another minute to combine all the ingredients. Serve hot.

Serves 2 to 4

¾ pound top sirloin steak

1½ tablespoons oyster sauce

1 tablespoon soy sauce

Black pepper to taste

1½ teaspoons cornstarch

½ cup raw, unsalted cashews

3 tablespoons vegetable or peanut oil, divided

1 teaspoon minced garlic

½ cup canned sliced water chestnuts, drained

½ cup canned sliced bamboo shoots, drained

½ teaspoon salt

½ pound flank steak

2 tablespoons burgundy

3 cloves garlic, chopped, divided

Black pepper to taste

3 tablespoons plus 2 teaspoons olive oil, divided

1½ teaspoons cornstarch

2 tablespoons tomato sauce

3 tablespoons water

1½ teaspoons granulated sugar

2 Japanese eggplants, cut on the diagonal into ½-inch-wide strips

½ cup chopped onion

¼ teaspoon nutmeg

¼ teaspoon cinnamon

¼ teaspoon ground allspice

1 tablespoon chopped fresh parsley

2 cups cooked rice

Stir-Fried "Moussaka"

Don't be put off by the lengthy ingredient list for this dish! This dish is very easy to make—most of the ingredients are used in the marinade and the sauce.

1. Cut the beef across the grain into thin strips approximately 2 inches long. Place the beef in a bowl and marinate in the burgundy, half of the chopped garlic, black pepper, 2 teaspoons olive oil, and cornstarch for 20 minutes.

2. Combine the tomato sauce, water, and sugar in a bowl. Set aside.

3. Heat a wok or skillet on medium-high heat until it is nearly smoking. Add 1½ tablespoons oil. When the oil is hot, add the eggplant. Stir-fry, stirring and moving the eggplant around the pan, for 3 minutes. Remove the eggplant from the pan and drain in a colander or on paper towels.

4. Heat 1½ tablespoons oil in the wok or skillet. When the oil is hot, add the remainder of the garlic. Stir-fry for about 10 seconds then add the onion. Sprinkle the nutmeg, cinnamon, and ground allspice over the onion. Stir-fry the onion for 2 minutes, or until it begins to soften.

5. Add the beef, laying it flat in the pan. Let sear (brown) briefly, then stir-fry the meat, stirring and tossing until it is no longer pink.

6. Add the eggplant back into the pan. Add the sauce. Stir in the parsley. Taste and adjust seasoning if desired. Cook for 2 to 3 more minutes to heat everything through. Serve hot over the cooked rice.

Easy Eggplant Preparation Japanese eggplant is less bitter than the thicker Western eggplant. This means that there is no need to degorge the eggplant by salting it before cooking. Nonetheless, Japanese eggplant still requires special care—it is one of the few vegetables that can't be completely cooked by stir-frying. After browning briefly, the eggplant is gently braised until it is cooked through.

Mexican Breakfast Burritos

If you enjoy different types of Mexican cheeses, feel free to replace the Monterey jack with your favorite type of hard Mexican cheese when preparing these burritos.

1. Heat the flour tortillas according to the package directions. Keep warm in a 250°F oven while stir-frying the chorizo.

2. Cut the chorizo on the diagonal into 1-inch pieces. Lightly beat the eggs, stirring in the chicken broth, sour cream, salt, pepper, and chopped onion.

3. Heat a wok or skillet on medium-high heat until it is nearly smoking. Add 1 tablespoon oil. When the oil is hot, add the sausage. Stir-fry, stirring and moving the chorizo around the pan, until it is cooked through. Remove the chorizo from the pan.

4. Heat 1 tablespoon oil in the wok or skillet. When the oil is hot, add the egg mixture. Scramble the eggs for about 1 minute, then add the chorizo. Continue scrambling until the eggs are almost cooked but are still moist. Remove from the heat.

5. Lay a tortilla out flat. Spoon one-fourth of the scrambled-egg mixture lengthwise in the center of the tortilla. Sprinkle 1 tablespoon of the shredded cheese over the filling. Fold up the tortilla in the standard burrito shape. Continue filling the rest of the tortillas.

Yields 4 burritos

4 soft flour tortillas

2 links chorizo (Spanish sausages)

4 large eggs

¼ cup chicken broth

1 tablespoon sour cream

¼ teaspoon salt, or to taste

¼ teaspoon black pepper, or to taste

¼ cup chopped red onion

2 tablespoons olive oil, divided

¼ cup shredded Monterey jack cheese

¾ pound flank steak

4½ teaspoons Japanese soy sauce

3 teaspoons Japanese mirin

1 teaspoon granulated sugar

1 pound broccoli florets

3 tablespoons vegetable oil, divided

1 tablespoon minced garlic

2 teaspoons minced ginger

¼ cup teriyaki sauce

Sizzling Beef with Teriyaki Sauce

Mirin, the Japanese version of rice wine, gives teriyaki dishes their rich flavor. If you can't find mirin, try substituting an equal amount of sake (available in many liquor stores) and increasing the amount of sugar in the marinade to 2 teaspoons.

1. Cut the beef into thin strips (it's easiest to do this if the beef is frozen for 15 to 20 minutes). In a small bowl, combine the soy sauce, mirin, and sugar. Add the beef strips. Marinate the beef for 20 minutes.

2. Blanch the broccoli florets in boiling water for 2 to 3 minutes, until the broccoli turns bright green. Plunge the broccoli into cold water to stop the cooking process. Drain thoroughly.

3. Heat a wok or skillet until it is nearly smoking. Add 1½ tablespoons oil. When the oil is hot, add the garlic. Stir-fry for 10 seconds, then add the steak, laying it flat in the pan. Let sear (brown) briefly, then stir-fry the meat, stirring and tossing until it is no longer pink. Remove and drain in a colander or on paper towels.

4. Heat 1½ tablespoons oil in the wok or skillet. When the oil is hot, add the ginger. As soon as the ginger starts sizzling, add the broccoli florets. Stir-fry for 1 minute, then add the teriyaki sauce. Bring to a boil. Add the beef back into the pan. Cook for another minute, stirring to mix everything together, then serve hot.

Appealing Japanese Cuisine   Designed to appeal to all the senses, a properly prepared Japanese dish should have a pleasing appearance, aroma, taste, and even texture. To enhance the appearance of Sizzling Beef with Teriyaki Sauce, try garnishing it with colorful pickled red ginger (called benishoga) before serving.

Beef and Bean Sprouts

*You can alter this basic recipe by replacing the carrot
with trimmed snow peas or strips of bell pepper.*

1. Cut the flank steak across the grain into thin strips. Place the beef in a bowl and add the soy sauce, rice wine or sherry, salt, white pepper, and cornstarch. Marinate the beef in the refrigerator for 15 minutes.

2. Combine the chicken broth and dark soy sauce in a small bowl. Set aside.

3. Heat a wok or skillet until it is almost smoking and add the oil. When the oil is hot, add the minced ginger and garlic. Stir-fry for 10 seconds, then add the beef. Sear the beef briefly, then stir-fry, stirring and moving the beef around the pan, until it is no longer pink and is nearly cooked.

4. Push the beef to the sides of the pan and add the carrot in the middle. Stir-fry the carrot until it darkens, then add the mung bean sprouts. Stir-fry for a minute or until the carrot is tender but still crisp. Add 1 tablespoon water if the vegetables begin to dry out during stir-frying.

5. Add the broth mixture and bring to a boil. Stir in the sugar. Stir-fry for 1 to 2 more minutes to heat everything through. Serve hot.

Serves 2

½ pound flank steak

2 teaspoons light soy sauce

2 teaspoons Chinese rice wine or dry sherry

¼ teaspoon salt

½ teaspoon freshly ground white pepper, or to taste

1 teaspoon cornstarch

3 tablespoons chicken broth

1 tablespoon dark soy sauce

2 tablespoons vegetable or peanut oil

1 thin slice ginger, minced

1 clove garlic, minced

1 carrot, julienned

2 cups mung bean sprouts

1 tablespoon water, if needed

½ teaspoon granulated sugar

1½ pounds beef short ribs

1½ teaspoons salt, divided

½ teaspoon black pepper

2 teaspoons cornstarch

4 tablespoons olive oil, divided

2 cloves garlic, crushed

1 medium white onion, chopped

½ teaspoon dried basil

½ teaspoon dried oregano

1 cup chopped carrots

1 cup beef broth, divided

1 cup broccoli florets

1 cup cauliflower florets

2 tablespoons tomato sauce

1 tablespoon Worcestershire sauce

1 teaspoon granulated sugar

Speedy Beef Stew

If you can't find beef short ribs, you can use stewing beef instead.
Be sure to cut the stewing beef into uniform pieces so it cooks evenly.

1. Cut the short ribs into 1- to 1½-inch cubes. Place the beef cubes in a bowl and toss with 1 teaspoon salt, black pepper, and cornstarch. Marinate the beef for 15 minutes.

2. Heat a wok or skillet over medium-high heat until it is nearly smoking. Add 2 tablespoons oil. When the oil is hot, add half the beef, laying it flat in the pan. Let sear (brown), then stir-fry the meat, stirring and tossing until it is no longer pink. Remove and drain in a colander or on paper towels. Repeat with the remainder of the beef.

3. Heat 2 tablespoons oil in the wok or skillet. When the oil is hot, add the garlic. Stir-fry for 10 seconds, then add the onion. Sprinkle the dried basil and oregano over the garlic and onion. Stir-fry for 2 minutes or until the onion begins to soften. Add the carrots and ½ teaspoon salt. Stir-fry the carrots for 2 minutes, splashing with 1 tablespoon beef broth if they begin to dry out. Add the broccoli and cauliflower. Stir-fry for 2 minutes.

4. Add ¾ cup beef broth. Cover and cook the vegetables for about 3 minutes, until they are tender but still crisp. Uncover and add the beef back into the pan. Add the remainder of the beef broth. Stir in the tomato sauce, Worcestershire sauce, and the sugar. Stir-fry for 1 to 2 more minutes to mix all the ingredients together. Serve hot.

Crisped Beef with Zucchini

This recipe shows you how to combine a meat dish with one of the vegetable stir-fry dishes in Chapter 10. Try to look for a balance of flavors when pairing recipes. For example, Crisped Szechuan Beef is already spicy, so you wouldn't want to pair it with a spicy vegetable dish.

Serves 2 to 4

¼ cup chicken broth

1 tablespoon chile paste, or to taste

1 tablespoon dark soy sauce

1 teaspoon granulated sugar

Crisped Szechuan Beef (page 194, but see step 2 below)

2 Stir-Fried Zucchini (page 250)

Freshly ground white pepper to taste

1. Combine the chicken broth, chile paste, dark soy sauce, and sugar in a bowl. Set aside.

2. Prepare the Crisped Szechuan Beef up through step 2, draining the dry-fried beef in a colander or on paper towels. Clean out the wok or skillet.

3. Use the same wok or skillet to prepare the Stir-Fried Zucchini (page 250). Pour the sauce over the stir-fried zucchini and bring to a boil. Add the Crisped Szechuan Beef. Stir in the white pepper. Stir-fry for another minute to mix the ingredients together and heat through. Serve hot.

1 pound ground beef

½ teaspoon salt

¼ teaspoon black pepper

2 teaspoons cornstarch

½ cup water

½ cup chicken broth

3½ tablespoons olive oil, divided

2 cloves garlic, crushed

½ cup chopped onion

1 green bell pepper, diced

1 tablespoon additional water, if needed

1 cup tomato sauce

½ teaspoon ground cumin

1 tablespoon brown sugar

1 tablespoon Worcestershire sauce

Salt and black pepper to taste

Hamburger buns, as needed

Sloppy Joes

Kids especially love the soupy texture of these Sloppy Joes. For extra protein, sprinkle some shredded cheese on top of the Sloppy Joes before serving.

1. Combine the ground beef with the salt, pepper, and cornstarch in a bowl. Let the ground beef stand for 15 minutes.

2. Combine the water with the chicken broth in a bowl. Set aside.

3. Heat a wok or skillet on medium-high heat until it is nearly smoking. Add 2 tablespoons oil. When the oil is hot, add the ground beef. Stir-fry the meat, stirring and moving it around the pan with a spatula, until it is no longer pink and is nearly cooked through. Remove the meat and drain in a colander or on paper towels. Clean out the pan.

4. Heat 1½ tablespoons oil in the wok or skillet. When the oil is hot, add the crushed garlic. Stir-fry for 10 seconds, then add the onion. Stir-fry the onion for 2 minutes or until it begins to soften. Add the green bell pepper. Stir-fry for 2 minutes. Splash the vegetables with 1 tablespoon water if they begin to dry out.

5. Stir in the broth mixture and the tomato sauce. Stir in the cumin, brown sugar, and Worcestershire sauce. Bring to a boil. Stir in the cooked beef. Stir-fry for 2 to 3 more minutes to combine all the ingredients and make sure the ground beef is cooked through. Taste and add salt and pepper if desired. Serve the Sloppy Joes on the hamburger buns.

The History of Sloppy Joes It's believed sloppy joes were invented during the Depression, when housewives were forced to make inexpensive cuts of meat stretch as far as possible. Sloppy joes, which used less ground beef than regular hamburgers and combined it with a thick tomato sauce, were the perfect solution.

Curried Beef

Rice wine makes a frequent appearance in Chinese stir-fries.
If you can't find rice wine, dry sherry can be used as a substitute.

Serves 4

1 pound sirloin steak

1½ tablespoons light soy sauce

1 tablespoon Chinese rice wine, more if necessary

1 teaspoon Asian sesame oil

2 teaspoons cornstarch

½ cup chicken broth

1 tablespoon dark soy sauce

1 teaspoon granulated sugar

3 tablespoons vegetable or peanut oil, divided

2 cloves garlic, crushed

1 medium onion, chopped

1 cup frozen peas

2 tablespoons curry powder

1 teaspoon salt

Black pepper to taste

1. Cut the sirloin across the grain into thin strips 1½ to 2 inches long. Place the beef in a bowl and add the light soy sauce, rice wine, Asian sesame oil, and cornstarch. Marinate the beef for 20 minutes.

2. Combine the chicken broth, dark soy sauce, and sugar in a bowl. Set aside.

3. Heat a wok or skillet over medium-high heat and add 2 tablespoons oil. When the oil is hot, add half the beef, laying it flat in the pan. Let sear (brown) briefly, then stir-fry the meat, stirring and tossing until it is no longer pink. Remove the meat and drain in a colander or on paper towels. Repeat with the other half of the beef. If the beef begins to dry out, add 1 tablespoon of rice wine instead of adding more oil.

4. Heat 1 tablespoon oil in the wok or skillet. When the oil is hot, add the garlic. Stir-fry until aromatic, then add the onion. Stir-fry the onion for about 2 minutes, until it starts to soften. Add the frozen peas and the curry powder. Stir-fry for a minute.

5. Pour in the sauce and bring to a boil. Add the beef back into the pan. Stir in salt and black pepper to taste. Stir-fry for another minute to heat everything through. Serve hot.

Serves 4

1 pound flank steak or filet
    mignon

1 tablespoon peppercorns,
    crushed

1 teaspoon sea salt

2 tablespoons olive oil

1 tablespoon fresh ginger,
    minced

1 tablespoon water, white
    wine vinegar, or balsamic
    vinegar, if needed

Stir-Fried French Peppered Steak

You may experiment with different combinations of peppercorns—
from fiery white peppercorns to milder green peppercorns,
which are picked before the berry has fully ripened.

1. Cut the beef across the grain into thin strips 1½ to 2 inches long. Use the palm of your hand to rub the crushed peppercorns and sea salt into the beef. Place the beef in a bowl and let stand for 20 minutes.

2. Heat a wok or skillet over medium-high heat until it is nearly smoking. Add the oil. When the oil is hot, add the fresh ginger. Stir-fry for 10 seconds, then add half the beef, laying it flat in the pan. Let sear (brown) briefly, then stir-fry the meat for 4 to 5 minutes, stirring and tossing until it is cooked through. If the beef begins to dry out, add 1 tablespoon water, white wine vinegar, or balsamic vinegar instead of adding more oil. Remove the meat and drain in a colander or on paper towels. Repeat with the other half of the beef.

3. Serve hot with vegetables and rice or noodles.

Crushing Peppercorns   You don't need a mortar and pestle to crush peppercorns. Just place the peppercorns in a plastic bag and place the bag underneath a heavy pot or skillet. Press down hard on the inside of the pan with the palm of your hand until the peppercorns are fully crushed.

Stir-Fried Beef with Onion

Onions are a great addition to a healthy stir-fry. Not only do they add plenty of flavor, but they do not contain any fat and are low in carbohydrates and calories.

1. Cut the steak across the grain into thin strips 1½ to 2 inches long. Place the beef in a bowl and add the soy sauce, 1 tablespoon Chinese rice wine or dry sherry, hoisin sauce, and cornstarch. Marinate the beef for 15 minutes.

2. In a small bowl, combine the dark soy sauce, 1 tablespoon Chinese rice wine or dry sherry, and the brown sugar. Set aside.

3. Heat a wok or skillet over medium-high heat until it is nearly smoking, and add 1 tablespoon oil. When the oil is hot, add the garlic. Stir-fry for 10 seconds, then add the onions. Stir-fry the onions for 3 to 4 minutes, until they are softened. Remove the onions and drain in a colander or on paper towels.

4. Heat 2 tablespoons oil in the wok or skillet. When the oil is hot, add the minced ginger. Stir-fry for about 10 seconds, then add the beef. Let the beef sear, then stir-fry, stirring and moving the beef around the pan, until it is no longer pink and is nearly cooked through.

5. Add the dark soy sauce mixture into the wok or skillet and bring to a boil. Add the onion back into the pan. Stir-fry for 1 to 2 minutes to heat everything through. Taste and adjust seasoning, adding salt or black pepper if desired. Serve hot.

Serves 3 to 4

1 pound sirloin or flank steak

1½ tablespoons light soy sauce

2 tablespoons Chinese rice wine or dry sherry, divided

2 teaspoons hoisin sauce

2 teaspoons cornstarch

3 tablespoons dark soy sauce

1½ teaspoons brown sugar

3 tablespoons vegetable or peanut oil, divided

1 teaspoon minced garlic

2 large red onions, thinly sliced

½ teaspoon minced ginger

Salt or black pepper to taste

1½ pounds beef short ribs

1 teaspoon salt

½ teaspoon black pepper

2 teaspoons cornstarch

3½ tablespoons olive oil, divided

2 cloves garlic, chopped

1 medium white onion, chopped

2 teaspoons paprika, or to taste

3 cups frozen stir-fry vegetable mix

½ cup beef broth

1 tablespoon Worcestershire sauce

1 teaspoon granulated sugar

Spicy Beef Short Ribs

This stir-fried version of stew takes less than 30 minutes to make and tastes as good as stew that has been simmering on the stovetop all afternoon.

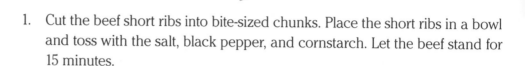

1. Cut the beef short ribs into bite-sized chunks. Place the short ribs in a bowl and toss with the salt, black pepper, and cornstarch. Let the beef stand for 15 minutes.

2. Heat a wok or skillet over medium-high heat until it is nearly smoking. Add 2 tablespoons oil. When the oil is hot, add half the garlic. Stir-fry for 10 seconds, then add half the short ribs. Let sear (brown) briefly, then stir-fry the meat, stirring and tossing until there is no pinkness and it is nearly cooked through. Remove the meat and drain in a colander or on paper towels. Repeat with the remainder of the beef.

3. Heat 1½ tablespoons oil in the wok or skillet. When the oil is hot, add the remaining garlic. Stir-fry for 10 seconds, then add the onion. Sprinkle the paprika over the garlic and onions. Stir-fry for 2 minutes, or until the onion begins to soften. Add the stir-fry vegetables. Stir-fry the vegetables according to the package directions, or until they are heated through (3 to 5 minutes).

4. Add the beef broth into the pan and bring to a boil. Add the beef back into the pan, stirring to mix it with the other ingredients. Stir in the Worcestershire sauce and the sugar. Stir-fry for 1 to 2 more minutes to mix everything together, and serve hot.

Beef Stew Around the World Every culture has its own version of a one-pot dish combining meat, vegetables, and seasonings, simmered for hours on the stovetop. Ancient Romans dined on a dish of lamb with seasonings, and Hungarian cattle drivers were dining on a mixture of dried meat mixed with water and seasonings (the forerunner to modern-day Hungarian goulash) by at least the sixteenth century.

Mexican Taco Salad

Stir-frying the vegetables for taco salad brings out their natural flavors.
Serve this salad with guacamole, sour cream, and salsa for dipping.

Serves 4 to 6

1. In a bowl, combine the ground beef with the salt, pepper, and cornstarch. Let the beef stand for 20 minutes.

2. Heat a wok or skillet on medium-high heat until it is nearly smoking, and add 2 teaspoons olive oil. When the oil is hot, add the ground beef. Stir-fry, stirring and tossing it in the pan, until there is no trace of pink. Remove the ground beef and drain in a colander or on paper towels. Clean out the pan.

3. Heat 3 teaspoons oil in the same wok or skillet. When the oil is hot, add the garlic. Stir-fry for about 15 seconds, then add the onion. Stir-fry the onion for about 2 minutes, until it begins to soften. Sprinkle the chili powder on the onion while stir-frying. Add the chopped bell peppers. Stir-fry for 1 minute, splashing the peppers with 1 tablespoon of water or broth if they begin to dry out. Add the lettuce and stir-fry briefly (less than 30 seconds).

4. Add the diced tomatoes with juice. Bring to a boil. Stir in the Worcestershire sauce and the chopped green onions. Add the ground beef back into the pan. Stir-fry for 1 to 2 more minutes to let the flavors blend together. Remove from the heat and stir in the shredded cheese. Serve with the taco chips.

1 pound ground beef

½ teaspoon salt

½ teaspoon pepper

2 teaspoons cornstarch

5 teaspoons olive oil, divided

2 cloves garlic, crushed

1 onion, chopped

1 tablespoon chili powder, or to taste

½ green bell pepper, seeded and cut into cubes

½ red bell pepper, seeded and cut into cubes

1 tablespoon water or chicken broth, if needed

1 cup lettuce leaves, shredded

1 cup diced tomatoes with juice

1 tablespoon Worcestershire sauce

2 green onions, chopped

2 cups shredded Cheddar cheese

1 package taco chips

Hungarian Goulash

For extra flavor, use canned diced tomatoes that are flavored with herbs. Serve this hearty stew over cooked egg noodles, with plenty of crusty bread for dipping.

Serves 4 to 6

1½ pounds stewing beef

1¼ teaspoons salt, divided

½ teaspoon black pepper

1 tablespoon cornstarch

¾ cup canned diced tomatoes

¾ cup beef broth

4 tablespoons olive oil, divided

2 cloves garlic, chopped

1 medium white onion, chopped

1 tablespoon paprika, or to taste

2 ribs celery, cut on the diagonal into ½-inch-thick pieces

1 tablespoon water, if needed

1 tomato, halved and thinly sliced

½ cup sour cream

1. In a large bowl, toss the stewing beef with 1 teaspoon salt, black pepper, and cornstarch. Combine the canned diced tomatoes and beef broth in a small bowl and set aside.

2. Heat a wok or skillet over medium-high heat until it is nearly smoking. Add 2 tablespoons oil. When the oil is hot, add half the stewing beef, laying it flat in the pan. Let sear (brown) briefly, then stir-fry the meat, stirring and tossing until it is no longer pink. Remove and drain in a colander or on paper towels. Repeat with the remainder of the stewing beef.

3. Heat 2 tablespoons oil in the wok or skillet. When the oil is hot, add the garlic. Stir-fry for about 15 seconds, then add the onion. Sprinkle the paprika over the onion. Stir-fry for 2 minutes or until the onion begins to soften. Add the celery. Sprinkle ¼ teaspoon salt over the celery and stir-fry until it begins to turn a brighter green (about 1 minute). Splash the celery with 1 tablespoon water if needed. Add the tomato slices. Stir-fry for 1 minute.

4. Add the broth mixture and bring to a boil. Add the beef back into the pan. Reduce the heat to medium and cook, stirring for a few more minutes to heat everything through. Taste and adjust the seasoning if desired. Stir in the sour cream just before serving.

Tomato Lore Tomatoes are one of the many foods Genoese explorer Christopher Columbus introduced to Spain following his voyages to the Americas. Although the French christened them *pommes d'amour*, or "apples of love," most Europeans were slow to embrace the tomato because of its acidic taste. Today, it's a different story—the tomato is the world's most popular fruit.

Beef with Cauliflower

Combining cauliflower with sweet red bell pepper provides an interesting combination of color, texture, and flavors. Serve this easy stir-fry over cooked basmati or jasmine rice.

Serves 3 to 4

½ pound flank or sirloin steak

2 tablespoons white wine vinegar

¼ cup chicken broth

2 teaspoons granulated sugar

2 tablespoons vegetable or peanut oil, divided

1 teaspoon minced garlic

1 teaspoon minced ginger

1 cup cauliflower florets

¼ teaspoon salt

1 red bell pepper, cut into cubes

1. Cut the flank steak across the grain into thin strips approximately 1½ to 2 inches long. Combine the white wine vinegar, chicken broth, and sugar in a small bowl. Set aside.

2. Heat a wok or skillet over medium-high heat until it is nearly smoking and add 1 tablespoon oil. When the oil is hot, add the garlic. Stir-fry the garlic for 10 seconds, then add the beef. Let sear briefly, then stir-fry the beef until it is no longer pink. Remove and drain in a colander or on paper towels.

3. Heat 1 tablespoon oil in the wok or skillet. When the oil is hot, add the minced ginger. Stir-fry for 10 seconds, then add the cauliflower. Stir-fry the cauliflower for 1 minute, sprinkling with the salt. Add the red bell pepper. Stir-fry for another minute, then add the broth mixture. Cover and cook for 1 to 2 minutes, until the cauliflower is tender but still crisp.

4. Add the beef back into the pan. Stir-fry for another 1 to 2 minutes to mix everything together. Serve hot.

¾ pound flank or sirloin steak

1 tablespoon soy sauce

1 tablespoon Chinese rice wine or dry sherry

1½ teaspoons cornstarch

3 tablespoons vegetable or peanut oil, divided

2 cloves garlic, minced

2 slices ginger, minced

2 cups green beans, trimmed

1 cup baby corn, drained, halved

½ teaspoon salt

Simple Stir-Fry Sauce (page 16)

Beef in Stir-Fry Sauce

For extra flavor, prepare the sauce earlier in the day to give the flavors more time to blend. Refrigerate the sauce in a sealed container until ready to use. For stir-frying, it's best to choose cuts of beef that are lean and tender. Flank steak and sirloin steak are the best choices for stir-frying.

1. Cut the flank steak across the grain into thin strips. Place the beef in a bowl and add the soy sauce, rice wine or sherry, and cornstarch. Marinate the beef for 15 minutes.

2. Heat a wok or skillet over medium-high heat until it is nearly smoking. Add 2 tablespoons oil. When the oil is hot, add the garlic. Stir-fry for 10 seconds, then add the beef. Let sear briefly, then stir-fry the beef, stirring and moving it around the pan until it is no longer pink. Remove and drain in a colander or on paper towels.

3. Heat 1 tablespoon oil in the wok or skillet. Add the ginger and stir-fry for 10 seconds. Add the green beans and stir-fry for 1 minute. Add the baby corn. Stir-fry the vegetables for 1 more minute, sprinkling with the salt.

4. Add the sauce and bring to a boil. Add the beef back into the pan. Stir-fry for 1 to 2 more minutes, to mix together the ingredients. Serve hot.

Roman-Style Lamb

If you've ever had Italy's take on fondue, bagna cauda, you'll know that anchovies have a distinguished place in Italian cuisine. Serve Roman Style Lamb with basic stir-fried noodles (page 200), with plenty of fresh parsley for garnish.

Serves 2 to 4

¾ pound lean lamb
½ teaspoon salt
Black pepper to taste
½ teaspoon dried rosemary
¼ teaspoon dried basil
1½ teaspoons cornstarch
3 tablespoons olive oil
2 shallots, sliced
2 cloves garlic, chopped
1 anchovy fillet, chopped
2 Roma tomatoes, thinly
   sliced
2 tablespoons chicken broth
2 tablespoons dry white wine

1. Cut the lamb across the grain into thin strips. Place the lamb in a bowl and add the salt, black pepper, dried rosemary, dried basil, and cornstarch. Let the lamb stand for 15 minutes.

2. Heat a wok or skillet over medium-high heat until it is nearly smoking. Add the oil. When the oil is hot, add the shallots and the garlic. Stir-fry for a minute, then add the anchovy, mashing it to mix it in with the garlic. Add the Roma tomatoes and stir-fry for a minute.

3. Push the shallots, garlic, and tomato to the sides of the wok and add the sliced lamb in the middle. Stir-fry the lamb for 2 to 3 minutes, until it is no longer pink and it is nearly cooked through.

4. Add the chicken broth and white wine and bring to a boil. Stir-fry for another minute to heat everything through. Taste and adjust seasoning, adding salt or pepper if desired. Serve hot.

Chapter 5

Fish and Shellfish Dishes

Serves 2 to 4

1 pound shrimp, shelled,
deveined

½ teaspoon salt

2 tablespoons chicken broth

2 tablespoons soy sauce or
fish sauce

1 teaspoon granulated sugar

3 tablespoons vegetable or
peanut oil

2 teaspoons minced ginger

1 tablespoon Chinese rice
wine or dry sherry

6 ounces snow peas,
trimmed

1 green onion, finely
chopped

Stir-Fried Shrimp with Snow Peas

This is a simple shrimp stir-fry that would go nicely with cooked jasmine or basmati rice.

1. Rinse the shrimp under cold running water and pat dry with paper towels. Place the shrimp in a bowl and toss with the salt.

2. In a bowl, combine the chicken broth with the soy sauce or fish sauce and the sugar.

3. Heat a wok or skillet over medium-high heat until it is nearly smoking and add the oil. When the oil is hot, add the ginger. Stir-fry for 10 seconds, then add the shrimp. Stir-fry the shrimp briefly until they turn bright pink. Splash the shrimp with the rice wine or sherry while stir-frying.

4. Push the shrimp to the sides of the pan. Add the snow peas in the middle. Stir-fry in the hot oil for about 1 minute, until the snow peas turn a darker green and are tender but still crisp.

5. Add the chicken broth mixture into the pan and bring to a boil. Stir in the green onion. Stir-fry for another minute, to heat everything through. Serve hot.

Fish Sauce As the name implies, fish sauce is made from small fresh fish that are fermented in salt for about 18 months. The salty brown liquid is a staple ingredient in Thai cooking, taking the place of salt as a seasoning. Fish sauce is also found in Vietnamese cuisine and occasionally in southern Chinese dishes.

Crabmeat with Spring Vegetables

This light and simple dish is a great way to celebrate spring. To add a bit of spice to the dish, try adding ¼ teaspoon cayenne pepper with the ginger.

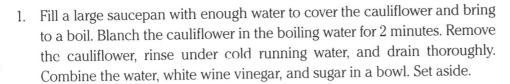

Serves 2 to 3

½ pound cauliflower

5 tablespoons water

3 tablespoons white wine vinegar

1 tablespoon granulated sugar

2 tablespoons vegetable or peanut oil

1 tablespoon minced ginger

1 zucchini, cut on the diagonal into ¼-inch slices

¾ pound crabmeat, fresh or canned

1. Fill a large saucepan with enough water to cover the cauliflower and bring to a boil. Blanch the cauliflower in the boiling water for 2 minutes. Remove the cauliflower, rinse under cold running water, and drain thoroughly. Combine the water, white wine vinegar, and sugar in a bowl. Set aside.

2. Heat a wok or skillet over medium-high heat until it is nearly smoking. Add the oil. When the oil is hot, add the ginger. Stir-fry for 10 seconds, then add the cauliflower and the zucchini. Stir-fry for 1 minute, then pour in the vinegar mixture. Stir-fry for another minute, turning down the heat to medium if needed and stirring quickly so as not to brown the cauliflower. Stir in the crabmeat and stir-fry for another minute or until the cauliflower is tender but still crisp. Serve immediately.

1 pound large shrimp,
    shelled and deveined

½ teaspoon salt

3 tablespoons vegetable or
    peanut oil

1 teaspoon minced garlic

1½ tablespoons red curry
    paste

1 shallot, chopped

1 green bell pepper, cut into
    bite-sized chunks

1 red bell pepper, cut into
    bite-sized chunks

1 tablespoon soy sauce

1 tablespoon Chinese rice
    wine or dry sherry

½ teaspoon granulated
    sugar, or to taste

Curried Shrimp

*As always, feel free to turn the heat up or down on this
dish by using more or less curry paste if desired.*

1. Rinse the shrimp under cold running water and pat dry with paper towels. Place the shrimp in a bowl and toss with the salt.

2. Heat a wok or skillet over medium-high heat until it is nearly smoking. Add the oil. When the oil is hot, add the shrimp. Stir-fry briefly until they turn pink.

3. Push the shrimp up the sides of the pan. Add the garlic and curry paste into the hot oil. Stir-fry for 30 seconds, then add the shallot. Stir-fry, mixing the shallot in with the curry paste, for about 1 minute or until the shallot begins to soften.

4. Add the green bell pepper. Stir-fry briefly, then add the red bell pepper. Stir-fry for 2 minutes, or until the green bell pepper is tender but still crisp. Splash the peppers with the soy sauce while stir-frying.

5. Stir-fry for another minute, mixing the shrimp with the vegetables and stirring in the rice wine or sherry and the sugar. Serve hot.

Red or Green Curry Paste   Red chili peppers are the main ingredient in red curry paste, while green chilies are used to make green curry paste. The heat level of the paste will depend on the specific type of chili pepper used and whether the seeds (which are the hottest part of the pepper) are included.

Sweet and Sour Fish

*Cod or sole would both be good choices for this recipe. Garnish the
fish with lemon wedges and fresh cilantro before serving.*

1. Rinse the fish fillets, pat dry, and cut into bite-sized pieces.

2. Add the chopped bell peppers to the sauce. Warm the sauce on low heat
   while cooking the fish.

3. Heat a wok or skillet over medium-high heat until it is almost smoking. Add
   the oil. When the oil is hot, add the ginger slices and the chopped green
   onions. Stir-fry for about 10 seconds, then add the fish cubes. Stir-fry the fish
   cubes until they are opaque. Splash with soy sauce and continue cooking,
   stirring gently, until the fish cubes are cooked through. Season with black
   pepper if desired.

4. Bring the sweet and sour sauce to a boil, stirring. Pour over the stir-fried fish
   and serve.

Serves 4

1 pound white fish fillets

½ red bell pepper, seeded
and cut into bite-sized
pieces

½ green bell pepper, seeded
and cut into bite-sized
pieces

Simple Sweet and Sour Sauce
(page 28)

2 tablespoons vegetable or
peanut oil

4 thin slices ginger

2 green onions, cut into
thirds

1½ tablespoons soy sauce

Black pepper to taste

1 pound shrimp, peeled and
deveined

1 teaspoon salt

1 tablespoon red wine
vinegar

1 tablespoon soy sauce

1 tablespoon water

1 teaspoon granulated sugar

2 tablespoons vegetable or
peanut oil

2 teaspoons minced ginger

2 green onions, finely
chopped

6–8 small red chilies, seeded
and chopped

½ cup peanuts

Spicy Shrimp with Peanuts

*For seafood lovers, this recipe is an interesting
variation on classic Easy Kung Pao Chicken (page 33).*

1. Rinse the shrimp under cold running water. Place the shrimp in a bowl and soak in warm water with the salt for 15 minutes. Remove. Pat the shrimp dry with paper towels.

2. Combine the red wine vinegar, soy sauce, water, and sugar in a bowl. Set aside.

3. Heat a wok or skillet over medium-high heat until it is nearly smoking and add the oil. When the oil is hot, add the ginger, green onion, and the chopped chilies. Stir-fry for about 30 seconds, then add the shrimp. Stir-fry the shrimp for 1 minute or until they turn pink, then add the sauce. Stir in the peanuts. Cook for another 2 minutes to heat through, then serve hot.

Enhancing Shrimp Flavor   To add extra flavor, let the shrimp stand in warm salted water for 10 to 15 minutes after rinsing. This firms up the shrimp and enhances its natural flavor. Pat the shrimp dry with paper towels before stir-frying.

Shrimp Scampi

There's a good chance that the "fresh shrimp" displayed at your local supermarket has previously been frozen. Refreezing shrimp alters the flavor, so don't attempt to freeze it at home unless you are certain that it is truly fresh and hasn't been frozen.

Serves 2 to 4

1 pound jumbo shrimp, peeled and deveined

½ teaspoon salt

2 tablespoons olive oil

1 teaspoon minced ginger

2 teaspoons lemon juice

3 tablespoons butter

2 shallots, chopped

2 cloves garlic, chopped

2 teaspoons paprika

1. Rinse the shrimp under cold running water and pat dry with paper towels. Place the shrimp in a bowl and toss with the salt.

2. Heat a wok or skillet over medium-high heat until it is nearly smoking and add the oil. When the oil is hot, add the minced ginger. Stir-fry for 10 seconds, then add the shrimp. Stir-fry the shrimp briefly, until they turn bright pink. Splash the shrimp with the lemon juice during stir-frying.

3. Push the shrimp up the sides of the wok or skillet. Add the butter, shallots, and garlic to the middle of the pan. Stir-fry for about 1 minute, until the shallots begin to soften. Sprinkle the paprika over the shallots while you are stir-frying.

4. Mix the shrimp with the shallots, garlic, and seasonings. Stir-fry for another minute to heat through. Serve hot.

Serves 3 to 4

1 pound scallops

½ teaspoon salt

1 tablespoon cornstarch

2 tablespoons vegetable or peanut oil

1 teaspoon minced ginger

2 teaspoons soy sauce

¼ teaspoon chile paste, or to taste

½ teaspoon granulated sugar

3 green onions, chopped

Basic Stir-Fried Scallops

If you are using large sea scallops, be sure to pull off the hard muscle on the side and cut the scallops in half after rinsing.

1. Rinse the scallops in cold running water and pat dry with paper towels. Place the scallops in a bowl and toss with the salt and the cornstarch.

2. Heat a wok or skillet over medium-high heat until it is nearly smoking. Add the oil. When the oil is hot, add the ginger. Stir-fry for 10 seconds, then add the scallops.

3. Stir-fry the scallops for 1 minute, then splash with the soy sauce. Stir in the chile paste, sugar, and green onions. Continue stir-frying until the scallops are white but not too firm (total stir-frying time should be 2 to 3 minutes). Serve hot.

Serves 3 to 4

1 pound medium shrimp, shelled, deveined

½ teaspoon salt

2 teaspoons cornstarch

2 tablespoons vegetable or peanut oil

2 slices ginger

1 tablespoon soy sauce

2 teaspoons granulated sugar

Simple Stir-Fried Shrimp

Take care not to overcook the shrimp, or they will be tough. You may splash the shrimp with Chinese rice wine instead of soy sauce if that's what you have on hand.

1. Rinse the shrimp and pat dry with paper towels. Place the shrimp in a bowl and stir in the salt and cornstarch. Let the shrimp sit for at least 5 minutes.

2. Heat a wok or skillet over medium-high heat until it is nearly smoking. Add the oil. When the oil is hot, add the sliced ginger. Let brown for 2 to 3 minutes, and then remove. (This is to flavor the oil.)

3. Add the shrimp. Stir-fry, stirring and moving the shrimp around the pan until it turns pink and begins to curl. Stir in the soy sauce and sugar while stir-frying. Serve hot.

Shrimp in Black Bean Sauce

Pungent black bean sauce lends a rich flavor to shellfish dishes. If you like, spice up this dish by adding a small amount of chile paste to the garlic and black bean sauce.

1. Rinse the shrimp in cold running water and drain. Place the shrimp in a bowl and toss with the cornstarch.

2. Heat a wok or skillet over medium-high heat until it is nearly smoking. Add the oil. When the oil is hot, add the black bean sauce and the garlic. Stir-fry for 30 seconds, mixing the garlic and black bean sauce together. Add the shrimp, minced ginger, and the green onion. Stir-fry the shrimp until they turn pink and the edges begin to curl, mixing in with the sauce.

3. Add the chicken broth and bring to a boil. Taste and adjust seasoning if desired. Serve hot over rice.

Serves 2 to 4

1 pound shrimp, shelled, deveined

2 teaspoons cornstarch

2 tablespoons vegetable or peanut oil

2 tablespoons Chinese black bean sauce

1 teaspoon minced garlic

2 slices ginger, minced

2 green onions, quartered

¼ cup chicken broth

Scallops with Garlic and Red Pepper

This dish is especially delicious when served with cooked rice and a stir-fried green vegetable or a salad.

1. Rinse the scallops under cold running water and pat dry. Cut the scallops into quarters.

2. Heat a wok or skillet over medium-high heat until it is nearly smoking. Add the oil. When the oil is hot, add the garlic and the chile paste. Stir-fry for 10 seconds, mixing the chile paste in with the garlic.

3. Add the onion and stir-fry until it begins to soften (about 2 minutes). Add the scallops. Stir-fry for about 2 minutes, until they begin to brown, splashing with the rice wine or dry sherry. Add the red bell pepper. Stir-fry for a minute or until the scallops are cooked through. Taste and adjust seasoning if desired. Serve immediately.

Serves 2 to 4

1 pound sea scallops

2 tablespoons vegetable or peanut oil

2 cloves garlic, chopped

½ teaspoon chile paste, or to taste

½ cup chopped yellow onion

1 tablespoon Chinese rice wine or dry sherry

2 red bell peppers, cut into bite-sized cubes

1 pound bay scallops

Freshly ground white pepper to taste

3 tablespoons chicken broth

1 tablespoon oyster sauce

1 teaspoon granulated sugar

3 tablespoons vegetable or peanut oil, divided

½ teaspoon minced garlic

3–5 ounces snow peas, trimmed

1 large red bell pepper, cut into bite-sized chunks

½ teaspoon minced ginger

Scallops with Snow Peas

In this recipe the vegetables are stir-fried first and then returned to the pan to mix with the sauce in the final stages of cooking.

1. Rinse the scallops in cold running water and pat dry with paper towels. Place the scallops in a bowl and toss with the white pepper.

2. Combine the chicken broth, oyster sauce, and sugar in a bowl. Set aside.

3. Heat a wok or skillet over medium-high heat until it is nearly smoking. Add 2 tablespoons oil. When the oil is hot, add the garlic. Stir-fry for 10 seconds, then add the snow peas. Stir-fry the snow peas for 1 minute, then add the red bell pepper. Stir-fry for 1 minute or until the snow peas have turned a darker green and the vegetables are tender but still crisp. Remove the vegetables and drain in a colander or on paper towels.

4. Heat 1 tablespoon oil in the wok or skillet. When the oil is hot, add the ginger. Stir-fry for 10 seconds, then add the scallops. Stir-fry the scallops until they turn white and are just starting to firm up.

5. Add the broth mixture and bring to a boil. Add the vegetables back into the pan. Stir-fry for 1 to 2 more minutes to mix everything together. Serve hot.

Ketchup Shrimp

If you've purchased frozen shrimp for use in this recipe, rinse the shrimp under cold running water until they have thawed. Be sure to drain the shrimp thoroughly.

1. Rinse the shrimp and pat dry with paper towels. Combine the ketchup, dark soy sauce, white vinegar, and sugar in a bowl. In another small bowl, dissolve the cornstarch into the water. Set aside.

2. Heat a wok or skillet over medium-high heat until it is nearly smoking. Add the oil. When the oil is hot, add the chopped garlic. Stir-fry for about 15 seconds, until it is aromatic; then add the shrimp.

3. Stir-fry the shrimp briefly until they start to turn pink. Push the shrimp to the sides of the pan. Add the sauce in the middle and bring to a boil.

4. Add the dissolved cornstarch and water into the sauce, stirring to thicken. As soon as the sauce has thickened, stir to combine it with the shrimp. Serve hot.

Ketchup History It's hard to picture a bottle of ketchup as anything but red, but originally the word referred to salty sauces made with everything from blueberries to mushrooms. Tomato-based ketchup recipes didn't become popular until the nineteenth century.

Serves 3 to 4

¾ *pound medium shrimp, shelled, deveined*

3 *tablespoons ketchup*

1 *tablespoon dark soy sauce*

1 *tablespoon white vinegar*

2 *teaspoons sugar*

½ *teaspoon cornstarch*

1 *tablespoon water*

2 *tablespoons vegetable or peanut oil*

1 *tablespoon chopped garlic*

Serves 2 to 4

1 pound jumbo shrimp (16–20 shrimp), shelled and deveined

½ teaspoon salt

2 ribs celery

3 tablespoons vegetable or peanut oil

2 slices ginger

½ cup chopped red bell pepper

1 cup canned baby corn, drained

½ cup Simple Sweet and Sour Sauce (page 28)

2 green onions, quartered

Sweet and Sour Shrimp

The combination of red bell pepper with celery and baby corn in this dish provides an interesting contrast in color and texture.

1. Rinse the shrimp under cold running water. Pat dry with paper towels, place in a bowl, and toss with the salt.

2. Cut the celery into ½-inch slices on the diagonal. Fill a medium saucepan with enough water to cover the celery and bring to a boil. Blanch the celery in boiling water for 2 to 3 minutes, until it is tender but still crisp. Rinse the celery in cold water and drain in a colander.

3. Heat a wok or skillet over medium-high heat until it is nearly smoking. Add the oil. When the oil is hot, add the ginger. Stir-fry for 10 seconds, then add the shrimp. Stir-fry the shrimp until they turn pink. Push the shrimp up the sides of the pan.

4. Add the celery. Stir-fry briefly, then add the red bell pepper. Stir in the baby corn. Stir-fry until the vegetables are tender but still crisp (total stir-frying time should be 2 to 3 minutes).

5. Push the vegetables to the sides and add the sauce in the middle, stirring quickly to thicken. When the sauce has thickened, stir to mix the sauce with the other ingredients. Stir in the green onions. Cook for another minute, mixing everything together. Serve hot.

How to Devein Shrimp Deveining shrimp isn't as difficult as you may imagine. Using a sharp knife, make a shallow cut along the back of the shrimp. Remove the vein by hand or hold the shrimp under a strong stream of cold running water to rinse it out.

Lemon-Flavored Shrimp

If using large shrimp, cut them in half before marinating.
Serve with cooked carrots and brown rice for a nutritious meal.

Serves 3 to 4

1 pound shrimp, shelled and
    deveined

1 tablespoon lemon juice

½ teaspoon salt

3 teaspoons cornstarch,
    divided

2 tablespoons ketchup

¼ cup plus 4 teaspoons
    water, divided

3 tablespoons olive oil,
    divided

2 slices ginger

½ medium red onion, cut
    into rings

1 zucchini, cut on the
    diagonal into ½-inch
    slices

1 tablespoon soy sauce

1 red bell pepper, seeded and
    cut into bite-sized chunks

1 teaspoon granulated sugar

Fresh cilantro leaves, to
    garnish

1. Rinse the shrimp under cold running water and pat dry. Place the shrimp in a bowl and add the lemon juice, salt, and 2 teaspoons cornstarch. Marinate the shrimp for 10 minutes.

2. In a small bowl, stir the ketchup into ¼ cup water and set aside. In a separate small bowl, dissolve 1 teaspoon cornstarch into 4 teaspoons water and set aside.

3. Heat a wok or skillet over medium-high heat until it is nearly smoking. Add 2 tablespoons oil. When the oil is hot, add the ginger slices. Let brown for 2 to 3 minutes and then remove. Add the shrimp and stir-fry until it just begins to turn pink. Remove the shrimp from the pan.

4. Heat 1 tablespoon oil in the wok or skillet. When the oil is hot, add the onion. Stir-fry until softened, then add the zucchini. Stir-fry for 2 minutes, splashing the soy sauce over the zucchini. Add the red bell pepper. Stir-fry for a minute, then push to the sides and add the ketchup mixture in the middle. Bring to a boil, then add the cornstarch and water mixture, stirring to thicken. Stir in the sugar. Add the shrimp back into the pan. Stir-fry briefly to mix all the ingredients together. Garnish with the cilantro and serve.

Stir-Frying Shrimp When stir-frying shrimp, it's important not to overcook them. If overcooked, shrimp become tough. Stir-fry the shrimp just until they turn pink and the edges begin to curl.

1 pound shelled, deveined
    medium shrimp

1½ teaspoons salt, divided

1 egg white

2 teaspoons cornstarch

1 cup tomatoes, undrained

3½ tablespoons tomato
    paste

3½ tablespoons olive oil,
    divided

3 slices ginger

½ cup chopped red onion

1 teaspoon cayenne pepper,
    or to taste

½ teaspoon dried thyme

4 ribs celery, cut into ½-inch
    slices

Additional water, if needed

Black pepper to taste

2 green onions, finely
    chopped

1 teaspoon granulated sugar

Shrimp Creole

*You may vary the vegetables in this popular southern dish, reducing the
celery and adding chopped green bell pepper or sliced okra if desired.*

1. Rinse the shrimp under cold running water and pat dry with paper towels. Cut the shrimp in half lengthwise. Place the shrimp in a bowl and mix in 1 teaspoon salt, egg white, and cornstarch. Marinate the shrimp for 10 minutes.

2. In a small bowl, combine ⅓ cup juice from the canned tomatoes with the tomato paste. Discard the remainder of the juice.

3. Heat a wok or skillet over medium-high heat until it is nearly smoking. Add 2 tablespoons oil. When the oil is hot, add the shrimp. Stir-fry until they turn pink and the ends have begun to curl. Remove the shrimp from the pan and drain in a colander or on paper towels.

4. Heat 1½ tablespoons oil in the same wok or skillet. When the oil is hot, add the ginger. Let the ginger brown for 2 to 3 minutes, then remove from the pan. Add the chopped onion. Stir-fry until it begins to soften (about 2 minutes), sprinkling with the cayenne pepper and dried thyme. Push to the sides and add the celery in the middle. Stir-fry for 2 minutes, sprinkling with up to ½ teaspoon salt and adding 1 to 2 tablespoons water if the celery begins to dry out.

5. Add the tomatoes, sprinkling with a bit of black pepper. Stir-fry for 1 minute, then add the tomato juice mixture. Bring to a boil, then add the shrimp back into the pan. Stir in the green onions and the sugar. Stir-fry for another minute to heat through and blend all the ingredients. Taste and adjust seasoning, adding salt or pepper if desired. Serve hot over rice.

Cucumber with Prawns

In this recipe, you can replace the chile paste with a small fresh red chili pepper, seeded and chopped.

Serves 2 to 4

1 pound prawns, shelled, deveined

2 teaspoons salt, divided

Black pepper to taste

2½ teaspoons Asian sesame oil, divided

1 egg white

2 teaspoons cornstarch

1 large cucumber

2 tablespoons vegetable or peanut oil

2 teaspoons minced ginger

1 green onion, cut into 1-inch sections

½ teaspoon chile paste, or to taste

1 tablespoon red wine vinegar

1 teaspoon granulated sugar

1. Rinse the prawns under cold running water and pat dry with paper towels. Place the prawns in a bowl and add 1 teaspoon salt, black pepper, ½ teaspoon Asian sesame oil, egg white, and cornstarch. Marinate the prawns for 15 minutes.

2. Cut the cucumber lengthwise into quarters (do not peel). Use a spoon to remove the seeds in the middle and cut diagonally into slices about ½ inch thick. Place the sliced cucumber strips in a colander and sprinkle 1 teaspoon salt over them. Let the cucumbers sit for 30 minutes. Pat dry with paper towels to remove the excess water.

3. Heat a wok or skillet over medium-high heat until it is nearly smoking. Add the vegetable or peanut oil. When the oil is hot, add the prawns. Stir-fry the prawns, stirring and moving them around the pan, until they change color. Remove the prawns and drain in a colander or on paper towels.

4. Heat 2 teaspoons sesame oil in the same wok or skillet. When the oil is hot, add the minced ginger, green onion, and the chile paste. Stir-fry briefly until aromatic, then add the cucumber. Stir-fry for about 20 seconds or until the cucumber is heated through.

5. Add the shrimp back into the pan. Stir in the red wine vinegar and the sugar. Stir briefly to mix everything together and serve hot.

Prawn or Shrimp? Prawns and shrimp are two different species of crustacean. If you look closely, you'll see slight differences in their legs and pincers. However, in cooking, the two are used interchangeably—what Americans call jumbo shrimp would be considered prawns in Britain. Whenever a recipe calls for prawns, feel free to substitute large shrimp.

Serves 2 to 4

1 pound medium to large
   shrimp, shelled, deveined

½ teaspoon salt

1/3 cup chicken broth

1½ teaspoons Chinese rice
   vinegar

2 teaspoons chopped garlic

½ teaspoon chili sauce, or
   to taste

1 teaspoon cornstarch

4 teaspoons water

4 tablespoons vegetable or
   peanut oil, divided

2 thin slices ginger

½ teaspoon minced ginger

½ cup chopped onion

2 cups chopped broccoli

½ teaspoon granulated
   sugar

1–2 tablespoons additional
   water, if needed

Shrimp with Broccoli in Garlic Sauce

*If you like, add extra heat to this dish by replacing the
chili sauce with 2 teaspoons chopped red chili peppers.*

1. Rinse the shrimp under cold running water and pat dry with paper towels.
    Place the shrimp in a bowl and toss with the salt.

2. In a bowl, combine the chicken broth, rice vinegar, garlic, and chili sauce.
    In a separate small bowl, dissolve the cornstarch in the water.

3. Heat a wok or skillet over medium-high heat until it is nearly smoking. Add
    2 tablespoons oil. When the oil is hot, add the sliced ginger. Let the ginger
    brown for 2 to 3 minutes, then remove from the oil. Add the shrimp. Stir-fry
    until they turn pink and the edges begin to curl. Remove the shrimp and
    drain in a colander or on paper towels.

4. Heat 2 tablespoons oil in the wok or skillet. Add the minced ginger. Stir-fry
    for 10 seconds, then add the onion. Stir-fry the onion for about 2 minutes,
    until it begins to soften. Add the broccoli and sprinkle the sugar over the
    vegetable mixture. Stir-fry the broccoli until it turns a darker green and is
    tender but still crisp (about 3 minutes). Add 1 to 2 tablespoons water if the
    broccoli begins to dry out during stir-frying.

5. Push the vegetables to the sides of the wok or skillet. Add the sauce into the
    middle of the pan and bring to a boil. Stir the cornstarch and water mixture
    and add to the sauce, stirring quickly to thicken. When the sauce has thick-
    ened, add the shrimp back into the pan. Stir-fry shrimp with the vegetables
    for another minute to blend the flavors. Serve hot.

Simple Stir-Fried Fish

*As with meat and poultry, adding egg white to a seafood
marinade helps protect the fish from the hot oil.*

Serves 2 to 4

1 pound fish fillets

½ teaspoon salt

Black pepper to taste

1 egg white

2 tablespoons Chinese
rice wine or dry sherry,
divided

2 teaspoons cornstarch

2 tablespoons vegetable or
peanut oil

2 thin slices ginger

1 green onion, finely
chopped

1 tablespoon soy sauce

1 teaspoon Asian sesame oil

1. Cut the fish fillets into 1½- to 2-inch squares that are about ½ inch thick. Place the fish cubes in a bowl and add the salt, black pepper, egg white, 1 tablespoon Chinese rice wine or sherry, and the cornstarch. Marinate the fish for 15 minutes.

2. Heat a wok or skillet over medium-high heat until it is nearly smoking. Add the oil. When the oil is hot, add the ginger and green onion. Stir-fry for 10 seconds, then add the fish. Let the fish sit in the pan briefly, then gently stir-fry the fish cubes, moving them around the wok, until they turn white and are firm.

3. Splash the fish cubes with 1 tablespoon rice wine or sherry and the soy sauce. Let the fish cook for another minute, remove it from the heat, and stir in the sesame oil. Serve hot.

Storing Fresh Fish While fresh fish should be eaten the same day you purchase it, it can be stored overnight. Always store fresh fish in the coldest part of the refrigerator—the temperature should not rise above 35°F or 2°C. To store fresh fish, remove the packaging that it came in, rinse the fish under cold water, and wrap it loosely in plastic wrap.

2 tablespoons vegetable or peanut oil

3 slices ginger, cut into thin strips

1 onion, chopped

1 teaspoon cayenne powder, or to taste

1 green bell pepper, cut into bite-sized chunks

1 red bell pepper, cut into bite-sized chunks

1 tablespoon soy sauce

1 pound crabmeat

½ cup crushed tomatoes, undrained

1 tablespoon chopped fresh basil

1 teaspoon granulated sugar

Black pepper to taste

Crab Creole

If crabmeat is difficult to find in your area or proves to be too expensive, you may use imitation crabmeat such as surimi instead.

1. Heat a wok or skillet over medium-high heat until it is nearly smoking. Add the oil. When the oil is hot, add the ginger. Stir-fry for 10 seconds, then add the onion. Stir-fry until the onion begins to soften (about 2 minutes), then mix in the cayenne powder.

2. Add the green bell pepper. Stir-fry for a minute, then add the red bell pepper. Stir-fry for about 1 more minute, until the vegetables are tender but still crisp. Splash the vegetables with the soy sauce while stir-frying.

3. Add the crabmeat. Stir-fry for a minute, then add the crushed tomatoes. Bring to a boil, and stir in the basil, sugar, and black pepper. Stir-fry for another minute to heat through and blend all the ingredients. Taste and adjust seasoning if desired. Serve hot over rice.

Marsala Scallops

Use bay scallops (instead of sea scallops) if possible in this recipe because their smaller size makes them better suited for stir-frying.

Serves 3 to 4

1 pound scallops

2 tablespoons olive oil

2 thin slices ginger

1/3 cup Marsala wine

1/3 cup chicken broth

2 shallots, chopped

½ pound shiitake mushrooms, thinly sliced

1 tablespoon butter

2 tablespoons chopped fresh parsley

1 tablespoons chopped fresh basil

Freshly ground black pepper to taste

1. Rinse the scallops under cold running water and pat dry.

2. Heat a wok or skillet over medium-high heat until it is nearly smoking. Add the oil. When the oil is hot, add the ginger. Brown for 2 to 3 minutes, and then remove from the pan (this is to flavor the oil). Add the scallops and stir-fry until they turn white. Remove the scallops from the pan and drain in a colander or on paper towels.

3. Add the wine into the pan and bring to a boil. Deglaze the pan by using a spatula to scrape off the browned bits from the stir-fried scallops.

4. Add the chicken broth into the pan. Bring to a boil and add the shallots and the mushrooms. Cook for 2 to 3 minutes, until the shallots have softened. Stir in the butter, fresh parsley, fresh basil, and black pepper. Serve immediately.

Shiitake—the Miracle Mushroom Native to Japan and China, shiitake mushrooms symbolize longevity in Asian culture. Recent research shows that shiitake mushrooms have earned their health-giving reputation. The meaty-flavored mushroom is believed to contain powerful antioxidants that can help fight off cancer-causing agents. It is also believed to help lower blood pressure and is a good source of protein.

Serves 2 to 4

¾ pound prawns shelled, deveined

¼ cup chicken broth

1 tablespoon Chinese rice wine or dry sherry

1 teaspoon granulated sugar

2 tablespoons vegetable or peanut oil

½ teaspoon salt

1 teaspoon minced ginger

1 cup baby corn, halved

1 cup sliced water chestnuts

2 green onions, quartered

Black pepper to taste

½ teaspoon Asian sesame oil

Prawns with Two Kinds of Vegetables

If you're using canned baby corn and water chestnuts, be sure to rinse them under running water to remove any "tin" taste from the can. Thicken the chicken broth mixture by whisking in 2 teaspoons cornstarch if desired.

1. Rinse the prawns under cold running water and pat dry with paper towels. Combine the chicken broth, rice wine or sherry, and sugar in a bowl.

2. Heat a wok or skillet over medium-high heat until it is nearly smoking. Add the oil. When the oil is hot, add the salt and the prawns. Stir-fry the prawns until they turn pink and the edges begin to curl.

3. Push the prawns to the sides of the wok or skillet. Add the ginger, baby corn, and water chestnuts in the middle. Stir-fry briefly, then stir in the green onions.

4. Add the sauce and bring to a boil. Add the black pepper and stir-fry for another minute to blend the flavors. Remove from the heat and stir in the sesame oil. Serve hot.

Coconut Shrimp

For an extra touch, garnish the shrimp with 3 tablespoons unsweetened coconut flakes that have been toasted in the oven at 350°F until they turn golden brown.

Serves 3 to 4

1 pound large shrimp

½ teaspoon salt

¼ cup coconut milk

2 tablespoons chicken broth

1 teaspoon palm sugar or brown sugar

1 teaspoon cornstarch

4 teaspoons water, or as needed

3 tablespoons vegetable or peanut oil, divided

½ teaspoon minced ginger

1 teaspoon minced garlic

¼ teaspoon chile paste with garlic

2 shallots, chopped

1 green bell pepper, seeded and cut into bite-sized cubes

1. Rinse the shrimp in cold running water and pat dry with paper towels. Place the shrimp in a bowl and toss with the salt.

2. Combine the coconut milk, chicken broth, and palm or brown sugar in a bowl. In a separate small bowl, dissolve the cornstarch into 4 teaspoons water.

3. Heat a wok or skillet over medium-high heat until it is nearly smoking. Add 2 tablespoons oil. When the oil is hot, add the ginger. Stir-fry for 10 seconds, then add the shrimp. Stir-fry the shrimp until they turn pink, taking care not to overcook. Remove the shrimp from the pan and drain in a colander or on paper towels.

4. Heat 1 tablespoon oil in the wok or skillet. When the oil is hot, add the garlic and the chile paste. Stir-fry for 10 seconds and add the shallots. Stir-fry the shallot until softened, then add the bell pepper. Stir-fry the bell pepper for 2 minutes, or until it is tender but still crisp.

5. Push the vegetables to the sides of the pan. Add the coconut milk and chicken broth mixture in the middle and bring to a boil. Stir the cornstarch and water mixture, and pour into the coconut milk and broth, stirring to thicken. When the sauce has thickened, add the shrimp back into the pan. Stir-fry for 1 to 2 more minutes to combine all the ingredients. Serve hot.

Why Devein Shrimp at All? If you look closely at a shrimp, you'll see a gray thread running down its back. This is the shrimp's digestive tract or "vein." While eating the vein can't harm you, removing it improves the appearance of the dish. In addition, the veins of larger-sized shrimp may contain dirt or grit.

1 pound large prawns

1 sprig fresh curry leaves
(about 15 leaves)

2 tablespoons vegetable or
peanut oil

1 teaspoon minced ginger

2 teaspoons Chinese rice
wine or dry sherry

2 tablespoons butter

2 large green chilies, or to
taste

2 teaspoons minced garlic

¼ cup coconut milk

1 teaspoon granulated sugar

1 teaspoon fish sauce

1 tablespoon sweetened
coconut flakes, for garnish

Chopped fresh cilantro, for
garnish

Butter Prawns

*The indescribable aroma of fresh curry leaves is the secret behind many Indian dishes.
You can either leave the curry leaves in the stir-fry or remove them before serving.*

1. Rinse the prawns under cold running water and pat dry with paper towels.
    (Do not remove the shells.) If using fresh curry leaves, strip the sprigs from
    the stem.

2. Heat a wok or skillet over medium-high heat until it is nearly smoking
    and add the oil. When the oil is hot, add the minced ginger. Stir-fry for 10
    seconds, then add the prawns. Stir-fry the prawns briefly, until the shells
    turn a bright pink. Splash the prawns with the rice wine or sherry during
    stir-frying.

3. Push the prawns to the sides of the wok or skillet. Add the butter, green
    chilies, curry leaves, and the garlic in the middle of the pan. Stir-fry for
    about 1 minute, mixing the seasonings with the butter. Add the coconut
    milk and bring to a boil. Stir in the sugar and fish sauce. Stir-fry for another
    minute to mix the prawns with the coconut milk and seasonings. Garnish
    with the coconut flakes and cilantro before serving.

Curry Leaves Curry leaves play a prominent role as a flavor enhancer in Indian cuisine, in the same way that bay leaves do in the West. While dried curry leaves can be used
in long-simmered dishes, it's best to stick with fresh curry leaves for stir-fries. If the fresh
leaves are unavailable, you can substitute fresh basil.

Scallops with Black Beans

*Chinese fermented black beans are available at Asian markets. If unavailable,
Chinese black bean sauce can be used instead—follow the instructions
for adding the sauce in Shrimp in Black Bean Sauce (page 113).*

(page 113)

1. Rinse the scallops under cold running water and pat dry with paper towels. Rinse the black beans under cold running water for 10 minutes, drain, and chop. Place the black beans in a bowl and mash with a fork.

2. Heat a wok or skillet over medium-high heat until it is nearly smoking. Add 2 tablespoons oil. When the oil is hot, add the ginger. Stir-fry for 10 seconds, then add the scallops. Stir-fry for 2 to 3 minutes, until the scallops are white but not too firm. Splash the scallops with the rice wine or sherry while stir-frying. Remove the scallops and drain in a colander or on paper towels.

3. Heat 1 tablespoon oil in the wok or skillet. When the oil is hot, add the garlic and the mashed black beans. Stir-fry for 30 seconds, mixing the garlic with the beans. Add the tomato. Stir-fry for a minute, then add the chicken broth. Bring to a boil.

4. Add the scallops back into the pan. Stir in the soy sauce and brown sugar. Stir in the green onions. Stir-fry briefly to blend the flavors and serve hot.

Serves 2 to 4

1 pound bay scallops

2 tablespoons fermented black beans

3 tablespoons vegetable or peanut oil, divided

1 teaspoon minced ginger

1 tablespoon rice wine or dry sherry

1 teaspoon chopped garlic

1 tomato, cut into thin wedges, each wedge halved

¼ cup chicken broth

1 tablespoon soy sauce

½ teaspoon brown sugar

2 green onions, chopped on the diagonal into 1-inch sections

1 pound (16–20) extra-
large shrimp, shelled and
deveined

2 tablespoons cornstarch, or
as needed

3 tablespoons vegetable or
peanut oil, divided

1 teaspoon minced ginger

2 teaspoons chopped red
chilies

1 tablespoon five-spice
powder

Five-Spiced Shrimp

*This spicy shrimp dish is especially tasty when
served with plain cooked white rice and a salad.*

1. Rinse the shrimp under cold running water and pat dry with paper towels. Place the shrimp in a bowl and dust with the cornstarch.

2. Heat a wok or skillet over medium-high heat until it is nearly smoking. Add 2 tablespoons oil. When the oil is hot, add the minced ginger. Stir-fry for 10 seconds, then add the shrimp. Stir-fry briefly until they turn pink. Remove from the pan and drain in a colander or on paper towels.

3. Heat 1 tablespoon oil in the wok or skillet. When the oil is hot, add the chopped chilies and the five-spice powder. Stir-fry for 30 seconds, then add the shrimp back into the pan. Stir-fry briefly, coating the shrimp with the five-spice powder. Serve hot.

Classifying Shrimp The seafood industry uses a combination of size and number to classify shrimp. Whether shrimp are classified as medium, large, or jumbo depends on the number of that type of shrimp that is needed to make up 1 pound. A 1-pound bag of jumbo shrimp will contain only 16 to 20 shrimp, while a 1-pound bag of medium shrimp will hold between 35 and 40 shrimp.

Shrimp and Asparagus

*For an extra touch, try garnishing the shrimp and asparagus
with 2 tablespoons white sesame seeds before serving. Toast
the seeds first if you want to add a nutty flavor to the dish.*

1. Rinse the shrimp under cold running water and pat dry. Place the shrimp in a bowl and add the rice wine or sherry, salt, and cornstarch. Marinate the shrimp for 15 minutes.

2. Heat a wok or skillet over medium-high heat until it is nearly smoking. Add the oil. When the oil is hot, add the ginger. Let the ginger brown for 2 to 3 minutes, then remove it from the pan.

3. Add the shrimp into the wok or skillet. Stir-fry briefly until the shrimp turns pink and the edges begin to curl. Push the shrimp to the sides of the pan, and add the asparagus in the middle. Stir-fry for a minute, stirring in ½ teaspoon salt if desired. Stir-fry the asparagus until it is tender but still crisp (about 2 minutes total).

4. Stir the Sesame Sauce and add in the middle of the pan, stirring to thicken. Stir-fry briefly to combine all the ingredients and allow the flavors to blend and serve hot.

Serves 2 to 4

1 pound large shrimp, shelled, deveined

1 tablespoon Chinese rice wine or dry sherry

½ teaspoon salt

2 teaspoons cornstarch

3 tablespoons vegetable or peanut oil

2 slices fresh ginger

½ pound fresh asparagus, sliced on the diagonal into 1-inch pieces

½ teaspoon salt, optional

½ recipe Sesame Sauce (page 19)

1 pound fish fillets

2 tablespoons light soy sauce

1 tablespoon Chinese rice wine or dry sherry

½ teaspoon Asian sesame oil

3 teaspoons cornstarch, divided

1/3 cup chicken broth

1 tablespoon oyster sauce

1 teaspoon granulated sugar

4 teaspoons water

3 tablespoons vegetable or peanut oil, divided

2 teaspoons minced ginger, divided

2 ribs celery, cut on the diagonal into ½-inch pieces

¼ teaspoon salt, or to taste

1 red bell pepper, seeded and cut into bite-sized cubes

1–2 tablespoons additional water, optional

Stir-Fried Fish

Firm fish fillets that hold their shape during stir-frying,
such as cod or whitefish, work best in this recipe.

1. Cut the fish into cubes. Place the cubes in a bowl, and add the light soy sauce, rice wine or sherry, Asian sesame oil, and 2 teaspoons cornstarch. Marinate the fish for 15 minutes.

2. Combine the chicken broth, oyster sauce, and sugar in a bowl. In a separate small bowl, dissolve 1 teaspoon cornstarch into the water. Set aside.

3. Heat a wok or skillet over medium-high heat until it is nearly smoking, and add 2 tablespoons oil. When the oil is hot, add half the ginger. Stir-fry for 10 seconds, then add the fish cubes. Stir-fry the fish cubes for about 2 minutes or until they begin to brown. Remove the fish and drain in a colander or on paper towels.

4. Heat 1 tablespoon oil in the wok or skillet. When the oil is hot, add the remainder of the ginger. Stir-fry for 10 seconds, then add the celery. Stir-fry the celery for 1 minute, sprinkling with the salt. Add the red bell pepper, and stir-fry for another minute. Splash the vegetables with 1 to 2 tablespoons of water if they begin to dry out.

5. Push the vegetables to the sides of the pan. Add the chicken broth mixture and bring to a boil. Stir the cornstarch and water and add into the sauce, stirring quickly to thicken. Once the sauce has thickened, add the fish back into the pan. Stir-fry for another minute to mix the ingredients. Serve hot.

Fresh Fish Facts Nothing beats a meal prepared with freshly caught fish. To make sure the fish doesn't lose that fresh flavor by the time you're ready to stir-fry, store it in the coldest part of the refrigerator. Leave the fish refrigerated until you're ready to use it in the recipe.

Salt and Pepper Shrimp

Leaving the shells on the shrimp enhances the attractiveness of this dish, as the shrimp shells turn a vivid orange color. It also helps prevent the shrimp from overcooking.

1. Rinse the shrimp under cold running water and pat dry with paper towels. Dredge the shrimp with the cornstarch. Place the dredged shrimp on a plate next to the stove. Combine the salt and pepper in a small bowl.

2. Heat a wok or skillet over medium-high heat and add the oil. When the oil is hot, carefully add the shrimp. Cook until the shrimp turns pink and the edges begin to curl (about 1 minute). Remove the shrimp and drain in a colander or on paper towels.

3. Remove all but 1½ tablespoons oil from the wok or skillet. Add the ginger, garlic, and shallot. Stir-fry until the shallot begins to soften, then add the shrimp. Stir in the salt and pepper mixture. Stir in the green onion. Stir-fry for another minute to combine the ingredients. Serve hot.

Serves 2 to 4

1 pound medium to large shrimp, shells on

2 tablespoons cornstarch, or as needed

¾ teaspoon kosher or sea salt

¾ teaspoon freshly ground black pepper

2 cups vegetable or peanut oil

1 teaspoon minced ginger

½ teaspoon minced garlic

1 shallot, chopped

1 green onion, finely chopped

1 pound fish fillets

½ teaspoon salt

1 egg white

1 tablespoon Chinese rice wine or dry sherry

3 teaspoons cornstarch, divided

1/3 cup plus 4 teaspoons water, divided

4½ teaspoons oyster sauce

1 teaspoon dark soy sauce

3 tablespoons vegetable or peanut oil, divided

2 thin slices ginger

1 teaspoon minced ginger

½ teaspoon minced garlic

1 green onion, finely chopped

¼ pound fresh mushrooms, thinly sliced

¼ teaspoon black pepper, optional

Stir-Fried Fish with Oyster Sauce

*Ginger and green onion are frequently added to seafood stir-fries
to remove any "fishy" odor that may arise as you cook the fish.*

1. Cut the fish fillets into 1½- to 2-inch squares that are about ½ inch thick. Place the fish cubes in a bowl and add the salt, egg white, rice wine or sherry, and 2 teaspoons cornstarch. Marinate the fish for 15 minutes.

2. Combine ⅓ cup water, oyster sauce, and dark soy sauce in a bowl. In a separate bowl, dissolve 1 teaspoon cornstarch into 4 teaspoons water.

3. Heat a wok or skillet over medium-high heat until it is nearly smoking. Add 2 tablespoons oil. When the oil is hot, add the sliced ginger. Let brown for 2 to 3 minutes, and remove from the pan. Add the minced ginger, stir-fry for 10 seconds, and then add the fish. Let the fish sit in the pan briefly, then gently stir-fry the fish cubes until they turn white and are firm. Remove the fish and drain in a colander or on paper towels.

4. Heat 1 tablespoon oil in the wok or skillet. When the oil is hot, add the garlic and the green onion. Stir-fry for 10 seconds, then add the mushrooms. Stir-fry the mushrooms for 2 minutes or until they begin to darken. Sprinkle ¼ teaspoon black pepper over the mushrooms while stir-frying if desired.

5. Push the mushrooms to the sides of the pan. Add the sauce in the middle of the pan and bring to a boil. Add the cornstarch and water mixture into the sauce, stirring quickly to thicken. When the sauce has thickened, add the fish back into the pan. Stir-fry for another minute to mix everything together. Taste and adjust seasoning if desired. Serve hot.

How to Separate an Egg First, start with eggs that are still cold from the refrigerator. Lightly crack the middle of the egg against the side of a bowl, and use both hands to pull the shell apart so that you are holding half of the shell in each hand. Then, simply move the egg yolk back and forth from one half shell to the other, letting the egg white fall into the bowl.

Shrimp and Spinach Stir-Fry

*Dried shrimp is more than able to hold its own against the pungent
flavor of garlic in this recipe. Be sure not to overcook the spinach.*

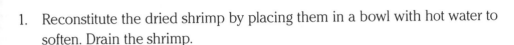

Serves 2 to 4

1 ounce dried shrimp

1½ tablespoons vegetable or
    peanut oil for stir-frying

3 garlic cloves, chopped

½ teaspoon red pepper
    flakes, or to taste

1 pound fresh spinach leaves,
    trimmed

1 tablespoon low-sodium soy
    sauce or fish sauce

1 teaspoon granulated sugar

1. Reconstitute the dried shrimp by placing them in a bowl with hot water to soften. Drain the shrimp.

2. Heat a wok or skillet over medium-high heat until it is nearly smoking. Add the oil. When the oil is hot, add the garlic and red pepper flakes. Stir-fry for 10 seconds, then add the shrimp. Stir-fry briefly (30 seconds to 1 minute), until they release their flavor.

3. Push the shrimp to the sides of the wok or skillet. Add the spinach leaves in the middle of the pan. Stir-fry for about 1 minute, then add the soy sauce and sugar. Continue stir-frying until the spinach turns a bright green, mixing the spinach in with the shrimp. Serve immediately.

Butterfly Shrimp with Mangetout

Butterflying shrimp gives it a more attractive appearance.
Mangetout, or "eat it all," is the French word for snow peas.

Serves 2 to 4

¾ pound large shrimp

1 teaspoon salt

2 teaspoons cornstarch

2 tablespoons chicken broth
    or water

1 tablespoon soy sauce

1 tablespoon Chinese rice
    wine or dry sherry

½ teaspoon brown sugar

3 tablespoons vegetable or
    peanut oil

2 thin slices ginger

1 cup snow peas, trimmed

1 red bell pepper, seeded and
    cut into thin strips

1. Rinse the shrimp under cold running water and pat dry with paper towels. Butterfly the shrimp, place in a bowl, and toss with the salt and cornstarch.

2. Combine the chicken broth or water, soy sauce, rice wine or sherry, and brown sugar in a bowl. Set aside.

3. Heat a wok or skillet over medium-high heat and add 3 tablespoons oil. When the oil is hot, add the ginger. Stir-fry for 10 seconds, then add the shrimp. Stir-fry the shrimp until they turn pink and the edges begin to curl.

4. Push the shrimp to the sides of the wok or skillet. Add the snow peas. Stir-fry for 1 minute, then add the red bell pepper. Stir-fry the vegetables for another minute or until the snow peas turn dark green and the vegetables are tender but still crisp.

5. Add the chicken broth mixture. Stir-fry for 1 to 2 more minutes to blend the flavors. Serve hot with rice or noodles.

How to Butterfly Shrimp   Remove the head and the shell around the body of the shrimp, but leave on the tail. Take a knife and carefully make an incision down the back of the shrimp, taking care not to cut right through. (If the shrimp has not already been deveined, devein it now.) Flatten the shrimp on either side of the cut, so that it fans out. Continue with the remainder of the shrimp.

Black Bean Squid

Scoring the squid tubes makes the edges curl up nicely when they are stir-fried. For extra color, feel free to add a sliced carrot to the stir-fry with the onion.

Serves 3 to 4

1 pound large squid tubes

2 tablespoons Chinese fermented black beans

2 cloves garlic, chopped

2 tablespoons water

¼ cup chicken broth

2 teaspoons dark soy sauce

1 tablespoon Chinese rice wine or dry sherry

4 tablespoons vegetable or peanut oil, divided

2 slices ginger, cut into thin strips

1 onion, thinly sliced

2 red bell peppers, seeded and chopped into large chunks

2 green onions, cut into 1-inch sections

1. Cut the squid tubes in half lengthwise. Score the squid tubes in a crisscross pattern by holding the knife at a 45-degree angle and making a series of cuts, and then holding the knife at a 120-degree angle and making a second series of cuts. Cut the scored squid into 1-inch squares.

2. Rinse the black beans under cold running water for 10 minutes, drain, and chop. Place the black beans in a bowl with the garlic and mash with a fork. Stir in the water. Combine the chicken broth, dark soy sauce, and rice wine or sherry in a bowl.

3. Heat a wok or skillet over medium-high heat until it is nearly smoking. Add 2 tablespoons oil. When the oil is hot, add half of the black bean mixture. Stir-fry for 30 seconds, then add the squid. Stir-fry the squid until it turns white and the edges begin to curl. Remove the squid and drain in a colander or on paper towels.

4. Heat 2 tablespoons oil in the wok or skillet. When the oil is hot, add the remaining black bean mixture and the ginger. Stir-fry for 30 seconds, then add the onion. Stir-fry the onion until it begins to soften, then add the bell pepper. Stir-fry for 1 minute.

5. Pour in the chicken broth mixture and bring to a boil. Add the squid back into the pan. Stir in the green onions. Stir-fry for another minute to blend the flavors. Serve hot.

4 Chinese dried black
    mushrooms

½ pound prawns, shelled,
    deveined

1 tablespoon Chinese rice
    wine or dry sherry

½ teaspoon salt

1 teaspoon cornstarch

¼ cup chicken broth

1½ tablespoons oyster sauce

1 teaspoon granulated sugar

2 tablespoons vegetable or
    peanut oil

1 teaspoon minced ginger

½ teaspoon minced garlic

¼ pound thinly sliced
    mushrooms

Black pepper to taste

1 teaspoon Asian sesame oil

Prawns with Two Kinds of Mushrooms

*If Chinese dried mushrooms are unavailable, you can experiment by using different
combinations of fresh mushrooms, such as button and porcini mushrooms.*

1. Reconstitute the dried black mushrooms by soaking them in boiling water
    for 20 to 30 minutes to soften. Squeeze the excess water out of the mush-
    rooms, remove the stems, and cut into thin strips.

2. Rinse the prawns under cold running water and pat dry with paper towels.
    Place the prawns in a bowl and add the rice wine or sherry, salt, and corn-
    starch. Combine the chicken broth, oyster sauce, and sugar in a bowl. Set
    aside.

3. Heat a wok or skillet over medium-high heat until it is nearly smoking. Add
    the oil. When the oil is hot, add the ginger and garlic. Stir-fry for 10 seconds,
    then add the prawns. Stir-fry the prawns until they turn pink and the edges
    begin to curl.

4. Push the prawns to the sides of the wok or skillet. Add the mushrooms. Stir-
    fry for 2 minutes, stirring in the black pepper. Add the sauce and bring to a
    boil. Stir-fry for another minute to blend the flavors. Remove from the heat
    and stir in the sesame oil. Serve hot.

How to Make Your Own Chicken Broth To make your own chicken broth,
place a whole chicken in a large pot. Add enough water to cover and bring to a boil. Add a
few slices of green onion, ginger, and black pepper. Simmer the chicken for 3 hours, strain,
and refrigerate the liquid in a sealed container until ready to use. (The chicken stock can
also be frozen.)

Shrimp Fried "Rice"

A food processor takes the work out of grating the cauliflower, turning this into a quick and easy dish. If you find the pan is getting a little overcrowded, scramble the eggs separately and add them back into the pan in the final stages of cooking.

1. Break off the florets from the cauliflower and chop into chunks. Chop the core into chunks. Process the florets and core in a blender or food processor, a few pieces at a time, using the "grate" function. Scrape out the bottom of the blender or food processor as needed. Continue until you have 3 cups of grated cauliflower.

2. Rinse the shrimp and pat dry. Lightly beat the eggs in a small bowl, stirring in the black pepper.

3. Heat a wok or skillet over medium-high heat until it is nearly smoking. Add the oil. When the oil is hot, add the garlic. Stir-fry for 10 seconds, then add the shrimp. Stir-fry the shrimp until they turn pink and the edges begin to curl. Push the shrimp to the sides of the pan. Add the onion in the middle, and sprinkle the paprika over the top. Stir-fry the onion for about 2 minutes, until it begins to soften.

4. Add the tomato. Stir-fry for a minute, stirring in the water if it begins to dry out. Push the vegetables to the sides of the pan. Add the eggs in the middle and scramble. Mix the eggs in with the other ingredients.

5. Add the cauliflower. Stir-fry for 1 minute, then stir in the soy sauce. Continue stir-frying, stirring and turning the ingredients over in the pan for 4 to 5 minutes, until the cauliflower is tender but still crisp. Taste and adjust seasonings if desired.

Serves 2 to 4

1 head cauliflower

10 large raw shrimp, deveined

2 eggs

Black pepper to taste

2 tablespoons vegetable or peanut oil

2 cloves garlic

1 onion, chopped

1 tablespoon paprika

1 tomato

1 tablespoon water

1 tablespoon soy sauce

Chapter 6

Pork Meals

½ pound boneless pork

2 tablespoons dark soy sauce, divided

4 teaspoons cider vinegar, divided

1 teaspoon brown sugar

Freshly cracked black or white pepper to taste

2 tablespoons vegetable or peanut oil, divided

½ teaspoon minced ginger

½ teaspoon minced garlic

1 green bell pepper, cut into bite-sized chunks

½ teaspoon salt

½ pound mung bean sprouts

1 tablespoon water or soy sauce, optional

1 teaspoon granulated sugar

Pork with Pepper and Bean Sprouts

To make a meal out of this simple pork dish, serve it with basic stir-fried noodles (page 200) and sliced fresh tomato.

1. Cut the pork into thin strips. Place the pork strips in a bowl and add 1 tablespoon dark soy sauce, 2 teaspoons cider vinegar, brown sugar, and cracked pepper. Marinate the pork for 20 minutes.

2. Heat a wok or skillet over medium-high heat until it is nearly smoking. Add 1 tablespoon oil. When the oil is hot, add the minced ginger. Stir-fry for 10 seconds, then add the pork. Stir-fry the pork for about 2 minutes, or until it is no longer pink and is nearly cooked. Remove the pork from the pan and drain in a colander or on paper towels.

3. Heat 1 tablespoon oil in the same wok or skillet. When the oil is hot, add the minced garlic. Stir-fry for 10 seconds, then add the green pepper and the salt. Stir-fry for 1 minute, then add the mung bean sprouts. Stir-fry for 30 seconds to 1 minute, taking care not to overcook the sprouts. Splash the vegetables with 1 tablespoon water or soy sauce during stir-frying if desired.

4. Push the vegetables to the sides and add the pork back into the pan. Stir in 1 tablespoon dark soy sauce, 2 teaspoons cider vinegar, and the granulated sugar. Stir-fry for 1 to 2 more minutes to heat everything and serve hot.

Using Pork in Stir-Fries Pork butt is an excellent choice for stir-fries, lean but with just enough fat to lend flavor and moisture to the dish. Leaner cuts of pork such as the shoulder and pork tenderloin don't add as much flavor. Use them in recipes that require only a small amount of pork or that have a rich sauce.

Stuffed Green Peppers with Asian Seasonings

In this dish, make sure to use green bell peppers, which are firmer than red bell peppers and hold their shape better during stir-frying.

1. Place the ground pork in a bowl. Stir in the sugar, light soy sauce, dark soy sauce, ginger, and cornstarch. Marinate the pork for 15 minutes.

2. Sprinkle a bit of cornstarch on the inside of the pepper halves (this will help the pork mixture stick to the pepper).

3. Heat a wok or skillet over medium-high heat until it is nearly smoking. Add 1 tablespoon oil. When the oil is hot, add the ground pork. Stir-fry the ground pork until it is no longer pink and is nearly cooked through. Remove from the pan.

4. Spoon a heaping portion of ground pork into each of the green pepper halves.

5. Heat 1 tablespoon oil in the wok. When the oil is hot, add the stuffed green peppers, meat-side down. Let cook for a minute, then add the chicken broth.

6. Bring to a boil. Turn down the heat, cover, and simmer for 5 minutes, adding more broth if needed. Serve hot.

Serves 4

½ pound ground pork

1 teaspoon sugar

1 tablespoon light soy sauce

2 teaspoons dark soy sauce

1 teaspoon minced ginger

1 teaspoon cornstarch

Extra cornstarch, as needed

4 green bell peppers, cut in half and seeded

2 tablespoons vegetable or peanut oil, divided

½ cup chicken broth

¾ pound pork

1 teaspoon salt

1 green bell pepper

1 leek

1 tablespoon light soy sauce

2 teaspoons dark soy sauce

1 tablespoon dry sherry

1 teaspoon granulated sugar

2 tablespoons vegetable or
peanut oil

1 tablespoon chile paste with
garlic

Twice-Cooked Pork

Instead of a regular leek, you can use Chinese leeks in this recipe, also called Chinese chives. Available year-round at Asian markets, they can also sometimes be found in the produce section of local supermarkets during the spring and summer months.

1. Cook the pork in a pot of boiling water for 20 minutes. Drain and allow to cool. Rub the salt over the pork and cut it into thin strips about 2 inches long and 1 inch wide.

2. Seed the bell pepper and cut into thin strips. Cut the leek in half lengthwise and cut into thin strips to match the bell pepper.

3. Combine the light soy sauce, dark soy sauce, sherry, and sugar in a small bowl. Set aside.

4. Heat a wok or skillet over medium-high heat and add oil. When the oil is hot, add the leek. Stir-fry for a minute, then add the green bell pepper.

5. Push the vegetables to the sides of the pan and add the chile paste in the middle. Let cook for about 30 seconds, then add the pork in the middle. Stir-fry, mixing all the ingredients together. Add the sauce. Stir-fry for another minute to heat everything through. Serve hot.

A Classic Szechuan Dish Twice-cooked pork is an example of Szechuan cuisine, known for its liberal use of chilies and spices. Traditionally, the dish is made with pork belly, but pork loin or shoulder can be used instead. Bean sauce, made with soybeans and salt, is frequently added to enhance the "beany" flavor.

Pork Goulash

*Although goulash is frequently made with sour cream, leaving it out makes
this a much healthier dish. A mere 2 tablespoons of sour cream has 50 calories!*

Serves 4 to 6

1 pound lean boneless pork

½ teaspoon salt

¼ teaspoon black pepper

1½ teaspoons cornstarch

6 tablespoons tomato juice

6 tablespoons beef broth

3½ tablespoons olive oil,
   divided

2 cloves garlic, chopped

1 medium white onion,
   chopped

1 tablespoon paprika, or to
   taste

1 cup canned sauerkraut,
   drained

¼ cup sour cream, optional

1. Cut the lean boneless pork into 1-inch cubes. In a large bowl, toss the pork with the salt, black pepper, and cornstarch. Set aside.

2. Combine the tomato juice and beef broth in a small bowl and set aside.

3. Heat a wok or skillet over medium-high heat until it is nearly smoking. Add 1½ tablespoons oil. When the oil is hot, add the pork, laying it flat in the pan. Let sear (brown) briefly, then stir-fry the meat, stirring and tossing until it is no longer pink and is nearly cooked through. Remove the meat from the pan and drain in a colander or on paper towels.

4. Heat 2 tablespoons oil in the wok or skillet. When the oil is hot, add the garlic. Stir-fry for 10 seconds, then add the onion. Sprinkle the paprika over the onion. Stir-fry the onion for 2 minutes or until it begins to soften. Add the sauerkraut. Stir-fry for a minute, mixing the sauerkraut in with the onion.

5. Add the tomato juice and beef broth and bring to a boil. Add the pork back into the pan. Reduce the heat to medium and stir for another 2 minutes to blend all the ingredients together. Taste and adjust the seasoning if desired. If using the sour cream, stir it in just before serving.

Stew Fit for a Cowboy The Hungarian version of stew, goulash, was invented over 1,000 years ago by cowboys looking for a way to cook the dried meat that they carried with them. But it wasn't until paprika was introduced to Hungary in the seventeenth century that Hungarian goulash took on the characteristic sweet and pungent flavor that we know today.

Easy Herbed French Pork Chops

Serve with Stir-Fried Cauliflower (page 260) or Double Nutty Fiddlehead Greens with Sesame (page 257) for a complete meal.

1. Cut the pork into bite-sized cubes. Place the pork cubes in a bowl and add 1½ tablespoons balsamic vinegar, dried rosemary, garlic salt, and the black pepper. Marinate the pork for 15 minutes.

2. Heat a wok or skillet over medium-high heat and add the oil. When the oil is hot, add the crushed garlic. Stir-fry for 10 seconds, then add the pork. Let brown for a minute, then stir-fry the pork, moving it around the pan for 6 to 8 minutes, until it is thoroughly cooked through. Splash the pork chops with 1 tablespoon balsamic vinegar during stir-frying. Serve hot.

Easy Teriyaki Marinated Pork Chops

Teriyaki marinade works well in pork dishes. To increase the flavor, marinate the pork for 30 minutes.

1. Cut the pork chops into cubes. Place the pork in a bowl and add the marinade. Marinate the pork for 15 minutes.

2. Heat a wok or skillet over medium-high heat and add the oil. When the oil is hot, add the minced ginger. Stir-fry until it is aromatic, then add the pork. Let brown for a minute, then stir-fry the pork until it is no longer pink and is nearly cooked. Splash the pork with the rice wine and stir in the green onions. Continue stir-frying for another minute or until the pork is cooked through.

Orange Pork Chops

Sake is the Japanese version of rice wine. If both Chinese rice wine and Japanese sake are unavailable, substitute 2 teaspoons of lemon juice in the marinade.

1. Cut the pork chops into cubes. Place the pork cubes in a bowl and add the soy sauce, rice wine or sake, and cornstarch. Marinate the pork in the refrigerator for 30 minutes.

2. Heat a wok or skillet on medium-high heat. Add 2 tablespoons oil. When the oil is hot, add the pork. Let it brown for a minute, then stir-fry, stirring and moving the pork around the pan until it is no longer pink and is nearly cooked through. Remove the pork and drain in a colander or on paper towels.

3. Heat 1 tablespoon oil in the wok or skillet. When the oil is hot, add the ginger. Stir-fry for 10 seconds, then add the carrots. Stir-fry for 2 minutes, stirring in the salt.

4. Add the Orange Sauce and bring to a boil. Add the pork back into the pan. Stir in the chopped green onions. Stir-fry until everything is mixed together and the pork is cooked through. Serve hot.

Serves 4

4 boneless pork chops

1 tablespoon soy sauce

1 tablespoon Chinese rice wine or Japanese sake

2 teaspoons cornstarch

3 tablespoons vegetable or peanut oil, divided

1 tablespoon minced ginger

4 carrots, cut on the diagonal into thin slices

1 teaspoon salt

Orange Sauce (page 17)

2 green onions, green parts only, finely chopped

Serves 4 to 6

1½ pounds boneless pork

1 teaspoon salt

½ teaspoon black pepper

1 tablespoon chile powder

1 tablespoon cornstarch

3 tablespoons olive oil, divided

1 teaspoon minced ginger

2 tablespoons chopped green chili peppers

1 teaspoon minced garlic

1 onion, chopped

1 green bell pepper, diced

¼ teaspoon salt, optional

1 cup black beans

1 cup diced tomatoes

1 teaspoon cumin

Skillet Chili Pork

Black beans are frequently featured in Mexican cooking. You shouldn't have any trouble finding black beans for this recipe—they are available at most local supermarkets.

1. Cut the pork into cubes. Place the pork cubes in a bowl and add the salt, black pepper, chili powder, and cornstarch. Set aside.

2. Heat a wok or skillet over medium-high heat and add 2 tablespoons oil. When the oil is hot, add the minced ginger. Stir-fry until aromatic, and add the pork. Let sit for a minute, then stir-fry the pork until it is no longer pink and is nearly cooked through. Remove from the pan and drain in a colander or on paper towels.

3. Heat 1 tablespoon oil. When the oil is hot, add the chopped chili peppers. Stir-fry for a few seconds, then add the minced garlic. Add the onion and stir-fry for about 2 minutes, until it is softened. Add the diced green pepper. Stir-fry for a minute, adding salt if desired.

4. Stir in the black beans and diced tomatoes. Stir in the cumin. Bring to a boil. Stir in the cooked pork. Turn down the heat, cover, and simmer for about 5 more minutes, until everything is heated through. Taste and adjust seasoning if desired. Serve hot.

Crying Onion Cure The next time you're peeling and chopping onions, try biting on the end of an unlit wooden match. The tip of the match is dipped in sulfur, which absorbs and neutralizes the sulfuric acid that escapes from the chopped onion before it reaches your nose.

Spicy Orange Pork Chops

Adjust the spiciness of this dish according to your own preference by using hotter or milder chili peppers. Serve Spicy Orange Pork Chops with Stir-Fried Bok Choy (page 264) and cooked rice or noodles for a complete meal.

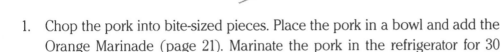

Serves 4

1 pound boneless pork chops

Orange Marinade (page 21)

2 tablespoons vegetable or peanut oil

1 tablespoon minced ginger

2 red chili peppers, chopped

1 teaspoon granulated sugar

3 green onions, green parts only, cut into thirds

1 teaspoon Asian sesame oil

1. Chop the pork into bite-sized pieces. Place the pork in a bowl and add the Orange Marinade (page 21). Marinate the pork in the refrigerator for 30 minutes.

2. Heat a wok or skillet on medium-high heat until it is nearly smoking. Add the oil. When the oil is hot, add the pork. Let it brown for a minute, then stir-fry, stirring and moving the pork around the pan until it is no longer pink and is nearly cooked through.

3. Push the pork to the sides of the wok and tilt the wok so that the remaining oil runs to the middle. Add the minced ginger and chopped chilies into the oil. Let cook for about 30 seconds, then mix with the pork. Stir in the sugar and green onions. Continue stir-frying until the pork is cooked through; remove from the heat and stir in the sesame oil. Serve hot.

¾ pound boneless pork

1 tablespoon light soy sauce

2 tablespoons Chinese
    rice wine or dry sherry,
    divided

1 teaspoon Asian sesame oil

1½ teaspoons cornstarch

½ cup unsalted cashews

2 tablespoons vegetable or
    peanut oil

1 teaspoon minced garlic

1 teaspoon minced ginger

1 teaspoon chile sauce, or to
    taste

1 tablespoon dark soy sauce

1 tablespoon water

1 teaspoon granulated sugar

2 green onions, chopped

Asian Chili Pork

*Chili sauce is available in Asian markets and can frequently be
found in the international section of local supermarkets. For extra
heat, replace the chili sauce with fresh or dried red chili peppers.*

1. Cut the pork into small cubes. Place the pork cubes in a bowl and add the light soy sauce, 1 tablespoon rice wine or dry sherry, the sesame oil, and the cornstarch. Marinate the pork for 15 minutes.

2. Roast the cashews in a heavy frying pan over medium heat, shaking the pan continuously so that the nuts do not burn. Roast until the cashews are browned (about 5 minutes) and remove the cashews from the pan to cool.

3. Heat a wok or skillet on medium-high heat until it is nearly smoking. Add the oil. When the oil is hot, add the garlic. Stir-fry for 10 seconds, then add the pork. Let it brown for a minute, then stir-fry, stirring and moving the pork around the pan until it is no longer pink and is nearly cooked through.

4. Push the pork to the sides of the wok or skillet and add the ginger and chile sauce in the middle. (Add more oil if needed.) Stir for about 30 seconds, then combine with the pork. Stir in 1 tablespoon rice wine or sherry, dark soy sauce, and water. Stir in the sugar and green onions. Add the roasted cashews and continue stir-frying until the pork is cooked through.

Preparing Pork for Stir-Frying Like other types of meat and poultry, pork is easiest to cut if it's partially frozen. Either place the pork in the freezer for 30 minutes to firm it up, or start cutting the pork before it's completely thawed.

Easy Pork and Paprika Stir-Fry

To make this simple stir-fry even easier, feel free to use a stir-fry vegetable mix from the produce section of the supermarket.

Serves 4 to 6

1 pound lean pork

¾ teaspoon salt

¼ teaspoon black pepper

2 teaspoons cornstarch

3½ tablespoons olive oil, divided

2 cloves garlic, chopped, divided

1 medium white onion, chopped

2 teaspoons paprika

1 cup sliced mushrooms

1 red bell pepper, seeded and cut into thin 1½-inch strips

1 cup snow peas, trimmed

½ cup beef broth

1 tablespoon Worcestershire sauce

1 teaspoon granulated sugar

1. Cut the pork into 1½- to 2-inch cubes. Place the pork cubes in a bowl and toss with the salt, black pepper, and cornstarch. Let the pork stand for 15 minutes.

2. Heat a wok or skillet over medium-high heat until it is nearly smoking. Add 2 tablespoons oil. When the oil is hot, add half the garlic. Stir-fry for 10 seconds, then add the pork. Let sit briefly, then stir-fry the pork, stirring and tossing until it is no longer pink and it is nearly cooked through. Remove the meat and drain in a colander or on paper towels.

3. Heat 1½ tablespoons oil in the wok or skillet. When the oil is hot, add the remaining garlic. Stir-fry for 10 seconds, then add the onion. Sprinkle the paprika over the onion and stir-fry for 2 minutes or until the onion begins to soften.

4. Add the mushrooms. Stir-fry for a minute, then add the red bell pepper and the snow peas. Stir-fry for another minute or until the mushrooms have darkened and the snow peas and red bell pepper are tender but still crisp. Splash the vegetables with a bit of the beef broth if they begin to dry out during stir-frying.

5. Add the beef broth into the pan and bring to a boil. Add the pork back into the pan, stirring to mix it with the other ingredients. Stir in the Worcestershire sauce and the sugar. Stir-fry for 1 to 2 more minutes to mix everything together. Serve hot.

1 pound boneless pork

1½ tablespoons soy sauce

1 tablespoon dry sherry

1 teaspoon Asian sesame oil

1 tablespoon minced ginger

5 teaspoons cornstarch,
    divided

½ cup chicken broth

1 tablespoon oyster sauce

3 tablespoons vegetable or
    peanut oil, divided

2 cloves garlic, crushed

6 ounces snow peas,
    trimmed

½ teaspoon salt, or to taste

1 red bell pepper, seeded and
    cut into bite-sized pieces

½ cup canned water
    chestnuts, drained and
    rinsed

2 tablespoons sesame seeds

Sesame Pork

*If you have trouble finding the snow peas called for in this recipe,
you may replace them with sugar snap peas or 1 green bell pepper.*

1. Cut the boneless pork into cubes. Place the pork cubes in a bowl and add the soy sauce, dry sherry, sesame oil, minced ginger, and 2 teaspoons cornstarch. Marinate the pork in the refrigerator for 30 minutes.

2. Combine the chicken broth and oyster sauce in a small bowl. Whisk in 3 teaspoons cornstarch.

3. Heat a wok or skillet on medium-high heat until it is almost smoking. Add 1½ tablespoons oil. When the oil is hot, add the crushed garlic. Stir-fry for 10 seconds and add the snow peas. Stir-fry for 1 minute, stirring in the salt. Add the red bell pepper and the canned water chestnuts. Stir-fry for another minute, then remove the vegetables.

4. Heat 1½ tablespoons oil in the same wok or skillet. When the oil is hot, add the marinated pork. Let sit briefly, then stir-fry until it is no longer pink and is nearly cooked. Push the pork to the sides of the pan.

5. Add the sauce into the middle, stirring quickly to thicken. When the sauce has thickened, add the stir-fried vegetables back into the pan. Stir-fry for another couple of minutes to heat everything through. Garnish with the toasted sesame seeds before serving.

Open Sesame! If you're familiar with only white sesame seeds, you might be surprised to learn that there are also yellow, beige, and black sesame seeds. All come from different varieties of the sesame plant. According to food historians, the expression "Open Sesame" may come from when the pods of the sesame plant burst open, spilling out the ripened sesame seeds.

Pineapple Pork

To lend extra color to this dish, use 1 red and 1 green bell pepper. Stir-fry the green bell pepper for a few seconds before adding the red bell pepper to the wok or skillet.

―――――

1. Cut the pork into thin strips 1½ to 2 inches long. Place the pork in a bowl and add the oyster sauce, rice wine or dry sherry, and cornstarch. Marinate the pork for 15 minutes.

2. Combine the chicken broth, dark soy sauce, and sugar in a bowl. Set aside.

3. Heat a wok or skillet on medium-high heat until it is nearly smoking. Add 1½ tablespoons oil. When the oil is hot, add the ginger. Stir-fry for 10 seconds, then add the pork. Let brown for a minute, then stir-fry the pork, moving it around the pan until it is no longer pink and is nearly cooked. Remove and drain in a colander or on paper towels.

4. Heat 1½ tablespoons oil in the wok or skillet. When the oil is hot, add the garlic and the green onions. Stir-fry for 10 seconds, then add the bell peppers. Stir-fry for 1 to 2 minutes, until the peppers are tender but still crisp. Stir in the pineapple chunks.

5. Pour the sauce over the vegetables and heat to boiling. Add the pork back into the pan. Stir-fry for 1 to 2 more minutes to heat everything through. Remove from the heat and stir in the Asian sesame oil. Serve hot.

Serves 3 to 4

- ¾ pound lean pork
- 1 tablespoon oyster sauce
- 1 tablespoon Chinese rice wine or dry sherry
- 1½ teaspoons cornstarch
- ¼ cup chicken broth
- 1 tablespoon dark soy sauce
- 1 teaspoon granulated sugar
- 3 tablespoons vegetable or peanut oil, divided
- 1 teaspoon minced ginger
- 1 teaspoon minced garlic
- 2 green onions, cut on the diagonal into 2-inch pieces
- 2 bell peppers, seeded and cut into thin strips
- 1 cup pineapple chunks, drained
- 1 teaspoon Asian sesame oil

Serves 2

½ pound lean boneless pork

2 teaspoons dark soy sauce

2 teaspoons light soy sauce

4 teaspoons cornstarch, divided

¼ cup reserved lychee juice

1½ tablespoons vegetable or peanut oil

1 teaspoon minced ginger

½ cup canned lychees

Romantic Pork with Lychees

Native to China, lychees have a soft, juicy flesh and sweet flavor that goes nicely with pork. Canned lychees are available year-round in Asian markets and in many local supermarkets.

1. Cut the pork into 1-inch cubes. Place the pork cubes in a bowl and add the dark soy sauce, light soy sauce, and 1 teaspoon cornstarch. Marinate the pork for 15 minutes. Whisk 3 teaspoons cornstarch into the reserved lychee juice.

2. Heat a wok or skillet over medium-high heat until it is nearly smoking. Add the oil. When the oil is hot, add the minced ginger. Stir-fry for 10 seconds, then add the pork. Stir-fry the pork until it is no longer pink and is nearly cooked through.

3. Add the lychees into the same wok or skillet. Stir the lychee juice and cornstarch and add into the pan, stirring to thicken. Stir-fry until the pork is cooked through and all the ingredients are mixed together. Serve hot.

Romantic Lychees The small red lychee nut, which is shaped like a heart and has sweet-tasting flesh, is a symbol of love in Chinese culture. Appropriately for a romantic fruit, lychees are also "heart healthy." Each lychee fruit contains less than 10 calories and is a good source of vitamin C and vitamins B2 and B3.

Stir-Fried Lychee Pork with Vegetables

If you can find fresh lychees, feel free to use them in this recipe—just peel the skin off the lychee and remove the seed in the middle. Instead of canned lychee juice, substitute ¼ cup water and 1 tablespoon granulated sugar.

1. Cut the pork into cubes. Place the pork cubes in a bowl and add 1½ tablespoons soy sauce, rice wine or sherry, Asian sesame oil, black pepper, and 2 teaspoons cornstarch. Marinate the pork for 20 minutes.

2. Combine the lychee juice and 1 tablespoon soy sauce in a bowl. Set aside. Dissolve 1 tablespoon cornstarch in the water. Set aside.

3. Heat a wok or skillet over medium-high heat until it is nearly smoking and add 2 tablespoons oil. When the oil is hot, add the garlic. Stir-fry for 10 seconds, then add the pork. Let brown for a minute, then stir-fry the pork, moving it around the pan until it is no longer pink and is nearly cooked. Remove and drain in a colander or on paper towels.

4. Heat 1 tablespoon oil in the same wok or skillet. When the oil is hot, add the minced ginger. Stir-fry for 10 seconds, then add the chopped shallot. Stir-fry, moving the shallot around the pan until it begins to soften, then add the red bell peppers. Stir-fry until they are tender but still crisp, then stir in the lychees.

5. Push the fruit and vegetables to the sides and add the lychee-juice mixture in the middle. Bring to a boil, and add the cornstarch and water mixture, stirring quickly to thicken. When the sauce thickens, add the pork back into the pan. Stir-fry for about 2 more minutes to mix the sauce in with the other ingredients. Stir in the green onions. Serve hot.

Serves 4

1 pound pork tenderloin

2½ tablespoons soy sauce, divided

1 tablespoon Chinese rice wine or dry sherry

1 teaspoon Asian sesame oil

Black pepper to taste

1 tablespoon plus 2 teaspoons cornstarch, divided

¼ cup reserved canned lychee juice

¼ cup water

3 tablespoons vegetable or peanut oil, divided

2 cloves garlic, minced

1 teaspoon minced ginger

1 shallot, chopped

2 red bell peppers, seeded and cubed

½ cup canned lychees

2 green onions, rinsed and finely chopped

1 pound boneless pork

1 teaspoon salt

½ teaspoon black pepper

1 tablespoon cornstarch

3 tablespoons chicken broth

1 tablespoon soy sauce

1 tablespoon dry sherry

3 tablespoons olive oil, divided

3 cloves garlic, chopped, divided

1 onion, chopped

1 teaspoon chile powder, or to taste

¼ teaspoon ground cumin, or to taste

6 tomatillos, thinly sliced

Black pepper to taste

Chile Verde Stir-Fry

Pork is paired with tomatillos, onion, and garlic in this easy stir-fried version of chile verde stew. Instead of chili powder, you may add either hot red jalapeño peppers or milder green Anaheim chilies.

1. Cut the boneless pork into cubes. Place the pork cubes in a bowl and add the salt, pepper, and cornstarch. Let the pork stand for 20 minutes. Combine the chicken broth, soy sauce, and dry sherry in a small bowl. Set aside.

2. Heat a wok or skillet over medium-high heat until it is nearly smoking. Add 2 tablespoons oil. When the oil is hot, add half the garlic. Stir-fry for 10 seconds, then add the pork. Lay flat for a minute, then stir-fry, moving the pork around the pan until it is no longer pink and is nearly cooked. Remove and drain in a colander or on paper towels.

3. Heat 1 tablespoon oil in the wok or skillet. When the oil is hot, add the remaining garlic. Stir-fry for 10 seconds, then add the onion. Stir-fry for about 2 minutes, until the onion begins to soften, stirring in the chili powder and ground cumin. Add the tomatillos. Stir-fry for 2 minutes, or until the tomatillos are tender but not too soft.

4. Add the pork back into the pan. Stir in the chicken broth mixture. Stir-fry for 1 to 2 more minutes, to combine all the flavors. Taste and adjust seasonings, adding black pepper if desired. Serve hot.

Terrific Tomatillos Sometimes called husk tomatoes, tomatillos are not tomatoes at all, but close relatives. Their papery outer husk makes tomatillos easy to distinguish from unripened green tomatoes, used to make Quick Fried Green Tomatoes (page 256). While fresh tomatillos can be hard to find, canned tomatillos are readily available in many supermarkets.

Asian Skillet Pork with Mushrooms

Instead of button mushrooms, you can use a combination of dried
Chinese black mushrooms and fresh mushrooms in this dish if desired.

1. Cut the pork chops into bite-sized cubes. Place the pork cubes in a bowl and add the oyster sauce, sherry, sesame oil, and cornstarch. Marinate the pork for 15 minutes.

2. Combine the chicken broth, dark soy sauce, and sugar in a small bowl. Set aside.

3. Heat a wok or skillet over medium-high heat until it is nearly smoking. Add 3 tablespoons oil. When the oil is hot, add the ginger. Stir-fry for 10 seconds, then add the pork cubes. Let sit for a minute, then stir-fry, moving the pork around the pan until it is no longer pink and is nearly cooked. Remove and drain in a colander or on paper towels.

4. Heat 1 tablespoon oil in the same wok or skillet. When the oil is hot, add the garlic and the chile paste. Stir-fry for 10 seconds, then add the mushrooms. Stir-fry for about 3 minutes, until the mushrooms have darkened, then add the sauce. Add the pork back into the pan. Heat everything through and serve hot.

Freezing Chicken Broth It's easy to freeze leftover chicken broth—just pour the unused broth into ice-cube trays and freeze until needed. For recipe measuring purposes, keep in mind that each frozen cube contains approximately 1 ounce of broth.

Serves 4

4 boneless pork chops

1½ tablespoons oyster sauce

1 tablespoons dry sherry

1½ teaspoons Asian sesame oil

1 tablespoon cornstarch

1/3 cup chicken broth

2 tablespoons dark soy sauce

1½ teaspoons granulated sugar

4 tablespoons vegetable or peanut oil, divided

2 teaspoons minced ginger

1 teaspoon minced garlic

½ teaspoon chile paste, or to taste

6 ounces button mushrooms, thinly sliced

¾ pound lean pork

1 tablespoon soy sauce

1 tablespoon rice wine or dry sherry

1 teaspoon granulated sugar

1 teaspoon Asian sesame oil

Freshly ground white pepper to taste

1½ teaspoons cornstarch

1 pound bok choy

3 tablespoons chicken broth

1 tablespoon oyster sauce

4 tablespoons vegetable or peanut oil, divided

1 teaspoon minced ginger

2 cloves garlic, crushed

½ teaspoon salt

2 green onions, cut on the diagonal into 1-inch pieces

Pork with Baby Bok Choy

If you like, thicken the sauce in this recipe by stirring in 1 teaspoon cornstarch mixed with 2 teaspoons water at the end of cooking. Stir quickly until the sauce has thickened, and serve immediately.

1. Cut the pork into cubes. Place the pork in a bowl and add the soy sauce, rice wine, sugar, sesame oil, white pepper, and cornstarch. Marinate the pork for 20 minutes.

2. Remove the base of the bok choy. Wash the bok choy and drain thoroughly. Separate the leaves from the stalks. Cut the stalks diagonally into 2-inch pieces. Cut the leaves crosswise into 2-inch pieces. Combine the chicken broth with the oyster sauce in a bowl. Set aside.

3. Heat a wok or skillet over medium-high heat until it is almost smoking. Add 2 tablespoons oil. When the oil is hot, add the ginger. Stir-fry for 10 seconds, then add the pork. Let sit briefly, then stir-fry the pork, stirring and moving it around the pan until it is no longer pink and is nearly cooked. Remove the pork and drain in a colander or on paper towels.

4. Add 2 tablespoons oil to the wok or skillet. When the oil is hot, add the crushed garlic. Stir-fry for 10 seconds, then add the bok choy stalks. Add the salt. Stir-fry for 1 minute, then add the leaves. Stir-fry for 1 more minute, or until the bok choy turns bright green.

5. Add the chicken broth/oyster sauce mixture into the wok. Bring to a boil. Add the pork back into the pan. Stir in the green onions. Stir-fry for another minute and serve hot.

Easy Mu Shu Pork

Traditionally, Mu Shu Pork is made with colorful Chinese vegetables such as dried mushrooms, cloud ear fungus, and lily buds. Canned bamboo shoots and fresh mushrooms make quick and easy alternatives while still providing color and texture.

Serves 2 to 3

½ pound pork tenderloin

1 tablespoon light soy sauce

2 teaspoons Chinese rice wine or dry sherry

½ teaspoon Asian sesame oil

1 teaspoon cornstarch

½ cup canned bamboo shoots

2 green onions

¼ cup water

1 tablespoon hoisin sauce

2 teaspoons dark soy sauce

1 teaspoon granulated sugar

3 eggs

Salt to taste

4½ tablespoons vegetable or peanut oil, divided

½ teaspoon minced ginger

½ cup thinly sliced fresh mushrooms

1. Cut the pork into thin shreds. Place the pork shreds in a bowl and add the soy sauce, rice wine or sherry, sesame oil, and cornstarch. Marinate the pork for 20 minutes.

2. Rinse the bamboo shoots under cold running water and drain thoroughly. Cut the slices into thin shreds. Rinse the green onions, drain, and shred. Combine the water, hoisin sauce, dark soy sauce, and sugar in a small bowl. Set aside. Lightly beat the eggs, stirring in the salt to taste.

3. Heat a wok or skillet over medium-high heat until it is nearly smoking. Add 2 tablespoons oil. When oil is hot, turn the heat down to medium and add the beaten eggs. Scramble quickly and remove. Clean out the pan.

4. Heat 1 tablespoon oil in the wok or skillet. When the oil is hot, add the minced ginger and the green onion. Stir-fry for 10 seconds, then add the pork. Stir-fry until the pork is no longer pink and is nearly cooked through. Remove and drain in a colander or on paper towels.

5. Heat 1½ tablespoons oil. Add the bamboo shoots and ¼ teaspoon salt. Stir-fry for a minute and add the mushrooms. Stir-fry for a minute, then add the sauce. Bring to a boil, then add the pork back into the pan. Stir in the eggs. Cook for another minute to mix everything together and serve hot.

Serving Mu Shu Pork In restaurants, this dish would be served with thin mandarin pancakes, green onion "brushes," and sweet and spicy hoisin sauce. Diners use the brushes to spread hoisin sauce on the pancake, add some mu shu pork, and roll up the pancake like a tortilla. When preparing Mu Shu Pork at home, you don't need to use green onion brushes, and store-bought tortillas make a convenient substitute for the pancakes.

1 pound lean pork

1 tablespoon dark soy sauce

1 tablespoon Chinese rice wine or dry sherry

1 teaspoon Asian sesame oil

2 teaspoons cornstarch

3½ tablespoons vegetable or peanut oil, divided

2 teaspoons minced garlic

1 tablespoon minced ginger

1 red bell pepper, cut into bite-sized cubes

3 plums, pits removed and cut in half

¼ cup water

¼ cup orange, peach, or plum juice

1 tablespoon granulated sugar

¼ teaspoon allspice

¼ teaspoon salt

Plum Pork

Allspice, which is an important element of this recipe, is not one single spice. As the name implies, allspice is a combination of spices, including nutmeg, cloves, and cinnamon.

1. Cut the pork into cubes. Place the pork cubes in a bowl and add the dark soy sauce, rice wine or dry sherry, sesame oil, and cornstarch. Marinate the pork for 20 minutes.

2. Heat a wok or skillet over medium-high heat until it is nearly smoking. Add 2 tablespoons oil. When the oil is hot, add the minced garlic. Stir-fry for 10 seconds, then add the pork. Stir-fry the pork until it is no longer pink and is nearly cooked through. Remove the pork from the pan and drain in a colander or on paper towels.

3. Add 1½ tablespoons oil in the wok or skillet. When the oil is hot, add the ginger. Stir-fry for 10 seconds, then add the red bell pepper. Stir-fry for a minute, or until the bell pepper is tender but still firm.

4. Add the plums and stir-fry for a minute. Add the water, fruit juice, and the sugar. Bring to a boil, stirring to dissolve the sugar. Add the pork into the pan. Stir in the allspice and the salt. Stir-fry for 1 to 2 more minutes to mix everything together. Taste and adjust seasoning if desired.

Pork Chop Suey

There are no hard-and-fast rules for how to make chop suey. Feel free to make substitutions using whatever vegetables you have on hand.

—————

1. Cut the pork into thin strips and place in a bowl. Add 1 tablespoon oyster sauce, rice wine or dry sherry, black pepper, and 1½ teaspoons cornstarch. Marinate the pork for 20 minutes. Combine the chicken broth and 2 tablespoons oyster sauce in a small bowl and whisk in 2 teaspoons cornstarch.

2. Heat a wok or skillet over medium-high heat until it is nearly smoking and add 2 tablespoons oil. When the oil is hot, add the garlic. Stir-fry for 10 seconds, then add the pork. Let sit for a minute, then stir-fry until the pork is no longer pink and is nearly cooked through. Remove the pork from the pan and drain in a colander or on paper towels.

3. Heat 1½ tablespoons oil in the wok or skillet. When the oil is hot, add the ginger. Stir-fry for 10 seconds, then add the onion and the celery. Stir-fry for a couple of minutes or until the onion is softened. Add the snow peas and the bell pepper. Stir-fry until the vegetables are tender but still crisp, adding more oil if needed.

4. Push the vegetables to the sides of the pan. Add the sauce in the middle, stirring continually to thicken. When the sauce has thickened, add the pork back into the pan. Stir-fry for 2 more minutes to mix everything together and make sure the pork is cooked through. Serve hot.

Chop Suey History There are several legends surrounding the origins of this popular American-Chinese dish. Some credit the chef of a visiting Chinese dignitary with creating the dish in the late 1800s. Others believe the idea of stir-frying bits of meat and vegetables in a flavorful gravy began with early Cantonese immigrants who came to North America to work on the railroads.

Serves 3 to 4

¾ pound lean pork

3 tablespoons oyster sauce, divided

1 tablespoon Chinese rice wine or dry sherry

Black pepper to taste

3½ teaspoons cornstarch, divided

1/3 cup chicken broth

3½ tablespoons vegetable or peanut oil, or as needed, divided

2 cloves garlic, chopped

2 thin slices ginger, chopped

½ onion, chopped

2 ribs celery, cut on the diagonal into ½-inch slices

4 ounces snow peas, trimmed

1 red bell pepper, cut into bite-sized chunks

¾ pound cooked ham

1 tablespoon vegetable or peanut oil

1 tablespoon minced ginger

1 tablespoon Chinese rice wine or dry sherry

2 cups mung bean sprouts, rinsed and drained

1 teaspoon granulated sugar

Ham with Mung Bean Sprouts

For a more attractive, neater appearance to this dish, trim the ends of the mung bean sprouts. Mung bean sprouts that have been trimmed in this way are called silver sprouts.

1. Slice the ham into thin strips about 1½ to 2 inches long.

2. Heat a wok or skillet over medium-high heat until it is almost smoking and add the oil. When the oil is hot, add the ginger. Stir-fry for 10 seconds, then add the cooked ham. Stir-fry for a minute, splashing the ham with the rice wine or sherry.

3. Add the mung bean sprouts. Stir-fry for 30 seconds to 1 minute, stirring in the sugar. Serve hot.

2 tablespoons vegetable or peanut oil

½ teaspoon minced garlic

½ teaspoon minced ginger

1 shallot, chopped

4 ounces pancetta, chopped

1 cup fresh peas

1–2 tablespoons chicken broth, if needed

Simple Peas and Pancetta

The sweet taste of the fresh peas nicely complements the salty taste of pancetta in this easy stir-fry dish.

1. Heat a wok or skillet over medium-high heat until it is nearly smoking and add the oil. When the oil is hot, add the garlic and the ginger. Stir-fry for 10 seconds, then add the shallot. Stir-fry for about 1 minute, until it begins to soften.

2. Add the pancetta. Stir-fry for 1 minute, then add the peas. Stir-fry for another minute, splashing the peas with the chicken broth if they begin to dry out during stir-frying. Serve hot.

Gingered Pork

The clean, sharp taste of ginger and its spicy scent add
wonderful flavor to the pork in this simple stir-fried dish.

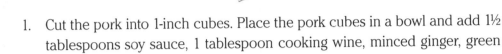

Serves 3 to 4

1 pound pork tenderloin

2½ tablespoons Japanese
    soy sauce (shoyu), divided

2 tablespoons cooking wine,
    divided

1 tablespoon minced ginger

2 green onions, finely
    chopped

2 teaspoons cornstarch

½ pound shiitake
    mushrooms

3 tablespoons vegetable or
    peanut oil, divided

1 clove garlic, crushed

Black pepper to taste

1. Cut the pork into 1-inch cubes. Place the pork cubes in a bowl and add 1½ tablespoons soy sauce, 1 tablespoon cooking wine, minced ginger, green onions, and the cornstarch. Marinate the pork for 20 minutes.

2. Remove the stems from the shiitake mushrooms and cut into wedges.

3. Heat a wok or skillet over medium-high heat until it is nearly smoking. Add 2 tablespoons oil. When the oil is hot, add the marinated pork. Let sit for a minute, then stir-fry until the pork is no longer pink and is nearly cooked. Remove from the pan and drain in a colander or on paper towels.

4. Heat 1 tablespoon oil in the same wok or skillet. When the oil is hot, add the crushed garlic. Stir-fry for 10 seconds, then add the mushrooms. Stir-fry the mushrooms until they have browned and most of the liquid has evaporated.

5. Add the pork back into the pan. Stir-fry the pork and mushrooms for another minute, splashing with 1 tablespoon cooking wine and 1 tablespoon soy sauce. Season with black pepper if desired. Serve hot.

Japanese Soy Sauce Like Chinese soy sauce, Japanese soy sauce is divided into two main varieties—light and dark. However, while Chinese soy sauce is made with soybeans, Japanese soy sauce is made with wheat. This gives Japanese soy sauce, also called shoyu, a more intense flavor. While Chinese soy sauce can be used instead of Japanese soy sauce in a pinch, the two aren't really interchangeable.

Serves 4 to 6

1 pound boneless pork

½ teaspoon dried parsley

½ teaspoon dried basil

1 teaspoon dried rosemary

½ teaspoon salt

Black pepper to taste

2 teaspoons cornstarch

6 tablespoons burgundy

6 tablespoons beef broth

3 tablespoons olive oil, divided

1 teaspoon minced ginger

½ pound fresh button mushrooms, sliced

1 teaspoon minced garlic

2 shallots, chopped

Pork Chops with Burgundy Mushrooms

Fresh parsley or rosemary makes the perfect garnish for this dish. Either one will add a bit of color and an additional layer of flavor. Serve with cooked white or brown rice.

1. Cut the pork into 1-inch cubes. Place the pork cubes in a bowl and add the dried parsley, basil, rosemary, salt, pepper, and cornstarch. Combine the burgundy and beef broth in a small bowl and set aside.

2. Heat a wok or skillet over medium-high heat until it is nearly smoking. Add 1 tablespoon oil. When the oil is hot, add the minced ginger. Stir-fry for 10 seconds, then add the mushrooms. Stir-fry for about 2 minutes, until the mushrooms have browned. Remove the mushrooms from the pan.

3. Heat 2 tablespoons oil in the wok or skillet. When the oil is hot, add the garlic. Stir-fry for 10 seconds, then add the cubed pork. Let brown for a minute, then stir-fry, stirring and moving the pork around the pan, until it is no longer pink and is nearly cooked. Remove the pork and drain in a colander or on paper towels.

4. Add the broth mixture and bring to a boil. Deglaze the pan, using a spatula to scrape up the browned bits of food. Add the mushrooms and the shallots. Stir-fry for a couple of minutes, then add the pork. Cook, stirring occasionally, until the liquid is almost evaporated (4 to 5 minutes). Taste and adjust seasoning, adding salt or pepper if desired. Serve hot.

Pork with Peking Sauce

Vary the vegetables in this dish as desired. Both Stir-Fried Zucchini (page 250)
or ½ green bell pepper and ½ red bell pepper would work well in this recipe.

Serves 2 to 4

1. Prepare the Peking Sauce up through step 2.

2. Cut the pork into bite-sized cubes. Place the pork cubes in a bowl and add the rice wine or sherry, dark soy sauce, white pepper, and the cornstarch. Marinate the pork for 20 minutes.

3. Heat a wok or skillet over medium-high heat until it is nearly smoking and add 2 tablespoons oil. When the oil is hot, add half the minced ginger and garlic. Stir-fry for 10 seconds, then add the pork. Stir-fry the pork until it is no longer pink and is nearly cooked through. Remove the pork from the pan and drain in a colander or on paper towels.

4. Heat 1 tablespoon oil in the wok or skillet. When the oil is hot, add the remaining ginger and garlic. Stir-fry for 10 seconds, then add the shallots. Stir-fry the shallots for about 1 minute, until they begin to soften. Add the baby corn. Stir-fry for a minute, splashing with 1 tablespoon soy sauce if the corn begins to dry out.

5. Add the Peking Sauce and bring to a boil. Add the pork back into the pan. Stir-fry for 1 to 2 more minutes to heat everything through and make sure the pork is cooked. Taste and adjust seasoning if desired.

What Is a Shallot? In the culinary world the shallot is viewed as an upscale version of an onion, although both come from the lily family. Shallots are smaller and milder than onions because of the way the shallot propagates—each shallot bulb divides into several smaller bulbs. The matured shallots have a more delicate flavor and a less pronounced "oniony" smell than regular onions.

Peking Sauce (page 22, but
    see instructions in step 1)

¾ pound lean pork

1 tablespoon Chinese rice
    wine or dry sherry

2 teaspoons dark soy sauce

¼ teaspoon freshly ground
    white pepper, or to taste

1½ teaspoons cornstarch

3 tablespoons vegetable or
    peanut oil, divided

2 slices ginger, minced,
    divided

2 cloves garlic, minced,
    divided

2 shallots, chopped

1 (8-ounce) can baby corn,
    drained

1 tablespoon soy sauce, if
    needed

Yields 4 omelets

12 eggs

¾ cup milk

½ teaspoon salt, or to taste

½ teaspoon black pepper, or to taste

Vegetable or peanut oil, as needed

2 thin slices ginger

1 cup finely chopped onion

1 teaspoon chili powder, or to taste

½ cup diced green bell pepper

½ cup diced red bell pepper

3½ ounces cooked ham, diced (about ⅔ cup)

Spicy Stir-Fried Omelet with Ham

Stir-frying the vegetables seals in their juices, adding extra flavor to this omelet recipe. Try stir-frying vegetables first whenever you're planning to add them to a fried egg dish, from the classic French omelet to a Mexican frittata.

1. In a large bowl, lightly beat the eggs and milk. Stir in the salt and black pepper.

2. Heat a wok or skillet over medium-high heat until it is nearly smoking and add 2 tablespoons oil. When the oil is hot, add the ginger. Brown the ginger for 2 to 3 minutes, and then remove it from the pan.

3. Add the onion to the wok or skillet. Sprinkle the chili powder over the onion and stir-fry until the onion begins to soften (about 2 minutes). Add the green bell pepper. Stir-fry briefly, then add the red bell pepper. Stir-fry for a minute, then add the cooked ham. Stir-fry for another minute or until the vegetables are crisp but tender. Remove the ham and vegetables from the pan. Drain in a colander or on paper towels.

4. Add the stir-fried meat and vegetables to the egg mixture.

5. Heat 1 tablespoon oil in the wok or skillet. Pour in one-quarter of the egg mixture. Cook until the edges begin to firm, tilting the pan so that the egg mixture is evenly distributed throughout the pan. Turn down the heat to medium if the bottom is cooking too quickly.

6. When the omelet is evenly cooked, carefully use a spatula to fold it over. Slide the omelet out of the pan and onto a plate. Continue cooking the remaining omelets, cleaning out the pan and adding more oil as needed.

Roast Pork Omelet

Pork is not often used in American omelets, but you may want to give it a try.
Roast pork and Chinese oyster sauce lend a savory flavor to this quick and easy omelet.

Yields 2 omelets

6 large eggs

6 tablespoons milk

¼ teaspoon salt

¼ teaspoon black pepper

2 tablespoons oyster sauce

4 tablespoons vegetable or
   peanut oil, or as needed,
   divided

2 thin slices ginger

¼ cup finely chopped onion

¾ cup diced roast pork

1. In a medium bowl, lightly beat the eggs and milk. Stir in the salt, black pepper, and oyster sauce.

2. Heat a wok or skillet over medium-high heat until it is nearly smoking and add 2 tablespoons oil. When the oil is hot, add the ginger. Brown the ginger for 2 to 3 minutes, and remove it from the pan. (This is to flavor the oil.) Add the onion and stir-fry until it begins to soften (about 2 minutes). Add the roast pork and stir-fry briefly (less than a minute). Remove the onion and roast pork from the pan. Drain in a colander or on paper towels.

3. Add the stir fried pork and onion to the egg mixture.

4. Heat 2 tablespoons oil in the wok or skillet. Pour in half of the egg mixture. Cook until the edges begin to firm, tilting the pan so that the egg mixture is evenly distributed throughout the pan. Turn down the heat to medium if the bottom is cooking too quickly.

5. When the omelet is evenly cooked, carefully use a spatula to fold it over. Slide the omelet out of the pan and onto a plate. Cook the second omelet, cleaning out the pan and adding more oil as needed.

1 pound lean pork

2 portions Korean-Inspired
Marinade (page 18),
divided

2 tablespoons vegetable oil

1 tablespoon Korean chile
paste

2 cloves garlic, crushed

2 medium zucchini, cut on
the diagonal into ¼-inch
slices

1 tablespoon toasted sesame
seeds

Korean-Style Pork Stir-Fry

*Made with red chili peppers and soybean paste, Korean chile paste (called
gochujang) is similar to Japanese miso and adds a distinct taste to this stir-fry.*

1. Cut the pork into thin strips, about 1½ inches long and ⅛ inch wide. Place
   the pork strips in a large resealable plastic bag. Pour in 1 portion of the
   marinade. Marinate the pork for at least 2 hours, turning the bag occasionally so that all the pork is evenly coated.

2. Heat a wok or skillet over medium-high heat until it is nearly smoking and
   add the oil. When the oil is hot, add the pork. (Discard the marinade.) Stir-
   fry the pork until it is no longer pink, then add the chile paste and garlic.
   Stir-fry briefly, then push the pork to the sides of the pan.

3. Add the zucchini to the wok or skillet. Stir-fry for a minute, then add the
   remaining portion of marinade. Bring to a boil and continue stir-frying until
   the zucchini turns a darker green and is tender but still crisp and the pork
   is cooked through. Remove from the pan and garnish with the toasted
   sesame seeds.

Pork and Apple Stir-Fry

Paprika lends a vivid red color and strong flavor to this quick and easy stir-fry. Be sure to use fresh paprika that you've purchased within the last six months, because stale paprika can develop a bitter taste.

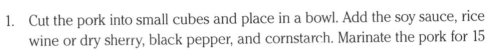

Serves 2 to 4

¾ pound boneless pork

1 tablespoon soy sauce

1 tablespoon Chinese rice wine or dry sherry

¼ teaspoon black pepper, or to taste

2 teaspoons cornstarch

4½ tablespoons vegetable or peanut oil, divided

2 thin slices ginger, chopped

2 cloves garlic, chopped

1 onion, chopped

1 tablespoon paprika

1½ cups cooked rice

1 cup chopped apple

1 tablespoon brown sugar

1 cup apple juice

1 teaspoon chopped fresh thyme

1 teaspoon chopped fresh parsley

Salt to taste

1. Cut the pork into small cubes and place in a bowl. Add the soy sauce, rice wine or dry sherry, black pepper, and cornstarch. Marinate the pork for 15 minutes.

2. Heat a wok or skillet on medium-high heat until it is nearly smoking, and add 2 tablespoons oil. When the oil is hot, add the ginger. Stir-fry for 10 seconds, then add the cubed pork. Stir-fry, stirring and tossing it in the pan, until the pork is no longer pink and is nearly cooked through. Remove the pork and drain in a colander or on paper towels.

3. Heat 1½ tablespoons oil. When the oil is hot, add the garlic. Stir-fry for 10 seconds and add the onion. Stir-fry the onion until it begins to soften (about 2 minutes), sprinkling the paprika over the onion while you are stir-frying.

4. Add 1 tablespoon oil in the middle of the pan. Add the rice and stir-fry, stirring it in the oil for a minute until it turns golden brown. Push to the sides and add the apple in the middle of the pan, stir-frying for 1 minute or until it begins to brown. Stir in the brown sugar. Stir to mix the apple with the onion and rice.

5. Add the apple juice and bring to a boil. Stir in the stir-fried pork. Stir in the fresh thyme and parsley. Continue stir-frying for 2 to 3 minutes to mix all the ingredients together. Taste and adjust seasoning, adding salt if desired. Serve hot.

Pungent Paprika Paprika, the spice that defines Hungarian cuisine, comes from the chili pepper plant. The taste and strength of paprika varies depending on the type of chili pepper used to make it and whether the seeds (the hottest part of the chili pepper) are included. In North America, paprika is normally brighter red and has a sweeter flavor than Hungarian paprika, which can be quite hot.

4 Chinese sausages

4 Napa cabbage leaves

1 tablespoon vegetable or peanut oil

¼ teaspoon salt

1 cup leftover mashed potatoes

1 tablespoon dark soy sauce

¼ cup chicken broth

Salt and black pepper to taste

Stir-Fried Bubble and Squeak

Traditionally, British bubble and squeak is made with leftover cabbage and potatoes from Sunday-night dinner. In this recipe, Chinese sausages (lop cheong) take the place of regular sausages or boiled beef. You can add extra flavor to this simple dish by using garlic-flavored mashed potatoes.

1. Cut the sausages on the diagonal into ½-inch pieces. Shred the cabbage leaves crosswise into thin strips.

2. Heat a wok or skillet over medium-high heat and add the oil. When the oil is hot, add the sausages. Stir-fry, moving the sausages around the pan, until they are nearly cooked through.

3. Push the sausages to the sides of the pan and add the shredded cabbage in the middle. Stir-fry for 1 minute, sprinkling salt over the cabbage leaves.

4. Add the leftover potatoes. Stir-fry, mixing the potatoes with the cabbage and sausage. Splash with the dark soy sauce.

5. Add the chicken broth into the pan. Stir-fry for another minute to heat everything through. Sprinkle with salt or pepper if desired. Serve hot.

Perfect Pancetta   The Italian version of bacon, pancetta is made from pork belly that is preserved with salt, pepper, and a number of other spices. Pancetta is much lighter in color than American bacon, due to the fact that it is not smoked. A mainstay of Italian cuisine, pancetta is a key ingredient in several pasta dishes, and it is also added to risotto.

Pork with Celery Cabbage

If you can't find celery cabbage in the produce section at the local supermarket, look for Napa cabbage, the name by which it is commonly known in the West. If you like, you can thicken the sauce by stirring in 1 teaspoon cornstarch dissolved in 2 teaspoons water.

1. Cut the pork into thin strips, about 1½ to 2 inches long. Place the pork in a bowl and toss with the salt and cornstarch.

2. Shred the celery cabbage crosswise into thin strips. Combine the water, rice wine or sherry, hoisin sauce, and chile paste in a bowl. Set aside.

3. Heat a wok or skillet over medium-high heat until it is nearly smoking. Add 2 tablespoons oil. When the oil is hot, add half the garlic and ginger. Stir-fry for 10 seconds, then add the pork. Let sit briefly, then stir-fry the pork, stirring and moving it around the pan until it is no longer pink and is nearly cooked through. Remove the pork and drain in a colander or on paper towels.

4. Heat 1½ tablespoons oil in the wok or skillet. When the oil is hot, add the remainder of the garlic and ginger. Stir-fry for 10 seconds, then add the cabbage. Stir-fry the cabbage until it is tender but still crisp (about 2 minutes). Sprinkle the cabbage with the sugar and ½ teaspoon salt if desired.

5. Add the sauce and bring to a boil. Add the pork back into the pan. Stir in the green onion. Stir-fry for another minute to heat everything through. Serve hot over cooked rice.

Serves 2 to 3

½ pound lean pork

½ teaspoon salt

1½ teaspoons cornstarch

½ pound (2 cups) celery cabbage

2 tablespoons water

1 tablespoon Chinese rice wine or dry sherry

1½ tablespoons hoisin sauce

¼ teaspoon chile paste, or to taste

3½ tablespoons vegetable or peanut oil, divided

1 teaspoon chopped garlic, divided

1 teaspoon chopped ginger, divided

1 teaspoon granulated sugar

½ teaspoon salt, optional

1 green onion, finely chopped

Oil for deep-frying

1 pound lean pork

1 tablespoon dark soy sauce

1 tablespoon Chinese rice wine or dry sherry

3 tablespoons cornstarch, divided

3 tablespoons water, divided

2 tablespoons oyster sauce

3½ tablespoons vegetable or peanut oil, divided

1 teaspoon minced garlic, divided

1 teaspoon minced ginger, divided

2 cups prepackaged shredded cabbage and carrot mix

½ teaspoon salt, or to taste

½ teaspoon granulated sugar, or to taste

1 cup mung bean sprouts

1 tablespoon water, optional

2 green onions, finely chopped

1 teaspoon sesame oil

1 package egg roll wrappers

Pork Egg Rolls

A prepackaged vegetable mix takes the work out of shredding cabbage and carrots in this recipe. To speed up the process even further, feel free to use barbecued pork from the Asian market.

1. Fill a deep-fat fryer, wok, or heavy deep-sided skillet with enough oil to cover the rolls and heat to 375°F.

2. Julienne the pork. Place the pork in a bowl and add the dark soy sauce, rice wine or sherry, and 2 teaspoons cornstarch. Marinate the pork for 15 minutes.

3. In a small bowl, combine 2 tablespoons water with the oyster sauce. In a separate small bowl, combine the remainder of the cornstarch with 1 tablespoon water to make a paste.

4. Heat a wok or skillet over medium-high heat until it is nearly smoking. Add 2 tablespoons oil. When the oil is hot, add half the garlic and ginger. Stir-fry for 10 seconds, then add the pork. Stir-fry until the pork is no longer pink and is nearly cooked. Remove and drain in a colander or on paper towels.

5. Heat 1½ tablespoons oil in the wok or skillet. When the oil is hot, add the remainder of the garlic and ginger. Stir-fry for 10 seconds, then add the shredded cabbage mixture. Stir-fry, sprinkling with the salt and sugar, for 2 minutes. Stir in the mung bean sprouts and stir-fry briefly (30 seconds to 1 minute). Add 1 tablespoon water if the vegetables begin to dry out during stir-frying.

6. Add the oyster sauce mixture. Add the pork back into the pan. Stir in the green onions. Stir-fry for 1 to 2 more minutes to blend all the ingredients together. Remove from the heat and stir in the sesame oil. Allow the filling to cool.

7. To make the egg rolls, take an egg roll wrapper and lay it out in front of you. Spoon about 2 tablespoons of the filling in the middle of the wrapper. Dip your finger in the cornstarch paste and trace the edges of the wrapper. Lift the bottom of the wrapper up and over the filling, fold the left and right sides over, and roll up the egg roll. Press down firmly on the edges to seal. To deep-fry the egg rolls, slide the rolls into the hot oil and deep-fry until they are golden brown and crispy (about 4 minutes). Remove the rolls with a slotted spoon and drain on paper towels. Don't stack the rolls before or after cooking.

Korean Sesame Pork

While it is most closely associated with Chinese cuisine, sesame oil is also a popular ingredient in both Korean and Thai dishes.

1. Cut the pork into thin strips about 1½ inches long.

2. Heat a wok or skillet over medium-high heat until it is nearly smoking and add the oil. When the oil is hot, add the pork. Stir-fry the pork until it is no longer pink, then add the chile paste and garlic. Stir-fry briefly, then push the pork to the sides of the pan.

3. Add the red bell peppers to the wok or skillet. Stir-fry for a minute, then add the sauce. Bring to a boil and continue stir-frying until the red bell peppers are tender but still crisp and the pork is cooked through. Remove from the pan and garnish with the toasted sesame seeds.

Serves 2 to 4

1 pound lean pork

2 tablespoons vegetable oil

1 tablespoon Korean chile paste

2 cloves garlic, crushed

2 red bell peppers, seeded and cut into thin strips

2 portions Korean-Inspired Sesame Sauce (page 26)

1 tablespoon toasted sesame seeds

¾ pound lean pork

1 tablespoon dark soy sauce

1 tablespoon Chinese rice
   wine or dry sherry

2 teaspoons cornstarch

3 tablespoons vegetable or
   peanut oil

1 teaspoon minced garlic

2 leeks, cut on the diagonal
   into ½-inch pieces

½ teaspoon salt, optional

Peking Sauce (page 22)

Peking Pork

*Serve Peking Pork with Stir-Fried Bok Choy (page 264)
and plenty of cooked rice for a complete meal.*

1. Cut the pork into thin strips about 1½ inches long. Place the pork in a bowl and add the soy sauce, rice wine or dry sherry, and cornstarch. Marinate the pork for 15 minutes.

2. Heat a wok or skillet over medium-high heat and add oil. When the oil is hot, add the garlic. Stir-fry for 10 seconds, then add the pork. Stir-fry the pork until it is no longer pink and is nearly cooked through.

3. Push the pork to the sides of the pan. Add the leeks and salt in the middle. Stir-fry the leeks for 1 minute, until they turn a darker green.

4. Add the Peking Sauce. Bring to a boil. Continue stir-frying for 1 to 2 more minutes, to blend the flavors and make sure the pork is cooked through. Serve hot.

Choosing Oil for Stir-Frying When stir-frying, it's important to choose an oil that won't break down at high temperatures. Chinese cooks traditionally use peanut oil, both because of its high smoke point and its nutty flavor. Canola oil and olive oil, which both contain a high degree of heart-healthy monounsaturated fat, are also good choices. Another option is coconut oil, commonly used in Thai stir-fry dishes.

Chapter 7

Stir-Fry Classics

Beef with Broccoli

It's hard to go wrong with this popular restaurant dish. If you'd like to add extra color to the dish, add a carrot, cut on the diagonal into thin slices.

1 pound flank steak

1 tablespoon Chinese rice wine or dry sherry

1 egg white

½ teaspoon salt

2 teaspoons cornstarch

1 cup plus 2 tablespoons vegetable or peanut oil, divided

2 thin slices ginger, chopped

2 cloves garlic, chopped

1 small onion, peeled and cut into wedges

2 cups broccoli florets

½ teaspoon granulated sugar

1–2 tablespoons water, if needed

Oyster-Flavored Brown Sauce (page 21)

1. Cut the steak across the grain into thin strips 1½ to 2 inches long. Place the beef strips in a bowl and add the rice wine or sherry, egg white, salt, and cornstarch. Marinate the beef for 15 minutes.

2. Heat a wok or skillet over medium-high heat until it is nearly smoking and add 1 cup oil. When the oil is hot, carefully slide half the beef into the hot oil. Cook the beef until it is no longer pink (about 1 minute), using a spatula to separate the strips. Remove the beef with a slotted spoon and drain in a colander or on paper towels. Repeat with the remainder of the beef. Clean out the pan.

3. Heat 2 tablespoons oil in the wok or skillet. Add the ginger and garlic. Stir-fry for 10 seconds, then add the onion. Stir-fry the onion for about 2 minutes, until it begins to soften. Add the broccoli and sprinkle the sugar over the mixture. Stir-fry the broccoli until it turns a darker green and is tender but still crisp (about 3 minutes). Add 1 to 2 tablespoons water if the broccoli begins to dry out during stir-frying.

4. Push the vegetables to the sides of the wok or skillet. Stir the brown sauce and add it into the middle of the pan. Bring the sauce to a boil, stirring quickly to thicken. When the sauce has thickened, add the beef back into the pan. Stir-fry for 2 more minutes to mix everything together and make sure the beef is cooked. Serve hot over rice.

Moo Goo Gai Pan

To enhance the savory flavor of this dish, replace half of the fresh mushrooms with Chinese dried mushrooms. Don't forget to soften the dried mushrooms in hot water before using.

Serves 2 to 4

- ¾ pound boneless, skinless chicken breast
- 1½ tablespoons light soy sauce
- 1 tablespoon dark soy sauce
- Black pepper to taste
- 3½ teaspoons cornstarch, divided
- 1½ tablespoons oyster sauce
- ⅓ cup water or chicken broth
- 4 tablespoons vegetable or peanut oil, divided
- 1 tablespoon minced ginger
- 1 onion, chopped
- 1 cup fresh button mushrooms, thinly sliced
- 1 tablespoon Chinese rice wine or dry sherry
- 2 ribs celery, cut thinly on the diagonal
- Salt, to taste
- 1 tablespoon minced garlic

1. Cut the chicken breast into thin strips 2 to 3 inches long. Place the chicken strips in a bowl and add the soy sauce, dark soy sauce, black pepper, and 1½ teaspoons cornstarch. Marinate the chicken in the refrigerator for 30 minutes.

2. Combine the oyster sauce and water or chicken broth in a bowl. Whisk in 2 teaspoons cornstarch. Set aside.

3. Heat a wok or skillet until it is nearly smoking. Add 2 tablespoons oil. When the oil is hot, add the ginger. Stir-fry for 10 seconds, then add the onion. Stir-fry the onion for about 2 minutes, until it begins to soften. Add the mushrooms and stir-fry for 1 minute, adding the rice wine or dry sherry. Add the celery, sprinkle the salt over, and stir-fry for another minute. Remove the vegetables from the pan.

4. Heat 2 tablespoons oil in the wok or skillet. When the oil is hot, add the garlic. Stir-fry for 10 seconds, then add the chicken. Let brown for a minute, then stir-fry until the chicken strips are white and nearly cooked through.

5. Push the chicken to the sides of the wok or skillet. Add the sauce in the middle of the pan and bring to a boil, stirring quickly to thicken. Add the vegetables back into the pan. Stir-fry for another minute to mix all the ingredients together and make sure the chicken is cooked through. Serve hot.

Moo Goo Gai Pan The name *Moo Goo Gai Pan* means "sliced chicken with fresh mushrooms." There are no hard-and-fast rules about what vegetables should accompany the chicken and mushrooms; while this recipe calls for peas, celery, onion, or red bell pepper could all be used instead.

1¼–1½ pounds boneless,
skinless chicken breasts

1½ tablespoons soy sauce

1 tablespoon Chinese rice
wine or dry sherry

2 tablespoons plus 2
teaspoons cornstarch,
divided

1/3 cup plus ¼ cup water,
divided

3 tablespoons vinegar

3 tablespoons granulated
sugar

1½ tablespoons dark soy
sauce

1½ tablespoons sesame oil

½ teaspoon chile paste, or
to taste

3 tablespoons vegetable or
peanut oil, divided

1 teaspoon minced garlic

1 teaspoon minced ginger

1 green bell pepper, seeded
and cut into cubes

2 tablespoons toasted
sesame seeds

Sesame Chicken

*The richness of dark soy sauce lends extra flavor to a standard
sweet-and-sour sauce in this popular dish. The toasted sesame
seeds are a nice final touch, but you can leave them out if desired.*

1. Cut the chicken into cubes (it's easiest to do this if the chicken is partially frozen). Place the chicken cubes in a bowl and add the soy sauce, rice wine or dry sherry, and 2 teaspoons cornstarch. Marinate the chicken for 20 minutes.

2. Combine ⅓ cup water, vinegar, sugar, dark soy sauce, sesame oil, and chile paste in a bowl. In a separate small bowl, dissolve 2 tablespoons cornstarch into ¼ cup water. Set aside.

3. Heat a wok or skillet over medium-high heat until it is nearly smoking. Add 2 tablespoons oil. When the oil is hot, add half the garlic and ginger. Stir-fry for 10 seconds, then add half the chicken. Stir-fry the chicken until it turns white and is nearly cooked through. Remove the chicken and drain in a colander or on paper towels. Repeat with the remainder of the chicken.

4. Heat 1 tablespoon oil in the wok or skillet. Add the remainder of the garlic and ginger. Stir-fry for 10 seconds, then add the bell pepper. Stir-fry for about 2 minutes, until the bell pepper is tender but still crisp. Add the chicken back into the pan and stir-fry briefly.

5. Add the sauce into the pan and bring to a boil. Stir the cornstarch and water mixture and add to the sauce, stirring to thicken. Stir-fry for about 2 more minutes to blend the flavors. Remove from the pan and garnish with the toasted sesame seeds.

Friday Night Kung Pao Chicken

Although this dish is traditionally made with peanuts, heart-healthy cashews can be used instead. The bell peppers can be left out if desired.

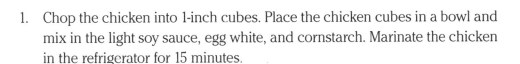

Serves 3 to 4

1 pound boneless, skinless chicken breasts

2 tablespoons light soy sauce

1 large egg white

1 tablespoon cornstarch

½ cup unsalted cashews

2 tablespoons dark soy sauce

1½ tablespoons water

1½ teaspoons granulated sugar

4 tablespoons vegetable or peanut oil, divided

1 tablespoon chopped garlic

1 tablespoon chopped red chili peppers

1½ sweet bell peppers, any color, chopped into cubes

1. Chop the chicken into 1-inch cubes. Place the chicken cubes in a bowl and mix in the light soy sauce, egg white, and cornstarch. Marinate the chicken in the refrigerator for 15 minutes.

2. While the chicken is marinating, roast the cashews in a heavy frying pan over medium heat, shaking the pan continuously so that the nuts do not burn. Roast until the cashews are browned (about 5 minutes). Remove the cashews from the pan to cool. Combine the dark soy sauce, water, and sugar in a bowl. Set aside.

3. Heat a wok or skillet over medium-high heat until it is nearly smoking. Add 2 tablespoons oil. When the oil is hot, add half the garlic. Stir-fry for 10 seconds, then add the chicken. Let the chicken brown briefly, then stir-fry until it is nearly cooked. Remove from the wok and drain in a colander or on paper towels.

4. Heat 2 tablespoons oil in the wok or skillet. When the oil is hot, add the remainder of the garlic, and the chopped chili peppers. Stir-fry for 15 seconds, then add the bell peppers. Stir-fry for a minute, then add the chicken. Stir-fry for another minute, combining the ingredients, then add the dark soy sauce mixture. Stir in the cashews. Stir-fry for another minute to combine the ingredients and serve hot.

A Dish with Two Names Kung Pao Chicken is named after a nineteenth-century Chinese official whose exact identity is unknown. Some claim he was an officer, while others claim he was the governor of Szechuan Province. Because of the dish's association with imperialism, revolutionaries during the Cultural Revolution renamed the dish Gong Bao Ji Ding, or "fast-fried chicken cubes."

¾ pound flank or sirloin steak

1 tablespoon Chinese rice wine or dry sherry

½ teaspoon salt

1½ teaspoons cornstarch

1 orange

Orange Sauce (page 17)

3 tablespoons vegetable or peanut oil, divided

1 teaspoon chopped ginger

1 teaspoon chopped garlic

½ teaspoon chile paste, or to taste

2 shallots, chopped

2 green onions, cut into 1-inch pieces

Beef with Orange Peel

Orange peel enhances the powerful orange flavor of this dish. To turn this into a one-dish meal, you can add other vegetables, such as colorful bell peppers.

1. Cut the beef across the grain into thin strips 1½ to 2 inches long. Place the beef strips in a bowl and add the rice wine or sherry, salt, and cornstarch. Marinate the beef for 15 minutes.

2. Peel the orange and use a paring knife to remove the white pith from the inside of the orange peel. Cut the orange peel into thin strips and stir it into the Orange Sauce.

3. Heat a wok or skillet over medium-high heat until it is nearly smoking and add 2 tablespoons oil. When the oil is hot, add half the ginger and garlic. Stir-fry for 10 seconds, then add the beef. Let sear briefly, then stir-fry the beef until it is no longer pink and is nearly cooked. Remove and drain in a colander or on paper towels.

4. Heat 1 tablespoon oil in the wok. When the oil is hot, add the remainder of the garlic and ginger and the chile paste. Stir-fry for 10 seconds, then add the shallots. Stir-fry for about 1 minute, until they begin to soften.

5. Add the sauce and bring to a boil. Add the beef back into the pan. Stir in the green onions. Stir-fry for 1 to 2 more minutes to heat through. Serve hot, garnished with orange segments if desired.

Sweet and Sour Pork

*Deep-frying the pork before stir-frying seals in the flavor and makes it
extra crispy. The amount of oil needed will depend on the size and shape
of the pan—make sure there is enough oil to cover the pork.*

Serves 4 to 6

½ cup cornstarch, or as
  needed, divided

4 tablespoons water

1 pound boneless pork

4 cups oil, or as needed

2 cloves garlic, crushed

1 carrot, cut on the diagonal
  into ½-inch slices

1 green bell pepper, seeded
  and cut into bite-sized
  chunks

Pineapple Sweet and Sour
  Sauce (page 25)

½ cup canned pineapple
  chunks, drained

Salt to taste

Black pepper to taste

1. In a small bowl, dissolve 1 tablespoon cornstarch in the water and set aside. Cut the pork into bite-sized cubes.

2. Heat oil for deep-frying in a deep-fat fryer or wok to 360°F to 375°F. Dredge the pork in the cornstarch. Deep-fry the pork until it is browned and crispy. Carefully remove the pork from the deep-fat fryer. Drain in a colander or on paper towels.

3. Heat a wok or skillet on medium-high heat. Add 2 tablespoons oil. When the oil is hot, add the garlic. Stir-fry until it is aromatic, then add the carrot and green bell pepper. Stir-fry for 2 minutes or until they are tender but still crisp.

4. Add the sauce and bring to a boil. Add the cornstarch and water mixture to the sauce, stirring to thicken. When the sauce thickens, add the pork and the pineapple into the pan. Stir-fry for 2 more minutes or until all the ingredients are heated through. Taste and adjust seasoning, adding salt and pepper if desired. Serve hot.

Restaurant-Style Sweet and Sour Pork It takes only a few simple adjustments to make this recipe taste like it came straight from your favorite Chinese restaurant. Instead of dredging the pork in cornstarch, dip it in a batter consisting of egg and equal parts flour, cornstarch, and water. After deep-frying the pork, reheat the oil and deep-fry the pork a second time to make it extra crispy.

1 pound lean beef

¼ cup chicken broth

1 tablespoon oyster sauce

1 tablespoon cornstarch

2 tablespoons water

4 tablespoons vegetable or peanut oil, divided

2 cloves garlic, crushed

2 thin slices ginger, chopped

1 medium onion, chopped

1 red bell pepper, seeded and cut into thin strips

6–8 ounces snow peas, trimmed

1 tablespoon soy sauce

1 cup mung bean sprouts

Salt and pepper to taste

Beef Chop Suey

To add extra flavor to this dish, season the vegetables with salt or sugar while stir-frying. If you run out of oil, add a bit of water or chicken broth to keep the vegetables from drying out.

1. Cut the beef across the grain into thin strips about 1½ to 2 inches long. Set aside.

2. Combine the chicken broth and oyster sauce in a small bowl. In a separate small bowl, dissolve the cornstarch into the water.

3. Heat a wok or skillet over medium-high heat until it is nearly smoking and add 2 tablespoons oil. When the oil is hot, add the garlic. Stir-fry for 10 seconds, then add the beef, laying it flat in the pan. Let sear (brown) briefly, then stir-fry the meat, stirring and tossing until it is no longer pink. Remove the meat and drain in a colander or on paper towels.

4. Heat 2 tablespoons oil in the wok or skillet and add the ginger. Stir-fry for 10 seconds, then add the onion. Stir-fry the onion for about 2 minutes, until it begins to soften. Add the bell pepper and the snow peas. Stir-fry for 1 minute, stirring in the soy sauce. Add the mung bean sprouts and stir-fry for about 30 seconds.

5. Push the vegetables to the sides of the pan and add the chicken broth mixture into the middle. Bring to a boil, then add the cornstarch and water mixture, stirring quickly to thicken. When the sauce has thickened, stir to mix in with the vegetables. Add the beef. Stir for another minute to heat everything through. Taste and season with salt and pepper if desired. Serve hot.

Broccoli with Oyster Sauce

*If you like, you can use Chinese broccoli, called gai lan, in this recipe.
Chinese broccoli has a slightly more bitter taste than regular broccoli,
so you may want to increase the amount of sugar to 2 teaspoons.*

Serves 4

1 pound broccoli

1 tablespoon oyster sauce

2 teaspoons cooking sherry

1 teaspoon granulated sugar

3 tablespoons chicken broth

2 tablespoons vegetable or
  peanut oil

1 clove garlic, crushed

2 thin slices ginger

1. Cut off the broccoli florets and cut in half. Cut the spears on the diagonal. Wash and drain the broccoli.

2. Whisk the oyster sauce, cooking sherry, and sugar into the chicken broth. Set aside.

3. Heat a wok or skillet over medium-high heat until it is nearly smoking. Add the oil. When the oil is hot, add the crushed garlic and ginger slices. Stir-fry for about 10 seconds, then add the broccoli. Stir-fry the broccoli for 1 minute.

4. Add the chicken broth mixture. Continue stir-frying, stirring and moving the broccoli around the pan until it turns a darker green and is tender but still crisp. Remove the garlic and ginger before serving.

Stir-Frying Broccoli You don't absolutely need to add liquid to a broccoli stir-fry. Broccoli can just be stir-fried in oil. But thick, low-moisture vegetables like broccoli benefit from being briefly boiled in the pan or wok after the initial stir-frying.

Serves 4 to 6

1 cup medium shrimp, peeled, deveined

1 tablespoon oyster sauce

½ teaspoon granulated sugar

1 teaspoon cornstarch

4 tablespoons vegetable or peanut oil, divided

2 thin slices ginger

1 stalk celery, cut on the diagonal into thin strips

½ red bell pepper, seeded and cut into thin slices

½ cup mung bean sprouts

¼ teaspoon salt

2 green onions, finely chopped

6 eggs

⅛ teaspoon freshly ground white or black pepper, or to taste

Shrimp Egg Foo Yung

Although it has been Westernized, egg foo yung is based on an authentic Chinese dish that is often described as a Chinese omelet.

1. Rinse the shrimp under cold running water and pat dry with paper towels. Place the shrimp in a bowl and add the oyster sauce, sugar, and cornstarch. Marinate the shrimp for 10 minutes.

2. Heat a wok or skillet over medium-high heat until it is nearly smoking. Add 2 tablespoons oil. When the oil is hot, add the ginger. Stir-fry for 10 seconds, then add the shrimp. Stir-fry the shrimp briefly until they turn pink and the edges begin to curl. Remove the ginger.

3. Push the shrimp to the sides of the wok or skillet and add the celery in the middle. Stir-fry for about 1 minute, until the celery begins to turn a brighter green. Add the red bell pepper and stir-fry for another minute. Add the mung bean sprouts and stir-fry briefly, sprinkling the sprouts with the salt. Stir in the green onions. Remove the shrimp and vegetables and drain in a colander or on paper towels.

4. In a large bowl, lightly beat the eggs, stirring in the pepper. Stir in the stir-fried shrimp and vegetables. Set aside.

5. Heat 2 tablespoons oil in the wok or skillet. When the oil is hot, add ½ cup of the egg mixture. Cook until the bottom is cooked, tilting the pan or lifting the egg mixture with a spatula so that runny uncooked portions flow underneath. When the bottom is cooked, turn over and cook the other side. Continue with the remainder of the egg, adding more oil while cooking if needed.

Egg Foo Yung with Brown Sauce

The savory flavor of brown sauce goes nicely with the cooked ham and vegetables, but you can also serve the egg foo yung alone or with standard condiments such as ketchup.

Serves 4 to 6

½ portion Oyster-Flavored Brown Sauce (page 21)

3 tablespoons vegetable or peanut oil, divided

¼ cup chopped onion or shallot

½ green bell pepper, seeded and cut into cubes

½ red bell pepper, seeded and cut into cubes

2 teaspoons Chinese rice wine or dry sherry

½ cup mung bean sprouts

¼ teaspoon salt

6 eggs

⅛ teaspoon black pepper, or to taste

½ cup cooked ham, diced

1. Warm the Oyster-Flavored Brown Sauce on low heat while making the egg foo yung.

2. Heat a wok or skillet over medium-high heat until it is nearly smoking and add 1 tablespoon oil. When the oil is hot, add the onion or shallot. Stir-fry briefly until it begins to soften, then add the green bell pepper. Stir-fry for a minute, then add the red bell pepper. Splash the peppers with the rice wine while stir-frying.

3. Add the mung bean sprouts and stir-fry briefly, sprinkling the sprouts with the salt. Remove the vegetables and drain in a colander or on paper towels.

4. In a large bowl, lightly beat the eggs with the black pepper. Stir in the stir-fried vegetables and the ham.

5. Heat 2 tablespoons oil in the wok or skillet. When the oil is hot, add ½ cup of the egg mixture. Cook until the bottom is cooked, tilting the pan or lifting the egg mixture with a spatula so that runny uncooked portions flow underneath. When the bottom is cooked, turn over and cook the other side. Continue with the remainder of the egg, adding more oil while cooking if needed.

Deep-Frying Egg Foo Yung Instead of pan-frying, you can deep-fry the egg foo yung. To deep-fry the egg foo yung, heat 2 cups of oil to 375°F. When the oil is hot, carefully add ½ cup of the egg mixture into the pan. Deep-fry for about 2 minutes, until the bottom is browned, then carefully ladle some oil over the top of the omelet so that it is cooked as well. Remove with a slotted spoon. Drain on paper towels before serving.

4 large Chinese dried black
mushrooms

4 tablespoons cloud ear
fungus

¼ cup golden lily buds,
optional

½ pound pork tenderloin,
julienned

1 tablespoon dark soy sauce

1 teaspoon cornstarch

6 tablespoons vegetable or
peanut oil, divided

3 eggs, lightly beaten

1 tablespoon Chinese rice
wine or dry sherry

1 teaspoon minced ginger

1 green onion, julienned

2 cups shredded Napa
cabbage

½ teaspoon granulated
sugar

½ cup bamboo shoots,
julienned

2 tablespoons light soy sauce

8–10 Chinese pancakes or
tortillas

¼ cup hoisin sauce, or as
needed

Restaurant-Style Mu Shu Pork

*Traditionally, mu shu pork is served with Chinese pancakes, but tortillas
make a handy substitute. Although the names sound exotic, cloud ears,
dried mushrooms, and lily buds are easy to find at Asian markets.*

1. Reconstitute the dried black mushrooms, cloud ear fungus, and golden
   lily buds by soaking them in boiling water for 15 to 20 minutes to soften.
   Squeeze the excess water out of the mushrooms, cut off the stems, and cut
   into thin strips. Cut the hard ends off the dried lily buds.

2. Place the pork strips in a bowl and add the dark soy sauce and
   cornstarch.

3. Heat 2 tablespoons oil and add the eggs. Scramble the eggs until they are
   almost dry and remove from the pan. Clean out the pan. Heat 2 tablespoons
   oil in the wok or skillet and add the pork. Stir-fry until the pork is no longer
   pink, splashing with the rice wine or dry sherry. Remove the pork and drain
   in a colander or on paper towels.

4. Heat 2 tablespoons oil. Add the ginger and green onion. Stir-fry for 10 seconds, then add the cabbage. Stir-fry for 2 minutes, sprinkling with the sugar.
   Add the mushrooms, cloud ear fungus, optional lily buds, and the bamboo
   shoots. Stir-fry for 2 more minutes, or until the cabbage is tender but crisp,
   splashing the vegetables with the soy sauce.

5. To assemble the mu shu pork, lay out a Chinese pancake or tortilla on a
   plate in front of you. Spread 1 to 2 teaspoons of hoisin sauce over the pancake or tortilla and spoon a portion of the mu shu pork in the center. Roll
   up the pancake or tortilla.

General Tso's Chicken

Chicken thighs are combined with hot chilies and a spicy sauce in this famous dish that is named after a nineteenth-century Chinese military officer.

¾–1 pound boneless, skinless chicken thighs

1 large egg white

2 teaspoons Chinese rice wine or dry sherry

½ teaspoon salt

1 tablespoon cornstarch

2 tablespoons plus 1 teaspoon dark soy sauce

1 tablespoon white wine vinegar

3 tablespoons water

1 teaspoon hoisin sauce

2 teaspoons granulated sugar

2 cups vegetable or peanut oil

1 teaspoon minced garlic

6 small dried red chili peppers

1. Cut the chicken into 1-inch cubes. In a bowl, stir together the egg white, rice wine or sherry, salt, and the cornstarch. Add the chicken and marinate in the refrigerator for 30 minutes.

2. Combine the dark soy sauce, white wine vinegar, water, hoisin sauce, and sugar in a small bowl. Set aside.

3. Heat a wok or skillet over medium-high heat until it is nearly smoking. Add 2 cups oil. When the oil is hot, add the chicken. Stir-fry the chicken cubes until they turn white (about 30 seconds), using a spatula to separate the cubes. Remove from the wok and drain in a colander or on paper towels.

4. Remove all but 1 tablespoon oil from the wok or skillet. When the oil is hot, add the garlic and chili peppers. Stir-fry for 10 seconds, then add the chicken back into a pan. Stir-fry the chicken for a minute, then push to the sides of the pan and add the sauce in the middle. Bring the sauce to a boil. Stir-fry for 1 to 2 more minutes to mix the sauce with the chicken. Serve hot.

Make-Ahead Velvet Chicken Don't feel up to making the velveting mixture when you come home from work? Velvet the chicken earlier in the day and refrigerate in a sealed container. Then when you come home, all that's left to do is quickly stir-fry the chicken in the sauce.

Serves 2 to 4

1 boneless, skinless chicken breast

2 teaspoons soy sauce

2 teaspoons rice wine or dry sherry

Black pepper to taste

2 teaspoons cornstarch, divided

¼ cup chicken broth

2½ teaspoons oyster sauce

3 tablespoons vegetable or peanut oil, divided

1 teaspoon minced garlic

1 teaspoon minced ginger

1 onion, chopped

1 green bell pepper, seeded, thinly sliced

¼ pound thinly sliced mushrooms

2 ribs celery, thinly sliced

1 cup mung bean sprouts

1 teaspoon salt, optional

1 teaspoon granulated sugar (optional)

Chicken Chop Suey

Chop suey is a great dish to make when it's time to clean out the vegetable-crisper section of your refrigerator. Of course, you can also use a prepackaged chop suey mix (use 3½ to 4 cups) instead of using your leftover vegetables.

1. Cut the chicken into thin strips about 1½ inches long. Place the chicken in a bowl and add the soy sauce, rice wine or sherry, black pepper, and 1 teaspoon cornstarch. Marinate the chicken for 20 minutes.

2. Combine the chicken broth and oyster sauce in a small bowl. Whisk in 1 teaspoon cornstarch. Set aside.

3. Heat a wok or skillet over medium-high heat until it is nearly smoking. Add 1½ tablespoons oil. When the oil is hot, add the garlic and ginger. Stir-fry for 10 seconds, then add the chicken. Let brown briefly, then stir-fry the chicken until it turns white and is nearly cooked through. Remove and drain in a colander or on paper towels.

4. Heat 1½ tablespoons oil in the wok or skillet. Add the onion. Stir-fry for 2 minutes or until it begins to soften. Add the green bell pepper and the mushrooms. Stir-fry for a minute, then add the celery. Stir-fry for another minute or until the mushrooms have darkened and the green vegetables are tender but still crisp. Stir in the mung bean sprouts and stir-fry for another 30 seconds. Stir in up to 1 teaspoon salt and 1 teaspoon sugar while stir-frying the vegetables, if desired.

5. Push the vegetables to the sides of the wok or skillet. Stir the chicken broth mixture and add in the middle. Bring to a boil, stirring to thicken. Once it has thickened, stir-fry for another minute to blend all the flavors. Serve hot.

Beef with Dried Tangerine Peel

Deep-frying the beef before stir-frying with the other ingredients makes it crisp and gives it a nice brown coating. If desired, you can deep-fry the beef a second time to make it extra crispy. Dried tangerine peel is available at Asian grocery stores.

1. Cut the beef across the grain into thin strips 1½ to 2 inches long. Place the beef strips in a bowl and add the egg white, rice wine or sherry, salt, and cornstarch. Marinate the beef for 20 minutes.

2. Reconstitute the dried tangerine peel by soaking it in hot water for 15 to 20 minutes. Cut the peel into thin strips.

3. Heat enough oil to cover the beef in a wok or heavy deep-sided skillet over medium-high heat. When the oil reaches 375°F, carefully slide the beef into the hot oil. Deep-fry the beef until it is browned on both sides, then remove and drain in a colander or on paper towels.

4. Remove all but 2 tablespoons oil from the wok or skillet. When the oil is hot, add the ginger, garlic, chile paste, and the tangerine peel. Stir-fry for 10 seconds, then add the shallots. Stir-fry for 1 minute or until the shallots begin to soften.

5. Add the sauce and bring to a boil. Add the beef back into the pan. Stir in the green onions. Stir-fry for 2 to 3 more minutes to combine all the flavors. Serve hot.

How to Make Dried Orange Peel It's easy to make dried orange peel at home to use in Beef with Dried Tangerine Peel. Use a sharp knife to cut away the white pith from an orange rind. Cut the rind into thin strips and leave out to dry for several days. For quicker drying, place the orange rind strips in a 250°F oven for 45 minutes or until they have hardened.

Serves 2 to 4

1 pound flank or sirloin steak

1 large egg white

1 tablespoon Chinese rice wine or dry sherry

½ teaspoon salt

1 tablespoon cornstarch

2 pieces (roughly 2 tablespoons) dried tangerine peel

3 cups vegetable or peanut oil, or as needed

1 teaspoon chopped ginger

1 teaspoon chopped garlic

½ teaspoon chile paste, or to taste

2 shallots, chopped

Orange Sauce (page 17)

2 green onions, cut into 1-inch pieces

½ pound lean pork

2 teaspoons Chinese rice wine or dry sherry

2 teaspoons dark soy sauce

2½ teaspoons cornstarch, divided

¼ cup water

1 tablespoon oyster sauce

1 teaspoon light soy sauce

½ teaspoon granulated sugar

¼ teaspoon black pepper, or to taste

4 tablespoons vegetable or peanut oil, divided

1 clove garlic, chopped

2 thin slices ginger, minced

1 medium shallot, chopped

1 cup snow peas, trimmed

1 cup mung bean sprouts

¼ teaspoon salt

10 ounces packaged chow mein noodles

Pork Chow Mein

Quick-cooking snow peas and packaged chow mein noodles make this recipe a great choice for busy weeknights.

1. Julienne the pork. Place the strips of pork in a bowl and add the rice wine or sherry, dark soy sauce, and 1 teaspoon cornstarch. Marinate the pork for 20 minutes.

2. In a small bowl, combine the water, oyster sauce, light soy sauce, sugar, and black pepper for the gravy. Whisk in 1½ teaspoons cornstarch.

3. Heat a wok or skillet over medium-high heat until it is nearly smoking. Add 2 tablespoons oil. When the oil is hot, add half the garlic and ginger. Stir-fry for 10 seconds, then add the pork. Let sit briefly, then stir-fry, stirring and moving the pork around the pan, until it turns white and is nearly cooked through. Remove from the pan and drain in a colander or on paper towels.

4. Heat 2 tablespoons oil in the wok. When the oil is hot, add the shallot and the remainder of the garlic and ginger. Stir-fry until the shallot begins to soften (about 1 minute). Add the snow peas and stir-fry until they turn dark green and are tender but still crisp (about 2 minutes). Stir in the mung bean sprouts, sprinkling with ¼ teaspoon salt if desired.

5. Push the vegetables to the sides of the wok or skillet. Add the sauce in the middle, stirring quickly to thicken. Add the pork back into the pan. Stir-fry for 1 to 2 more minutes to mix all the ingredients together. Pour over the chow mein noodles.

Grandmother Bean Curd (Mapo Doufu)

While ground pork is traditionally used to make mapo doufu, ground beef can be used as well. If Szechuan peppercorn is unavailable, you may substitute ground coriander or freshly ground white pepper.

Serves 3 to 4

½ pound ground pork

1 tablespoon soy sauce

1 teaspoon granulated sugar

Black pepper to taste

3 teaspoons cornstarch, divided

2 tablespoons plus 4 teaspoons water, divided

1 tablespoon Chinese fermented black beans

2 cloves garlic, minced

2 tablespoons vegetable or peanut oil

2 thin slices ginger, minced

½ tablespoon chile paste, or to taste

1 green bell pepper, chopped into bite-sized chunks

½ cup chicken broth

¾ pound firm tofu, drained and cut into ½-inch cubes

1 teaspoon freshly ground Szechuan peppercorn, or to taste

1. In a bowl, combine the ground pork with the soy sauce, sugar, black pepper, and 1 teaspoon cornstarch. Marinate the pork for 15 minutes. Dissolve 2 teaspoons cornstarch into 4 teaspoons water. Set aside.

2. Rinse the black beans under cold running water for 10 minutes, drain, and chop. Place the black beans in a bowl with the garlic and mash with a fork. Stir in 2 tablespoons water.

3. Heat a wok or skillet over medium-high heat until it is nearly smoking. Add the oil. When the oil is hot, add the minced ginger. Stir-fry for 10 seconds, then add the ground pork. Stir-fry the pork until it is no longer pink and is nearly cooked through.

4. Add the chile paste and the mashed black beans and garlic. Stir-fry for about 30 seconds, then add the bell pepper. Stir-fry for a minute, stirring to mix the bell pepper and pork in with the seasonings. Add 1 tablespoon of the chicken broth if the green pepper begins to dry out.

5. Add the chicken broth. Bring to a boil, then add the tofu cubes. Stir-fry for a minute, stirring gently. Stir in the ground Szechuan peppercorn. Stir the cornstarch and water mixture, then add into the pan, stirring to thicken. Serve hot.

Tofu Like Grandmother Used to Make The Szechuan name for this popular dish, Mapo Doufu, means "Pockmarked Grandmother Bean Curd." It is named after an old woman reputed to have invented the dish. While the exact identity of the woman is unknown, according to legend she was a grandmother whose face was scarred by smallpox.

½ pound firm tofu, drained
  and cut into ½-inch cubes

1 tablespoon dark soy sauce

1 tablespoon hoisin sauce

3 large eggs

½ teaspoon salt

Black pepper to taste

3 tablespoons vegetable or
  peanut oil, divided

2 thin slices ginger, chopped

1 clove garlic, chopped

¼ pound fresh mushrooms,
  thinly sliced

½ cup canned sliced bamboo
  shoots, drained

¼ cup plus 1 tablespoon
  water, divided

1 teaspoon granulated sugar

2 green onions, cut
  diagonally into 1-inch
  slices

Mu Shu Tofu

*Sweet and spicy hoisin sauce adds extra flavor to the tofu in
this vegetarian take on a classic northern Chinese recipe.*

1. In a medium bowl, combine the tofu cubes with the dark soy sauce and hoisin sauce. In a separate bowl, lightly beat the eggs, stirring in the salt and pepper.

2. Heat a wok or skillet over medium-high heat until it is nearly smoking. Add 1½ tablespoons oil. When the oil is hot, add the lightly beaten eggs. Scramble the eggs until they are cooked and remove from the pan. Clean out the pan.

3. Heat 1½ tablespoons oil in the wok or skillet. When the oil is hot, add the ginger and garlic. Stir-fry for 10 seconds, then add the mushrooms. Stir-fry for about 2 minutes or until they have browned. Add the canned bamboo shoots. Stir-fry for a minute, adding 1 tablespoon water if the vegetables begin to dry out.

4. Add the tofu. Stir-fry for 1 minute, then add ¼ cup water. Stir in the sugar and the green onions. Add the scrambled eggs. Stir-fry for another minute to mix everything together. Serve hot.

Thai Cuisine Sometimes called Asia's version of nouvelle cuisine, Thai cooking features a number of diverse culinary influences, from neighboring Malaysia to China and Indonesia. What sets Thai cuisine apart from other Asian cuisines is the extensive use of exotic ingredients such as tart tamarind fruit, galangal ginger (also called Siamese ginger), and Kaffir lime leaves.

Pad Thai

Probably Thailand's most famous dish, pad Thai is an intriguing combination of sweet, sour, spicy, and nutty flavors. Tamarind liquid is available at most Asian grocery stores, or you can substitute 6 tablespoons lemon juice mixed with 2 tablespoons tomato sauce.

8 ounces flat rice stick noodles

1 boneless, skinless chicken breast half

$1/3$ cup tamarind liquid

4 teaspoons lime juice

4 tablespoons fish sauce

4 teaspoons ketchup

4 teaspoons granulated sugar

2 eggs, lightly beaten

2 tablespoons vegetable or peanut oil

2 shallots, chopped

8–10 large prawns

1 tablespoon liquid, if needed

1 cup mung bean sprouts

1 tablespoon ground red chilies, or to taste

Salt and/or pepper to taste, optional

½ cup roasted peanuts, crushed

1. Soak the rice noodles in warm water for 20 minutes or until they have softened. Drain the noodles.

2. While the rice noodles are softening, prepare the other ingredients. Cut the chicken breast into thin strips about 2 inches long. In a bowl, combine the tamarind liquid, lime juice, fish sauce, ketchup, and sugar. In a separate bowl, lightly beat the eggs.

3. Heat a wok or skillet on medium-high heat until it is nearly smoking. Add the oil. When the oil is hot, add the chopped shallots and stir-fry for about 2 minutes, until they begin to soften. Add the prawns, stir-frying quickly until they turn pink. Push to the sides and add the chicken in the middle of the pan. Stir-fry the chicken until it turns white, adding 1 tablespoon water or fish sauce or chicken broth to the pan if needed.

4. Add the lightly beaten eggs in the middle and gently scramble. Stir-fry briefly to mix the bits of scrambled eggs with the other ingredients. Add the sauce and bring to a boil.

5. Add the noodles, stirring continually. Cook for a minute, then stir in the mung bean sprouts and the ground chilies. Stir-fry for another minute to mix everything through. Taste and adjust seasonings, adding more salt, pepper, or fish sauce if desired. Garnish with the crushed peanuts before serving.

½ pound lean pork

2 teaspoons dark soy sauce

2 teaspoons Chinese rice wine or dry sherry

Black pepper to taste

1 teaspoon plus 2 tablespoons cornstarch, divided

1 tablespoon water

2 tablespoons vegetable or peanut oil

½ teaspoon garlic

½ teaspoon ginger

½ cup shredded carrot

4 ounces fresh mushrooms, thinly sliced

½ teaspoon granulated sugar

1 red bell pepper, seeded and julienned

1 cup mung bean sprouts

1 tablespoon chicken broth

2 teaspoons light soy sauce

2 green onions, shredded

1 teaspoon Asian sesame oil

12 spring roll wrappers

Spring Rolls

Lighter than egg rolls, spring rolls were traditionally eaten in China during the annual festival celebrating the return of spring.

1. Cut the pork into very thin strips. Place the strips of pork in a bowl and add the dark soy sauce, rice wine or sherry, black pepper, and 1 teaspoon cornstarch. Marinate the pork for 15 minutes.

2. In a small bowl, combine 2 tablespoons cornstarch with the water to make a paste. Set aside.

3. Heat a wok or skillet over medium-high heat until it is nearly smoking. Add the oil. When the oil is hot, add the garlic and ginger. Stir-fry for 10 seconds, then add the pork. Stir-fry the pork until it is no longer pink and is nearly cooked through.

4. Push the pork to the sides of the wok or skillet and add the carrot and mushrooms in the middle. Stir-fry for a minute, stirring in the sugar, then add the red bell pepper and mung bean sprouts. Stir-fry for another minute, stirring in the chicken broth and soy sauce. Stir in the green onions.

5. Remove the filling from the heat and stir in the sesame oil. Allow the filling to cool briefly.

6. To fill the Spring Rolls, lay a wrapper on a plate in front of you. Place a tablespoon of filling in the middle of the wrapper. Dip your finger in the cornstarch paste and run it along the edges of the wrapper. Roll up the wrapper and seal in the edges.

7. Fill a deep-fat fryer, wok, or heavy deep-sided skillet with enough oil to cover the rolls and heat to 375°F. Carefully slide the rolls into the hot oil, a few at a time, and deep-fry until they are golden brown and crispy (about 2 to 4 minutes). Remove the rolls with a slotted spoon and drain on paper towels. Don't stack the rolls before or after cooking.

Beef Lettuce Wraps

*Deep-frying the rice vermicelli makes it puff up and turn crispy, making a
nice contrast in texture with the stir-fried meat and vegetables. The oil
used to deep-fry the rice noodles can be used to quickly "velvet" the beef.*

1. Cut the beef across the grain into thin strips that are about 1½ to 2 inches
   long. Lay the strips on top of one another and cut into thin matchsticks. In
   a bowl, combine the egg white, salt, and cornstarch. Mix in the beef strips
   and marinate in the refrigerator for 30 minutes.

2. In a small bowl, combine the hoisin sauce, water, sherry, rice vinegar, and
   chile paste. Set aside.

3. Heat 2 cups oil to 350°F in a preheated wok. When the oil is hot, add the
   rice vermicelli. Deep fry for about 30 seconds, until the noodles puff up and
   turn crispy. Carefully remove the noodles with a slotted spoon and drain on
   paper towels.

4. Add half the beef into the hot oil, and cook for about 30 seconds, until it is
   no longer pink. Remove and drain. Repeat with the remainder of the beef.

5. Remove all but 2 tablespoons oil from the wok. Add the garlic and green
   onions. Stir-fry for 10 seconds, then add the straw mushrooms and baby
   corn. Stir-fry for 1 minute, then add the sauce. Bring to a boil and add the
   beef back into the pan. Stir in the sugar. Stir-fry for 1 to 2 more minutes to
   mix everything together.

6. Lay a lettuce leaf on a plate. Add a small portion of the deep-fried rice
   vermicelli noodles onto the middle of the leaf. Spoon a small portion of
   the stir-fried beef and vegetables on top. Roll up the leaf. Continue with the
   remainder of the lettuce leaves until the noodles and filling are used up.

Yields 10 to 12 wraps

1 pound sirloin or flank steak

1 egg white

½ teaspoon salt

1 tablespoon cornstarch

2½ tablespoons hoisin sauce

2½ tablespoons water

1 tablespoon dry sherry

2 teaspoons rice vinegar

¼ teaspoon chile paste with
  garlic, or to taste

2 cups vegetable or peanut
  oil, or as needed

8 ounces rice vermicelli
  noodles

2 cloves garlic, chopped

2 green onions, chopped

1 (8-ounce) can straw
  mushrooms, drained

1 (8-ounce) can baby corn,
  drained

1 teaspoon granulated sugar

1 head iceberg lettuce or
  Bibb lettuce leaves

¾ pound flank steak

1 tablespoon soy sauce

5 teaspoons Chinese rice wine or dry sherry, divided

½ cup vegetable or peanut oil

1 tablespoon minced ginger

2 green onions, chopped

2 teaspoons chile paste, or to taste

1 tablespoon dark soy sauce

1 teaspoon granulated sugar

Freshly ground white pepper to taste

Crisped Szechuan Beef

If you like beef jerky, you'll love this Szechuan specialty, made by stir-frying strips of marinated beef until they are crisp and chewy.

1. Cut the flank steak across the grain into thin strips 1½ to 2 inches long. Add the soy sauce and 2 teaspoons Chinese rice wine or dry sherry. Marinate the beef for 20 minutes.

2. Heat a wok or skillet over medium-high heat until it is nearly smoking. Add ½ cup oil. When the oil is hot, add the beef, laying it flat in the pan. Let sear (brown) briefly, then stir-fry the meat for 10 minutes, or until the beef darkens and starts sizzling. (This is called dry-frying.) Remove the meat from the pan. Drain in a colander or on paper towels.

3. Remove all but 2 teaspoons oil from the wok or skillet. Add the minced ginger, green onions, and the chile paste. Stir-fry for 30 seconds, then add the beef back into the pan. Splash the beef with the dark soy sauce, 3 teaspoons rice wine or dry sherry, and sugar. Stir in the freshly ground white pepper. Serve hot.

Dry-Frying Beef isn't the only food that can be cooked using the dry-frying method. Chinese green beans, a popular restaurant dish, are also cooked by frying the beans until they are dried out. This gives the beans a browned skin and softer texture. Other foods that can be dry-fried include chicken, fish, and denser vegetables such as eggplant.

Black Bean Beef with Asparagus

In this recipe, you can substitute 2 tablespoons Chinese fermented black beans (also called salted black beans) for the black bean sauce. Rinse the fermented black beans and mash them together with the garlic and ginger. Both fermented black beans and Chinese black bean sauce are available at Asian grocery stores.

1. Cut the steak across the grain into thin strips 1½ to 2 inches long. Place the beef strips in a bowl and add the Easy Oyster-Flavored Marinade for Beef. Marinate the beef for 15 minutes.

2. Heat a wok or skillet over medium-high heat until it is nearly smoking and add 2 tablespoons oil. When the oil is hot, add half the ginger and garlic. Stir-fry for 10 seconds, then add half the beef. Stir-fry the beef until it is no longer pink and is nearly cooked. Remove and drain in a colander or on paper towels. Stir-fry the remainder of the beef.

3. Heat 1½ tablespoons oil in the wok or skillet. When the oil is hot, add the remainder of the garlic and ginger. Stir-fry for 10 seconds, then add the black bean sauce. Stir-fry for about 15 seconds, mixing with the garlic and ginger.

4. Add the asparagus in the wok or skillet. Stir-fry for 1 minute, then add the chicken broth and bring to a boil. Cover and cook until the asparagus turns a bright green and is tender but still crisp (about 2 more minutes). Uncover and add the beef back into the pan. Stir in the sugar. Stir-fry for 1 to 2 more minutes to mix everything together. Serve hot.

Serves 3 to 4

1 pound flank or sirloin steak

Easy Oyster-Flavored Marinade for Beef (page 17)

3½ tablespoons plus 2 teaspoons vegetable or peanut oil, divided

½ teaspoon minced ginger

½ teaspoon minced garlic

2 tablespoons Chinese black bean sauce

½ pound asparagus, cut on the diagonal into thin slices

¼ cup chicken broth

1 teaspoon granulated sugar

¾ pound boneless, skinless
chicken breast

1 tablespoon oyster sauce

1 tablespoon dry sherry

Freshly ground white pepper
to taste

1 teaspoon cornstarch

½ cup almonds

2 tablespoons vegetable or
peanut oil

1 teaspoon garlic

1 teaspoon ginger

1 onion, finely chopped

2 ribs celery, diced

¼ pound thinly sliced
mushrooms

½ teaspoon salt

2 tablespoons chicken broth

1 tablespoon soy sauce

½ teaspoon granulated
sugar

Almond Gai Ding

*Diced chicken and vegetables are combined with almonds in this popular
take-out dish. You can replace the almonds with cashews if you prefer.*

1. Dice the chicken into bite-sized cubes. Place the diced chicken in a bowl and add the oyster sauce, dry sherry, white pepper, and cornstarch. Marinate the chicken for 20 minutes.

2. Toast the almonds in a wok or skillet over medium heat, shaking the pan continuously so that the nuts do not burn. Toast until the almonds are golden (about 5 minutes). Remove the almonds from the pan to cool.

3. Heat a wok or skillet over medium-high heat until it is nearly smoking. Add the oil. When the oil is hot, add the garlic and ginger. Stir-fry for 10 seconds, then add the chicken. Stir-fry the chicken until it turns white and is nearly cooked.

4. Push the chicken to the sides of the wok or skillet. Add the onion in the middle and stir-fry for about 2 minutes, until it begins to soften. Add the celery, mushrooms, and salt. Stir-fry for about 2 minutes, until the mushrooms darken and the celery has turned a darker green and is tender but still crisp.

5. Stir in the chicken broth, soy sauce, and sugar. Stir-fry for another minute. Garnish with the almonds.

Almonds in Ancient Times You'll find several references to almonds in ancient writings. In Greek mythology, the gods take pity on Phyllis and turn her into an almond tree after she is deserted by her lover, Demophoon. In the Bible, the famous rod used by Aaron is made from the wood of an almond tree.

Korean Beef Lettuce Wraps

If you can't find Korean chile paste, try substituting chopped red chilies (fresh or dried), chili powder, or red pepper flakes.

Yields 10 to 12 wraps

1 pound sirloin or flank steak

2 tablespoons sesame oil

1 tablespoon soy sauce

1 tablespoon rice wine

¼ teaspoon black pepper, or to taste

2 teaspoons cornstarch

3 tablespoons vegetable oil, divided

1 teaspoon minced garlic

1 teaspoon minced ginger

1 tablespoon Korean chile paste (gochujang)

¼ cup chopped green onion

1 teaspoon granulated sugar

1 head iceberg lettuce or Bibb lettuce leaves

1. Cut the beef across the grain into thin strips 1½ inches long and ⅛ inch wide. Place the beef strips in a bowl and add the sesame oil, soy sauce, rice wine, pepper, and cornstarch. Marinate the beef for 30 minutes.

2. Heat a wok or skillet over medium-high heat until it is nearly smoking. Add 1½ tablespoons oil. When the oil is hot, add half the beef. Stir-fry the beef until it is no longer pink and is nearly cooked. Remove and drain in a colander or on paper towels. Stir-fry the remainder of the beef.

3. Heat 1½ tablespoons oil in the wok or skillet. Add the garlic, ginger, chile paste, and green onion. Add the beef back into the pan. Stir in the sugar. Stir-fry for 1 to 2 more minutes to combine the flavors and make sure the beef is cooked through.

4. Lay a lettuce leaf on a plate in front of you. Spoon out a portion of the beef mixture into the center of the leaf, and roll it up enchilada-style. Continue with the remainder of the beef and lettuce leaves.

Chapter 8

Noodles

2 quarts water

1 teaspoon salt

½ pound linguini or Chinese egg noodles

2 teaspoons vegetable, peanut, or Asian sesame oil, optional

Basic Noodles for Stir-Frying

Fresh noodles should be cooked until they are tender but still firm and a bit chewy in the middle—what the Italians call al dente, *or "to the teeth."*

1. In a large pot, bring the water to a boil with the salt. Add the noodles and cook until they are firm but tender.

2. Drain the noodles thoroughly. Stir in the oil if using.

3. Use the noodles as called for in a stir-fry recipe where they are added to the stir-fry at the end of cooking. Adding noodles to the stir-fry allows them to soak up the sauce.

Perfect Pasta Cooking Tips Always cook pasta in plenty of water. The pasta will taste better if it has plenty of room to move around during cooking. Wait for the water to come to a full rolling boil before adding the noodles. Stir the pasta to separate the strands. Finally, calculate the cooking time for the pasta from the moment the water returns to a rolling boil.

Chicken Lo Mein

For extra flavor, marinate the chicken strips in a bowl with 2 tablespoons oyster sauce, black or white pepper to taste, and 1 teaspoon cornstarch for 15 minutes before stir-frying. Cook the noodles and prepare the other ingredients while the chicken is marinating.

1. In a large pot, bring 2 quarts of water to a boil with 1 teaspoon salt. Add the noodles and cook until they are firm but tender. Drain the cooked pasta. Cut the chicken breasts into thin strips. Combine the chicken broth and soy sauce in a bowl and whisk in the cornstarch.

2. Heat a wok or skillet over medium-high heat until it is nearly smoking. Add 2 tablespoons oil. When the oil is hot, add the crushed garlic. Stir-fry the garlic for 10 seconds, then add the chicken. Let sit briefly, then stir-fry the chicken until it turns white and is nearly cooked. Remove the chicken from the pan and drain in a colander or on paper towels.

3. Heat 1 tablespoon oil in the wok or skillet. Add the mushrooms and snow peas, sprinkling ½ teaspoon salt on the vegetables if desired. Stir-fry for 1 minute, then add the red bell pepper. Stir-fry for 1 more minute or until the vegetables are tender but still crisp.

4. Add the sauce into the pan and bring to a boil. Add the noodles. Stir-fry for a minute to mix the noodles with the other ingredients. Add the chicken back into the pan. Stir-fry for 2 more minutes or until everything is heated through. Taste and add salt or pepper if desired. Serve hot.

Italian Pasta and Chinese Noodles Both Italian pasta and Chinese egg noodles are made with eggs and wheat flour. The main difference between the two is that Chinese noodles don't come in the variety of shapes Italian pasta comes in. However, long, thin Italian pasta such as spaghetti, fettuccini, and linguini can be used interchangeably with Chinese egg noodles in recipes.

Serves 4

- 1½ teaspoons salt, divided
- ½ pound fresh egg noodles or linguini
- ½ pound boneless, skinless chicken breast
- 1 cup chicken broth
- 2 tablespoons soy sauce
- 1 tablespoon cornstarch
- 3 tablespoons vegetable or peanut oil, divided
- 2 cloves garlic, crushed
- ¼ pound mushrooms, thinly sliced
- 6 ounces snow peas, trimmed
- 1 red bell pepper, thinly sliced
- Salt and pepper, to taste

1 pound flank steak

1½ tablespoons light soy sauce

1 tablespoon Chinese rice wine or dry sherry

Black pepper to taste

2 teaspoons cornstarch

4–5 ounces rice vermicelli noodles

1 tomato

3 tablespoons chicken broth

1 tablespoon dark soy sauce

¾ teaspoon granulated sugar

¼ teaspoon salt

¼ teaspoon chile paste

4 tablespoons vegetable or peanut oil, divided

2 cloves garlic, minced

2 thin slices ginger, minced

3 tablespoons curry powder, or to taste

1 onion, chopped

1 cup mung bean sprouts

Curried Rice Noodles with Beef

Thin rice vermicelli noodles soak up the curry flavor in this easy stir-fry recipe that makes a complete one-dish meal.

1. Cut the flank steak across the grain into thin strips that are about ½ inch wide, ⅛ inch thick, and 1½ to 2 inches long. Place the flank steak in a bowl and add the light soy sauce, rice wine or sherry, black pepper, and cornstarch. Marinate the steak for 15 minutes.

2. Soak the rice noodles in hot water for 15 to 20 minutes, until they are softened. Drain thoroughly and cut the noodles crosswise into thirds. Cut the tomato into thin slices and cut each slice in half. Combine the chicken broth, dark soy sauce, granulated sugar, salt, and chile paste in a small bowl.

3. Heat a wok or skillet over medium-high heat until it is nearly smoking and add 2 tablespoons oil. When the oil is hot, add half the minced garlic and ginger. Stir-fry for 10 seconds, then add half the beef. Let the meat sear for about 30 seconds before starting to stir-fry, then move the meat around quickly with a spatula, until it loses any pinkness and is nearly cooked through. Remove and drain in a colander or on paper towels. Repeat with the remainder of the beef.

4. Heat 2 tablespoons oil in the wok or skillet. When the oil is hot, add the remainder of the minced garlic and ginger and the curry powder. Stir-fry for 10 seconds, then add the chopped onion. Stir-fry the onion, mixing it in with the seasonings, until it begins to soften (about 2 minutes). Add the tomato and stir-fry for a minute.

5. Stir in the mung bean sprouts. Stir-fry for about 1 minute, then add the beef and the noodles. Pour in the chicken broth mixture. Stir-fry for another minute or until the noodles have absorbed the chicken broth mixture. Taste and adjust the seasonings if desired. Serve hot.

Singapore Noodles

Not sure which type of curry powder to use? Both Indian Madras curry powders and the milder Vietnamese brands would work in this recipe.

1. Soak the rice noodles in warm water for 15 minutes or until they have softened. Drain the noodles.

2. Rinse the shrimp under cold running water and pat dry. Combine the chicken broth, oyster sauce, and sugar in a bowl. Set aside.

3. Heat a wok or skillet over medium-high heat and add the oil. When the oil is hot, add the garlic, ginger, and curry powder. Stir-fry for 10 seconds, then add the snow peas. Stir-fry for about 2 minutes, until they are tender but still crisp.

4. Push the snow peas to the sides of the pan and add the shrimp in the middle. Stir-fry the shrimp until they turn pink, then add the sauce. Bring to a boil, then add the noodles. Stir-fry for a minute, then stir in the mung bean sprouts.

5. Stir in the black pepper. Stir-fry for another minute to heat everything through. Taste and adjust the seasoning if desired. Serve hot.

What Are Rice Stick Noodles? Made with rice flour and water, rice stick noodles are flat white noodles that come in varying widths. Like other types of noodles, rice noodles need to be softened in hot water before cooking. Rice stick noodles (also called rice noodles) are used in several Southeast Asian dishes, from Singapore noodles and pad Thai to Vietnamese pho bo soup.

Serves 4

½ pound flat stick rice noodles

1 pound small shrimp, shelled, deveined

½ cup chicken broth

2 tablespoons oyster sauce

1 tablespoon granulated sugar

3 tablespoons vegetable or peanut oil

2 cloves garlic, chopped

1 teaspoon minced ginger

1–2 tablespoons curry powder, or to taste

6 ounces snow peas, trimmed

2 cups mung bean sprouts, rinsed and drained

½ teaspoon black pepper, or to taste

1 (3¾-ounce) package rice
  vermicelli

¼ pound flank steak

2 tablespoons vegetable or
  peanut oil

2 cloves garlic, chopped

2 ribs celery, julienned

½ teaspoon salt

½ cup water or chicken broth

2 teaspoons dark soy sauce

½ teaspoon granulated
  sugar

Quick-Fried Beef with Celery for One

*Using a mandoline, which is a handy kitchen tool that thinly slices
vegetables and other ingredients, takes the work out of julienning the celery.*

1. Soak the rice noodles in a bowl filled with hot water until they are softened
   (15 to 20 minutes). Drain the noodles, lay them out horizontally on a cutting
   board, and cut crosswise into thirds. Cut the flank steak across the grain
   into thin strips 1½ inches long.

2. Heat a wok or skillet over medium-high heat until it is nearly smoking and
   add the oil. When the oil is hot, add the garlic. Stir-fry for 10 seconds, then
   add the beef. Let sear briefly, then stir-fry the beef until it is no longer pink
   and is nearly cooked (about 2 minutes).

3. Add the celery and stir-fry for 1 minute, sprinkling with the salt. Add the
   water or chicken broth and bring to a boil. Stir in the dark soy sauce and
   sugar. Reduce the heat to medium, cover, and cook for about 2 minutes,
   until the celery is tender but still crisp. Uncover, and stir in the noodles. Stir-
   fry for another 2 minutes. Serve hot.

Why Stir-fry with Olive Oil? Olive oil is thought to be one of the key factors in
the comparatively low rate of heart disease found in Mediterranean people. Olive oil contains monounsaturated fats, which scientists believe may help lower blood pressure, in
addition to reducing the risk of certain types of heart disease. Olive oil is also a good source
of vitamin E, thought to be an antioxidant.

Hunter's Chicken and Pasta for a Crowd

*If you don't have linguine on hand, spaghetti or other
types of thin egg noodles can also be used in this recipe.*

1. In a large pot, bring 3 quarts of water to a boil with 1½ teaspoons salt. Add the noodles and cook for 4 to 5 minutes, until they are firm but still tender. Drain the cooked pasta.

2. Cut the chicken into thin strips approximately 1½ to 2 inches long. Place the chicken strips in a bowl and add 3 tablespoons dry white wine, 1 teaspoon salt, black pepper, and cornstarch. Marinate the chicken for 20 minutes. Combine the chicken broth and 6 tablespoons white wine in a bowl. Set aside.

3. Heat a wok or skillet on medium-high heat until it is almost smoking. Add 3 tablespoons oil. When the oil is hot, add the chicken strips. Let them brown briefly, then stir-fry, stirring and tossing the chicken for 4 to 5 minutes, until it has changed color and is nearly cooked. Remove the chicken from the pan.

4. Heat 2 tablespoons oil in the pan. When the oil is hot, add the shallots. Stir-fry until they begin to soften, then add the sliced mushrooms. Stir-fry for about 1 minute, then add the chicken broth mixture. Stir in the tomato sauce. Bring to a boil, then add the chicken back into the pan. Stir in the chopped fresh basil and thyme. Stir-fry for 2 more minutes to blend all the ingredients and make sure the chicken is cooked. Taste and add salt or pepper if desired. Serve the chicken over the noodles. Garnish with extra thyme and basil leaves if desired.

Serves 4 to 6

2½ teaspoons salt, divided

¾ pound linguine

1½ pounds boneless, skinless chicken thighs

9 tablespoons dry white wine, divided

Freshly ground black pepper to taste

1 tablespoon cornstarch

6 tablespoons chicken broth

5 tablespoons olive oil, divided

2 shallots, chopped

½ pound fresh mushrooms, thinly sliced

¼ cup tomato sauce

1 tablespoon chopped fresh basil leaves

1 tablespoon chopped fresh thyme

Salt and pepper to taste

½ pound lean pork

1 tablespoon soy sauce

1 tablespoon Chinese rice
wine or dry sherry

1 teaspoon cornstarch

½ pound Japanese udon
noodles

2 tablespoons vegetable or
peanut oil

1 tablespoon chopped ginger

¼ cup finely chopped green
onion

½ cup chicken broth

½ teaspoon salt, optional

1 tablespoon Asian sesame
oil

Gingered Pork with Udon Noodles

*Used in Japanese cooking, udon noodles are made with wheat
flour, water, and salt. Feel free to use Japanese soy sauce in the
marinade and to replace the rice wine or dry sherry with mirin.*

1. Cut the pork into thin strips about 1½ inches long, ¼ inch wide, and ⅛ inch thick. Place the pork strips in a bowl and add the soy sauce, rice wine or sherry, and cornstarch. Marinate the pork for 15 minutes. Cook the udon noodles according to the package directions and drain.

2. Heat a wok or skillet over medium-high heat until it is nearly smoking. Add the oil. When the oil is hot, add the ginger and green onion. Stir-fry for 10 seconds, then add the pork. Stir-fry the pork until it is no longer pink and is nearly cooked.

3. Add the chicken broth and bring to a boil. Add the noodles. Stir-fry for 2 more minutes to blend all the ingredients. Taste and add the salt if desired. Stir in the sesame oil and serve hot.

Weeknight Lo Mein

Chicken, beef, and pork would all be good meat choices for this dish.
If you want to increase the vegetables, try adding ½ cup of shredded carrot.

1. In a large pot, bring 2 quarts of water to a boil with 1 teaspoon salt. Add the noodles and cook for 4 to 5 minutes, until they are firm but still tender. Drain the cooked pasta. Combine the chicken broth, oyster sauce, and soy sauce in a bowl. Set aside.

2. Heat a wok or skillet over medium-high heat until it is nearly smoking. Add the vegetable or peanut oil. When the oil is hot, add the ginger slices. Let brown for 2 to 3 minutes, then remove from the pan. (This is to flavor the oil.) Add the mung bean sprouts and ¼ teaspoon salt. Stir-fry for 30 seconds.

3. Add the cooked meat and noodles. Add the sauce. Stir in the green onions. Stir-fry for another minute to heat everything through. Stir in the sesame oil. Serve hot.

Mung Bean Safety The common name for salmonella poisoning, "hamburger disease," leads many people to mistakenly assume that uncooked meat is the only major source of food poisoning. However, vegetables and fruit, which are often eaten raw, can also carry the bacteria responsible for food-borne illness. For safety's sake, always rinse mung bean sprouts thoroughly before cooking.

Serves 2 to 4

1¼ teaspoons salt, divided

½ pound noodles

¼ cup chicken broth

1 tablespoon oyster sauce

1 tablespoon soy sauce

2 tablespoons vegetable or peanut oil

2 slices fresh ginger

1 cup mung bean sprouts

½ cup cooked meat

2 green onions, quartered

1 teaspoon Asian sesame oil

Serves 2 to 4

1¾ teaspoons salt, divided

¾ pound fusilli pasta

¼ cup water

1 tablespoon dark soy sauce

1 tablespoon rice vinegar

1 teaspoon Asian sesame oil

2 tablespoons vegetable or peanut oil

1 teaspoon minced garlic

2 green onions, quartered

Black pepper to taste

Sesame-Flavored Fusilli

To add extra color and flavor to this dish, try using vegetable-flavored fusilli, which are green, red, and yellow.

1. In a large pot, bring 3 quarts of water to a boil with 1½ teaspoons salt. Add the noodles and cook until they are firm but tender. Drain the noodles.

2. In a small bowl, combine the water, dark soy sauce, rice vinegar, and sesame oil. Set aside.

3. Heat a wok or skillet over medium-high heat until it is nearly smoking. Add the oil. When the oil is hot, add the garlic and green onions. Stir-fry for 10 seconds, then add the noodles. Stir-fry briefly, then add the sauce. Stir in ¼ teaspoon salt and the black pepper. Stir-fry for 1 to 2 more minutes to heat everything through. Serve hot or cold.

Replacing Fish Sauce in Vegetarian Recipes While Thai cuisine is largely vegetarian, the use of fish sauce can make some dishes non-vegetarian. The role of fish sauce is to lend a salty flavor to Thai dishes. (You'll frequently find it taking the place of salt as a table condiment in Thai restaurants.) Possible alternatives to fish sauce include Chinese or Japanese light soy sauce or a mixture of salt and water.

Vegetarian Pad Thai

If your vegetarian diet includes eggs, feel free to replace the egg substitute with 2 eggs. Add the eggs in the middle of the pan and lightly scramble before mixing with the other ingredients.

1. Soak the rice noodles in warm water for 15 minutes or until they have softened.

2. While the rice noodles are softening, prepare the other ingredients. Cut the tofu in half lengthwise and drain. Cut the drained tofu into bite-sized cubes. Combine the tamarind liquid, lime juice, tamari, ketchup, and sugar in a bowl. Set aside.

3. Heat a wok or skillet on medium-high heat until it is nearly smoking. Add the oil. When the oil is hot, add the chopped shallots and stir-fry until they begin to soften. Add the green bell pepper. Stir-fry for 2 minutes or until it is tender but still crisp. Add 1 tablespoon soy sauce if the bell pepper begins to dry out while stir-frying.

4. Add the egg substitute in the middle of the pan. Stir until it begins to set, then mix with the other ingredients. Add the tofu. Stir gently, then add the sauce and bring to a boil.

5. Add the noodles, stirring continually. Cook for a minute, then stir in the mung bean sprouts and the ground chilies. Stir-fry for another minute to mix everything through. Taste and adjust seasonings, adding salt or pepper if desired. Garnish with the crushed peanuts before serving.

Serves 3 to 4

8 ounces flat rice stick noodles

½ pound firm tofu

1/3 cup tamarind liquid

4 teaspoons lime juice

4 tablespoons tamari

4 teaspoons ketchup

4 teaspoons granulated sugar

2 tablespoons vegetable or peanut oil

2 shallots, chopped

1 large green bell pepper, chopped

1 tablespoon soy sauce, if needed

¼ cup egg substitute, or as needed

1 cup mung bean sprouts, rinsed

1 tablespoon ground red chilies, or to taste

½ cup roasted peanuts, crushed

1 pound fresh chow fun rice noodles

3 tablespoons vegetable or peanut oil, divided

1 clove garlic, crushed

1 medium onion, cut into rings

½ pound barbecued roast pork, thinly sliced

½ green bell pepper, seeded and cut into chunks

½ red bell pepper, seeded and cut into chunks

2 cups mung bean sprouts

½ teaspoon salt

1 tablespoon soy sauce

1 tablespoon oyster sauce

2 green onions, quartered

Roast Pork Chow Fun

This recipe features two popular ingredients in Cantonese cooking. Barbecued roast pork is the red pork seen hanging in Chinese meat markets, while chow fun are slippery rice noodles. Both can be found in Asian markets.

1. Separate the rice noodles to keep them from sticking together.

2. Heat a wok or skillet over medium-high heat until it is nearly smoking and add 2 tablespoons oil. When the oil is hot, add the chow fun noodles. Stir-fry the noodles until they are soft and translucent (about 4 minutes), adding a bit of water, soy sauce, or chicken broth if they begin to dry out. Remove the noodles from the pan.

3. Heat 1 tablespoon oil in the same wok or skillet. When the oil is hot, add the garlic. Stir-fry for 10 seconds, then add the onion. Stir-fry the onion until it begins to soften, then add the roast pork. Stir-fry for 1 minute, then add the bell peppers. Stir-fry for 1 minute, and add the mung bean sprouts. Sprinkle with the salt. Stir-fry briefly (for about 30 seconds), then add the noodles back into the pan. Stir in the soy sauce, oyster sauce, and green onions. Stir-fry briefly to heat everything through and serve hot.

Fried Macaroni and Cheese

This protein-packed variation on traditional "mac and cheese" is a good choice for busy weeknights. Feel free to garnish with additional shredded cheese and fresh parsley before serving.

1. Cook the macaroni according to the package directions. Drain the macaroni and stir in the butter or margarine.

2. Drain the tofu. Mash the tofu in a bowl, mixing in the fresh parsley.

3. Lightly beat the eggs, stirring in the salt and black pepper. Combine the cooked macaroni with the mashed tofu and the beaten eggs.

4. Heat a heavy skillet over medium-high heat until it is nearly smoking. Add the oil, tilting the skillet so that the oil covers the bottom of the pan.

5. Add the macaroni, tofu, and egg mixture to the pan. Stir-fry, quickly moving around the pan, for about 2 minutes, until the egg is cooked and the macaroni is just beginning to brown. Stir in the cheese and soy sauce. Stir-fry for another minute to melt the cheese. Serve hot.

Pasta Varieties There are over 350 different types of pasta, from long pastas such as spaghetti and linguine to tube-shaped macaroni, rigatoni, and manicotti. Some of the more unusual pasta shapes include corkscrew-shaped fusilli, and lumache pasta, which resembles a snail.

Serves 2 to 3

1 cup elbow or shell macaroni

1 tablespoon butter or margarine

3 ounces tofu

1 teaspoon minced fresh parsley

3 large eggs

½ teaspoon salt

1/8 teaspoon black pepper

½ cup shredded Parmesan cheese

2 tablespoons olive oil

1 tablespoon Kikkoman soy sauce

1 teaspoon salt

½ pound lo mein noodles, Italian spaghetti, or fettuccini

¾ cup chicken broth

2 tablespoons oyster sauce

1 tablespoon dark soy sauce

1 teaspoon granulated sugar

2 tablespoons vegetable or peanut oil

2 cloves garlic, chopped

2 thin slices ginger, chopped

1 cup chopped carrots

1 cup chopped red bell pepper

½ pound barbecued pork, sliced

1 tablespoon light soy sauce

2 green onions, quartered

1 teaspoon Asian sesame oil

Easy Pork Lo Mein

Using barbecued pork from an Asian market adds extra flavor to this simple stir-fry. Thin lo mein noodles are also available at Asian markets, but Italian spaghetti or fettuccini can be used instead.

1. In a large pot, bring 2 quarts of water to a boil with the salt. Add the noodles and cook until they are firm but tender. Drain the noodles.

2. Combine the chicken broth, oyster sauce, dark soy sauce, and sugar in a small bowl. Set aside.

3. Heat a wok or skillet over medium-high heat until it is nearly smoking and add the oil. When the oil is hot, add the chopped garlic and ginger. Stir-fry for 10 seconds, then add the chopped carrots. Stir-fry for 1 minute, then add the chopped bell pepper. Stir-fry for 1 minute or until the vegetables are tender but still crisp.

4. Add the barbecued pork. Stir-fry for a minute, splashing with the soy sauce. Add the noodles. Stir-fry briefly to mix the noodles with the vegetables, then add the sauce. Stir in the green onions. Stir-fry for another minute to heat through. Remove from the heat and stir in the sesame oil. Serve hot.

Noodle Cooking Times The amount of time needed to cook the noodles in the boiling water will vary depending on whether you are using fresh or dried noodles. Fresh noodles usually require about 3 minutes to reach al dente stage, while dried noodles need to cook for about 2 minutes longer.

Sesame Pork with Noodles

Thin Chinese noodles (sometimes called lo mein noodles), spaghetti, and linguini would all work well in this recipe. Remember to allow more time for the noodles to cook if you are using dried noodles.

1. In a large pot, bring 2 quarts of water to a boil with 1 teaspoon salt. Add the noodles and cook until they are firm but tender. Drain the noodles.

2. Cut the pork into thin strips about 1½ inches long. Place the pork in a bowl and add the dark soy sauce, rice wine or dry sherry, and cornstarch. Marinate the pork for 15 minutes.

3. Heat a wok or skillet over medium-high heat until it is nearly smoking. Add 1 tablespoon oil. When the oil is hot, add the garlic. Stir-fry for 10 seconds, and add the pork. Stir-fry the pork until it is no longer pink and is nearly cooked through.

4. Push the pork to the sides of the pan and heat 1 tablespoon oil in the middle. Add the ginger and stir-fry for 10 seconds. Add the carrot and the celery. Stir-fry for a minute, sprinkling ½ teaspoon salt over the vegetables. Stir to combine the vegetables with the pork.

5. Stir in the cooked noodles. Add the Sesame Sauce and bring to a boil. Stir-fry for 1 to 2 more minutes to mix all the ingredients together. Serve hot.

Serves 2 to 4

1½ teaspoons salt, divided

½ pound thin noodles, fresh or dried

½ pound lean pork

2 teaspoons dark soy sauce

2 teaspoons Chinese rice wine or dry sherry

1 teaspoon cornstarch

2 tablespoons vegetable or peanut oil, divided

½ teaspoon minced garlic

½ teaspoon minced ginger

1 cup shredded carrot

1 cup shredded celery

1½ portions Sesame Sauce (page 19)

2 teaspoons salt

1 pound linguine

2 tablespoons olive oil

1 teaspoon minced garlic

2 tomatoes, cut into thin
slices and halved

¼ teaspoon black pepper

Italian Pesto Sauce (page 23)

1 teaspoon granulated sugar

Italian Linguine with Pesto Sauce

*Briefly stir-frying the pesto sauce brings out the flavor of basil and garlic.
Feel free to use oblong Italian sun-dried tomatoes in this recipe.*

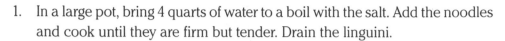

1. In a large pot, bring 4 quarts of water to a boil with the salt. Add the noodles and cook until they are firm but tender. Drain the linguini.

2. Heat a wok or skillet over medium-high heat until it is nearly smoking and add the oil. When the oil is hot, add the garlic. Stir-fry for 10 seconds, then add the tomatoes and the black pepper. Stir in the Italian Pesto Sauce. Add the noodles. Stir in the sugar. Stir-fry for 1 to 2 more minutes to blend the ingredients and heat everything through. Serve hot.

Choosing Olive Oil for Stir-Frying While unprocessed extra-virgin olive oil is the healthiest type of olive oil, its low smoke point makes it a poor candidate for stir-frying. Pure olive oil (also simply called olive oil) is the best choice for stir-frying.

Vegetable Chow Mein

Cashews take the place of meat or tofu in this healthy vegetarian recipe.
Instead of noodles, you could also substitute ¾ cup of cooked brown rice.

Serves 2 to 3

1 teaspoon salt

½ pound fresh wheat
noodles

1 cup unsalted cashews

2 tablespoons vegetable or
peanut oil

1 teaspoon chopped fresh
ginger

½ cup chopped onion

1 carrot, julienned

1 cup sliced mushrooms

1 cup snow peas

1 tablespoon soy sauce

$^1/_3$ cup Simple Stir-Fry Sauce
(page 16)

¾ teaspoon granulated
sugar

1. In a large pot, bring 2 quarts of water to a boil with the salt. Add the noodles and cook until they are firm but tender. Drain the noodles.

2. Roast the cashews in a heavy frying pan over medium heat, shaking the pan continuously so that the nuts do not burn. Roast until the cashews are browned (about 5 minutes). Remove the cashews from the pan to cool.

3. Heat a wok or skillet over medium-high heat until it is nearly smoking. Add the oil. When the oil is hot, add the ginger. Stir-fry for 10 seconds, then add the onion. Stir-fry for 2 minutes or until the onion begins to soften. Add the carrot. Stir-fry for 1 minute, then add the mushrooms. Stir-fry for another minute, then add the snow peas. Splash the vegetables with 1 tablespoon soy sauce during stir-frying.

4. Add the noodles. Stir in the Simple Stir-Fry Sauce and bring to a boil.

5. Stir in the roasted cashews and the sugar. Stir-fry for another minute to heat everything through, and serve hot.

4–5 ounces rice vermicelli
noodles

2 tablespoons vegetable or
peanut oil

2 cloves garlic, chopped

2 teaspoons chopped red
chilies, or to taste

2 green onions, chopped into
1-inch pieces

½ pound flank steak,
shredded

¼ cup Hot and Sour Sauce
(page 27)

½ teaspoon granulated
sugar

Spicy Shredded Beef with Rice Noodles

*Strips of beef are cooked in a spicy sauce with stir-fried
noodles in this tasty stir-fry that is great for busy weeknights.*

1. Soak the rice noodles in a bowl filled with hot water until they are softened (15 to 20 minutes). Drain the noodles thoroughly, lay them out horizontally on a cutting board, and cut crosswise into thirds.

2. Heat a wok or skillet over medium-high heat until it is almost smoking. Add the oil. When the oil is hot, add the garlic, red chilies, and green onions. Stir-fry for 10 seconds, then add the shredded beef. Stir-fry for about 2 minutes, until it is no longer pink and is nearly cooked through.

3. Add the noodles. Stir-fry for a few seconds, and add the Hot and Sour Sauce. Stir-fry for 2 minutes or until everything is heated through. Stir in the sugar. Serve hot.

Handling Rice Vermicelli These thin rice noodles can pose a challenge the first time you add them to a stir-fry. Once softened, rice vermicelli noodles are like sponges, drawing up the liquid around them. You can end up with globs of liquid-soaked noodles. Cut rice vermicelli crosswise into sections to make handling easier, and go sparingly on the sauce the first few times you use them in cooking.

Tomato Beef Chow Mein

If you're pressed for time and in too much of a hurry to prepare the noodles for this recipe, use packaged dried chow mein noodles, which are available in most supermarkets.

½ pound flank steak

2 teaspoons oyster sauce

1 tablespoon plus 2 teaspoons rice vinegar, divided

1 tablespoon plus ½ teaspoon cornstarch, divided

¼ cup chicken broth

2 tablespoons ketchup

1 tablespoon dark soy sauce

1 tablespoon sugar

4 tablespoons water

2 tablespoons vegetable oil

2 slices ginger

2 tomatoes, thinly sliced, each slice cut in half

2 ribs celery, cut on the diagonal into ½-inch slices

Homemade Chow Mein Noodles (page 220)

1. Cut the beef across the grain into thin strips that are approximately 2 inches long. Place the strips of beef in a bowl and add the oyster sauce, 2 teaspoons rice vinegar, and ½ teaspoon cornstarch. Marinate the beef for 15 minutes.

2. Combine the chicken broth, ketchup, 1 tablespoon rice vinegar, dark soy sauce, and sugar in a bowl. In a separate small bowl, dissolve 1 tablespoon cornstarch in the water. Set aside.

3. Heat a wok or skillet on medium-high heat until it is nearly smoking. Add the oil. When the oil is hot, add the ginger. As soon as the ginger sizzles, add the beef, laying it flat in the pan. Let sear (brown) briefly, then stir-fry the meat, stirring and tossing until it is nearly cooked through.

4. Push the beef to the sides of the pan. Add the tomato and celery in the middle. Stir-fry for 1 minute, or until the celery turns a darker green. Add the sauce in the middle and bring to a boil. Add the cornstarch and water mixture into the sauce, stirring continually. When the sauce thickens, stir-fry for 1 to 2 more minutes to mix it with the beef and vegetables. Pour the beef and vegetable stir-fry over the noodles.

Hoisin-Flavored Cellophane Noodles

1 bundle (about 3½ ounces) cellophane noodles

½ cup chicken broth

2 tablespoons hoisin sauce

¼–½ teaspoon chile paste

2 tablespoons vegetable or peanut oil

1 teaspoon minced garlic

½ teaspoon minced ginger

2 green onions, cut into 1-inch pieces

6 ounces fresh portobello mushrooms, cubed

1 red bell pepper, seeded and cubed

⅛ teaspoon freshly ground white pepper, or to taste

If you are using low-sodium chicken broth, feel free to add salt or a salt substitute for extra flavor.

1. Soak the rice noodles in a bowl filled with hot water until they are softened (15 to 20 minutes). Drain the noodles thoroughly, lay them out horizontally on a cutting board, and cut crosswise into thirds.

2. In a small bowl, combine the chicken broth, hoisin sauce, and chile paste. Set aside.

3. Heat a wok or skillet over medium-high heat until it is nearly smoking. Add the oil. When the oil is hot, add the garlic, ginger, and green onions. Stir-fry for 10 seconds, then add the mushrooms. Stir-fry for a minute, then add the red bell pepper. Stir-fry for another minute or until the mushrooms have darkened and the red bell pepper is tender but still crisp.

4. Add the noodles into the wok or skillet. Stir-fry briefly, then add the sauce. Bring to a boil, and stir-fry for another 1 to 2 minutes, until everything is heated through. Stir in the freshly ground white pepper. Serve hot.

Cellophane Noodles Made from mung bean flour, cellophane noodles are also called bean thread noodles and slippery noodles, due to their transparent appearance and slippery texture. Like rice vermicelli, mung bean noodles are very absorbent. Always soften the noodles in hot water for 15 to 20 minutes before cooking; otherwise, the noodles will quickly absorb most of the liquid in the dish.

Shanghai Noodles

*You can experiment with the flavors in this dish by
substituting white or red rice vinegar for the red wine vinegar.*

1. In a large pot, bring 3 quarts of water to a boil with 1½ teaspoons salt. Add the noodles and cook until they are firm but tender.

2. In a small bowl, combine the chicken broth, light soy sauce, dark soy sauce, red wine vinegar, and sugar. Set aside.

3. Heat a wok or skillet over medium-high heat until it is nearly smoking. Add the oil. When the oil is hot, add the garlic, ginger, and red pepper flakes. Stir-fry for 10 seconds, then add the onion. Stir-fry the onion for about 2 minutes, until it begins to soften. Add the Napa cabbage. Stir-fry for 1 minute, sprinkling with ½ teaspoon salt. Add the red bell pepper. Stir-fry for another minute, stirring in 1 to 2 tablespoons water or soy sauce if the vegetables begin to dry out.

4. Add the noodles into the wok or skillet. Stir-fry for a minute, then add the sauce. Bring to a boil. Stir-fry for 1 to 2 more minutes to heat through. Serve hot.

Serves 3 to 4

2 teaspoons salt, divided

¾ pound dried Chinese egg noodles or linguini

½ cup chicken broth

5 tablespoons light soy sauce

3 tablespoons dark soy sauce

5 tablespoons red wine vinegar

½ tablespoon granulated sugar

2 tablespoons vegetable or peanut oil

1 teaspoon minced garlic

½ teaspoon minced ginger

½ teaspoon red pepper flakes, optional

½ medium onion, chopped

2 cups shredded Napa cabbage leaves

1 cup chopped red bell pepper

1–2 tablespoons additional water or light soy sauce, if needed

Homemade Chow Mein Noodles

This recipe is also called noodle pancake or twice-browned noodles, but whatever the name, these fried noodles go well with a chow mein recipe such as Tomato Beef Chow Mein (page 217). Just pour the stir-fried meat and vegetables over the noodles.

1. In a large pot, bring 2 quarts of water to a boil. Add the noodles and cook until they are firm but tender. Drain the noodles and stir in the Asian sesame oil, salt, and sugar. Allow the noodles to dry in a colander for 1 hour.

2. Heat a large flat skillet over medium-high heat until it is nearly smoking. Add ¼ cup oil. When the oil is hot, carefully slide the dried noodles into the pan, spreading them out so that they cover the entire pan. Cook for 6 to 8 minutes, until the noodles are browned on the bottom. Turn the heat down to medium if the pan starts smoking.

3. Turn the noodle pancake over and brown on the other side (it should take less time to brown the bottom side). Slide the noodle pancake out of the pan. Use a knife to cut the noodle pancake into the number of serving portions needed.

How to Cook a Noodle Pancake Draining the noodles in a large colander for about an hour before cooking will cause them to naturally form into a pancake shape. Use a spatula to slide the noodles from the colander into the pan. To brown the bottom side of a noodle pancake, slide the noodle pancake out of the pan onto a large plate, invert it onto another plate, and slide it back into the pan.

Sesame-Flavored Fusilli with Scallops

Corkscrew-shaped fusilli pasta enhances the appearance of this simple noodle stir-fry. The pasta stays pleasantly chewy and the sauce sticks to it well.

Serves 2 to 4

1¼ teaspoons salt, divided

½ pound fusilli pasta

½ pound bay scallops

6 tablespoons water

1½ tablespoons dark soy sauce

1½ tablespoons rice vinegar

1½ teaspoons Asian sesame oil

3 tablespoons vegetable or peanut oil, divided

1 teaspoon minced garlic

1 zucchini, chopped on the diagonal into ½-inch slices

1 tablespoon light soy sauce

1 tomato, halved and thinly sliced

½ teaspoon minced ginger

Black pepper to taste

1. In a large pot, bring 2 quarts of water to a boil with 1 teaspoon salt. Add the noodles and cook until they are firm but tender. Drain the noodles.

2. Rinse the scallops in cold running water and pat dry with paper towels. Toss the scallops with ¼ teaspoon salt. In a small bowl, combine the water, dark soy sauce, rice vinegar, and sesame oil. Set aside.

3. Heat a wok or skillet over medium-high heat until it is nearly smoking. Add 2 tablespoons oil. When the oil is hot, add the garlic. Stir-fry for 10 seconds, then add the zucchini. Stir-fry for a minute, then stir in the soy sauce. Add the tomato. Stir-fry until the zucchini turns dark green and is tender but still crisp (about 3 minutes). Remove the vegetables and drain in a colander or on paper towels.

4. Heat 1 tablespoon oil in the wok or skillet. When the oil is hot, add the ginger. Stir-fry for 10 seconds, then add the scallops. Stir-fry the scallops until they turn white and are just starting to firm up. Add the noodles and the sauce. Stir in the black pepper.

5. Add the vegetables back into the pan. Stir-fry for 1 to 2 more minutes to heat everything through. Taste and adjust seasoning if desired. Serve hot.

1½ teaspoons salt, divided

½ pound fresh Chinese or Italian egg noodles

½ pound lean pork

1½ tablespoons light soy sauce

2½ tablespoons vegetable or peanut oil, divided

Black pepper to taste

½ cup chicken broth

¼ cup oyster sauce

2 tablespoons dark soy sauce

2 tablespoons rice wine or dry sherry

1 teaspoon granulated sugar

2 cloves garlic, chopped

2 thin slices ginger, chopped

2 cups chopped bok choy

1 red bell pepper, cubed

1 cup mung bean sprouts

Additional water, if needed

Oyster-Flavored Pork with Noodles

Bok choy and red bell pepper add extra color to this tasty dish, and the sauce flavors the egg noodles wonderfully.

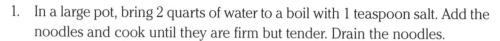

1. In a large pot, bring 2 quarts of water to a boil with 1 teaspoon salt. Add the noodles and cook until they are firm but tender. Drain the noodles.

2. Cut the pork into cubes. Place the pork in a medium bowl and add the light soy sauce, 1½ teaspoons vegetable oil, and pepper. Marinate the pork for 20 minutes. Combine the chicken broth with the oyster sauce, dark soy sauce, rice wine or sherry, and the sugar in a bowl. Set aside.

3. Heat a wok or skillet over medium-high heat until it is nearly smoking. Add 2 tablespoons oil. When the oil is hot, add the garlic and ginger. Stir-fry for 10 seconds, then add the pork. Stir-fry for 2 minutes or until the pork is no longer pink and is nearly cooked.

4. Push the pork to the sides of the wok or skillet and add the bok choy in the middle. Stir-fry the bok choy for 1 minute, sprinkling ½ teaspoon salt over the top. Add the red bell pepper. Add the mung bean sprouts. Stir-fry for another minute or until the bok choy turns bright green. Splash the vegetables with water if they begin to dry out during stir-frying.

5. Add the noodles. Stir-fry briefly, then add the sauce. Stir-fry for 1 to 2 more minutes to heat everything through. Serve hot.

Pasta Versus Noodles While pasta is normally made with durum wheat flour (with or without egg) and comes in an endless variety of shapes, a noodle is a long, ribbonlike piece of dough that can be made of everything from wheat flour to rice flour. So, while Chinese egg noodles can correctly be called pasta, the translucent cellophane noodles found in Hoisin-Flavored Cellophane Noodles (page 218) cannot.

Shrimp Chow Mein

*If you don't have leftover cooked ham, substitute 4 ounces of lean pork,
cut into thin strips, and stir-fry it separately. Don't increase the amount
of shrimp, as its strong flavor can overpower the other ingredients.*

1¼ teaspoons salt, divided

½ pound fresh egg noodles

¼ pound shelled, deveined
shrimp

¼ cup water

2 teaspoons oyster sauce

2 teaspoons Chinese rice
wine or dry sherry

1 teaspoon light soy sauce

3 tablespoons vegetable or
peanut oil

2 thin slices ginger, minced

4 ounces sliced mushrooms

1 rib celery, cut on the
diagonal into ½-inch
slices

1 red bell pepper, cubed

1 additional tablespoon soy
sauce, if needed

¼ pound cooked ham, cut
into chunks

Black pepper to taste

1. In a large pot, bring 2 quarts of water to a boil with 1 teaspoon salt. Add the noodles and cook until they are firm but tender. Drain the noodles.

2. Rinse the shrimp under cold running water and toss with ¼ teaspoon salt. Combine the water, oyster sauce, rice wine or sherry, and soy sauce in a bowl.

3. Heat a wok or skillet over medium-high heat until it is nearly smoking. Add the oil. When the oil is hot, add the ginger. Stir-fry for 10 seconds, then add the shrimp. Stir-fry the shrimp until they turn pink.

4. Push the shrimp to the sides of the wok or skillet. Add the mushrooms. Stir-fry for 1 minute, then add the celery and the red bell pepper. Stir-fry for another minute, until the mushrooms have darkened and the celery has turned a bright green. Splash the vegetables with 1 tablespoon soy sauce if they begin to dry out.

5. Add the noodles. Stir in the sauce and bring to a boil. Stir in the cooked ham. Stir-fry for 1 to 2 more minutes to mix everything together. Taste and adjust seasoning, adding black pepper if desired. Serve hot.

½ pound flank steak

1½ tablespoons ketchup

1½ tablespoons
Worcestershire sauce

1 tablespoon soy sauce

1½ tablespoons water, or as
needed

1½ teaspoons brown sugar

3 tablespoons vegetable or
peanut oil, divided

1 teaspoon minced garlic

2 shallots, peeled and
chopped

½ green bell pepper, cut into
thin strips

½ pound fresh mushrooms,
thinly sliced

½ red bell pepper, cut into
thin strips

1 tablespoon liquid, if
needed

2 ounces deep-fried rice
vermicelli

Easy Chinese Steak over Noodles

Rice vermicelli noodles puff up nicely when deep-fried. However, if you don't have any on hand, you can serve the steak and vegetables with tortilla or taco chips.

1. Cut the steak across the grain into thin strips, 1½ to 2 inches long, ⅛ inch wide, and ⅛ inch thick. Combine the ketchup, Worcestershire sauce, soy sauce, water, and brown sugar in a small bowl. Set aside.

2. Heat a wok or skillet over medium-high heat until it is nearly smoking. Add 1½ tablespoons oil. When the oil is hot, add half the garlic. Stir-fry for 10 seconds, then add the flank steak. Let sear briefly, then stir-fry the beef until it is no longer pink and is nearly cooked. Remove the beef and drain in a colander or on paper towels.

3. Heat 1½ tablespoons oil in the wok or skillet. Add the remaining garlic and stir-fry for 10 seconds. Add the shallots and stir-fry briefly, until they begin to soften. Add the green bell pepper and the mushrooms. Stir-fry for a minute, then add the red bell pepper. Splash the vegetables with 1 tablespoon water or dry sherry if they begin to dry out during stir-frying.

4. Add the sauce and bring to a boil. Add the beef back into the pan. Stir-fry for 2 to 3 more minutes to blend the flavors. Serve hot over the deep-fried rice vermicelli.

How to Deep-Fry Rice Vermicelli   To fry rice noodles, pour 2 inches of oil into a wok or deep-sided heavy skillet and heat to 375°F. When the oil is hot, remove the noodles from the package and use tongs to lower them into the hot oil. Cook briefly (for 1 second), turn over, and cook for 1 second more. Remove the noodles and drain in a colander or on paper towels.

Asian Noodles with Meat Sauce

For extra flavor, marinate the ground beef in 2 teaspoons light soy sauce and 2 teaspoons Chinese rice wine or dry sherry before stir-frying.

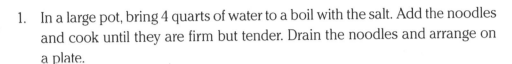

1. In a large pot, bring 4 quarts of water to a boil with the salt. Add the noodles and cook until they are firm but tender. Drain the noodles and arrange on a plate.

2. Combine the chicken broth, brown bean sauce, and hoisin sauce in a small bowl. Set aside.

3. Heat a wok or skillet over medium-high heat until it is nearly smoking. Add the oil. When the oil is hot, add the ginger, garlic, and the red pepper flakes. Stir-fry for 10 seconds, then add the ground beef. Stir-fry the beef until it is no longer pink and is nearly cooked.

4. Add the sauce and bring to a boil. Stir in the green onion and the sugar. Stir-fry for 2 more minutes to blend the flavors. Taste and adjust seasoning, adding salt and pepper if desired. Pour the meat sauce over the noodles and serve.

2 teaspoons salt

1 pound Chinese egg noodles or spaghetti

¼ cup chicken broth

3 tablespoons brown bean sauce

3 tablespoons hoisin sauce

2 tablespoons vegetable or peanut oil

1 teaspoon minced ginger

1 teaspoon minced garlic

¼ teaspoon red pepper flakes

½ pound ground beef

2 tablespoons chopped green onion

1 teaspoon granulated sugar

Salt and black pepper to taste

1 teaspoon salt

½ pound fresh egg noodles

1 teaspoon cornstarch

2 teaspoons water

1½ tablespoons vegetable or peanut oil

1 teaspoon chopped garlic

½ teaspoon chopped ginger

2 green onions, finely chopped

2 carrots, julienned

1 cup mung bean sprouts, drained

1 cup Strange Flavor Sauce (page 26)

Stir-Fried Dan Dan Noodles

There are many ways to make this popular Szechuan noodle dish. This recipe calls for the same sauce that is used in Strange Flavor Chicken Salad (page 42), the Szechuan take on cold chicken salad.

1. In a large pot, bring 2 quarts of water to a boil with the salt. Add the noodles and cook until they are firm but tender. Drain the noodles.

2. In a small bowl, dissolve the cornstarch into the water.

3. Heat a wok or skillet over medium-high heat until it is nearly smoking and add the oil. When the oil is hot, add the garlic, ginger, and green onions. Stir-fry for 10 seconds, then add the carrots. Stir-fry the carrots for 1 minute, then add the mung bean sprouts. Stir-fry briefly (30 seconds to 1 minute).

4. Push the vegetables to the side and add the Strange Flavor Sauce in the middle. Bring to a boil. Stir the cornstarch and water mixture and add to the sauce, stirring quickly to thicken. Add the noodles. Stir-fry for 1 to 2 more minutes to mix the flavors together. Serve hot.

Chinese Regional Cuisine   Cantonese cuisine is famed for its use of fresh ingredients and seafood, while northern Beijing cuisine is wheat-based, with a number of popular noodle dishes. Western China is home to Szechuan cuisine, famous for fiery dishes seasoned with Szechuan peppercorn and hot chili peppers. Eastern Shanghai cuisine is known for its liberal use of soy sauce and sugar and for its wide variety of seafood dishes.

Chapter 9

Rice Dishes

Basic Cooked Rice

Yields 3 cups

1½ cups water

1 cup long-grain rice

Unless the recipe calls for noodles, the majority of stir-fried dishes are meant to be served over a heaping plate of cooked rice. Feel free to use medium-grain or brown rice instead of long-grain rice. Remember to adjust the amount of water, as the liquid-absorption rate varies among different types of rice.

1. Bring the water and rice to a boil in a saucepan over medium heat.

2. When the water is boiling, partially cover and lower the heat to medium-low. Cook until most of the liquid is absorbed.

3. Cover and continue cooking the rice on low heat until the water is fully absorbed. Remove the rice from the heat and let sit, covered, for 5 minutes. Use a fork to fluff the rice before serving.

Coconut-Scented Rice

Yields 3 cups

¾ cup coconut milk

¾ cup water

1 cup long-grain rice

1 teaspoon sliced ginger

1 tablespoon brown sugar

Salt to taste

Replacing the water with coconut milk, chicken broth, or another liquid is a quick and easy way to add extra flavor to plain cooked rice. You could also use scented basmati or jasmine rice in this recipe for a different flavor.

1. Bring the coconut milk, water, rice, and ginger to a boil in a saucepan over medium heat. When the water is boiling, stir in the brown sugar and the salt. Partially cover the pot and lower the heat to medium-low. Cook until most of the liquid is absorbed.

2. Cover and continue cooking on low heat until the liquid is fully absorbed. Remove the rice from the heat and let sit, covered, for 5 minutes. Use a fork to fluff the rice before serving.

Basic Fried Rice

Nothing beats fried rice when you're looking for a creative way to serve leftovers.
If you're using frozen peas in this fried-rice recipe, be sure to thaw them first.

1. Lightly beat the eggs, stirring in the salt and pepper.

2. Heat a wok or skillet over medium-high heat until it is nearly smoking. Add 2 tablespoons oil. When the oil is hot, add the eggs. Stir the eggs until they are lightly scrambled. Remove the scrambled eggs and clean out the pan.

3. Heat 1 tablespoon oil. When the oil is hot, add the rice. Stir-fry for 2 minutes, stirring and tossing the rice. Stir in the soy sauce.

4. Stir in the peas. Stir-fry for about 30 seconds, then add the eggs back into the pan. Stir in the green onions and the sesame oil. Serve hot.

Basic Stir-Fried Glutinous Rice

Many people don't realize that glutinous rice, a staple of steamed
Asian snacks such as sticky rice wrapped in bamboo leaves, can also
be stir-fried. Here it makes a nice alternative to basic cooked rice.

1. Rinse the glutinous rice. Place the rice in a bowl with enough water to cover and soak for 5 to 6 hours. Drain the rice.

2. Heat a wok or skillet over medium-high heat until it is nearly smoking. Add 1 tablespoon oil. When the oil is hot, add the onion. Stir-fry the onion until it begins to soften (about 2 minutes).

3. Push the onion to the side and add 1 tablespoon oil in the middle. Add the rice. Stir-fry the rice for 2 to 3 minutes, until the grains are tender. Pour in the beef broth. Stir-fry until the rice has absorbed the liquid (about 2 minutes). Taste and add salt and pepper if desired. Serve hot.

½ cup raw shrimp, shelled, deveined

2 teaspoons curry powder

2 tablespoons Thai fish sauce

½ teaspoon coconut extract

½ cup unsalted cashews

2 tablespoons vegetable or peanut oil

2 tablespoons chopped garlic

2–3 red Serrano chilies, seeded and chopped

1 red bell pepper, seeded and diced

1 cup pineapple tidbits

3 cups cooked jasmine rice

½ teaspoon granulated sugar, or to taste

2 green onions, finely chopped

Salt or black pepper to taste

1–2 tablespoons shredded coconut

Piña Colada Fried Rice

Scented jasmine rice adds extra flavor to any fried-rice recipe. You can turn up the heat in this Thai-inspired dish by increasing the number of red chili peppers.

1. Rinse the shrimp under cold running water and pat dry. In a small bowl, combine the curry powder, fish sauce, and coconut extract. Set aside.

2. Roast the cashews in a skillet over medium heat, shaking the pan continuously so that the nuts do not burn. Roast until the cashews are browned (about 5 minutes). Remove the cashews from the pan to cool.

3. Turn the heat to medium-high and add 2 tablespoons oil, rotating the pan so that it coats the bottom. When the oil is hot, add the garlic and chopped chilies. Stir-fry quickly until they are fragrant, then add the shrimp. Stir-fry the shrimp, moving them quickly around the pan until they turn pink. Add the red bell pepper and the pineapple and continue stir-frying.

4. Add the rice and stir-fry for a minute, continually stirring the rice and turning it over. Add the curry powder mixture. Stir in the sugar. Stir in the green onions. Stir-fry for a minute more to mix the ingredients together. Do a taste test and add salt or black pepper if desired.

5. Sprinkle the shredded coconut over the top and garnish with the roasted cashews before serving.

The Science of Rice The main difference between long-, medium-, and short-grain rice isn't the length of the individual grains. It all comes down to two types of starch: amylose and amylopectin. Amylose produces a fluffier rice, while amylopectin makes the rice more sticky. Fluffy long-grain rice is rich in amylose, while short-grain rice (also called "sticky rice") contains more amylopectin.

Spanish Rice Side Dish

This easy and colorful side dish goes nicely with
everything from Beef in Stir-Fry Sauce (page 102) to tacos.

1. Bring the chicken broth and rice to a boil in a saucepan over medium heat.

2. When the broth is boiling, partially cover and lower the heat to medium-low.

3. When the broth is nearly absorbed, cover the rice and cook over low heat until the broth is completely absorbed.

4. Purée the tomatoes in a food processor or blender.

5. Heat a wok or skillet on medium heat until it is nearly smoking. Add the olive oil. Add the rice and stir-fry, stirring it in the oil until it turns golden brown.

6. Add the onion and garlic. Sprinkle the chili powder over the mixture. Stir the onion and garlic into the rice. Stir in the puréed tomato. Stir in the chopped parsley. Continue stir-frying for about 5 minutes, or until the onion is softened. Serve hot.

Rice Around the World Spain is the birthplace of paella Valencia—an elaborate dish with shellfish, meat, and rice that is flavored with saffron and a tomato-based sauce. Jambalaya is a Cajun/Creole adaptation of paella Valencia made with ingredients readily available in the southern United States. Japan's signature dish, sushi, is often served with a bowl of "sushi rice"—a sticky rice seasoned with rice vinegar and sugar.

Serves 3 to 4

1½ cups chicken broth

1 cup uncooked long-grain white rice

2 medium tomatoes, peeled, seeded, and quartered

2 tablespoons olive oil

¼ chopped onion

1 tablespoon chopped garlic

1 teaspoon chili powder

2 tablespoons chopped fresh parsley

2 teaspoons salt, divided

¼ teaspoon black pepper

1½ teaspoons cornstarch

¾ pound ground beef

3 tablespoons plus 2
    teaspoons vegetable or
    peanut oil, divided

1 teaspoon minced garlic

2 teaspoons minced ginger

2 cups chopped broccoli

½ cup water

1 cup cooked white rice

2 portions Basic Brown Sauce
    (page 20)

1 teaspoon granulated sugar

Ground Beef with Broccoli and Rice

Enjoy the flavor of Chinese Beef with Broccoli during the week with this easy one-pot dish.

1. In a bowl, mix 1 teaspoon salt, pepper, and cornstarch in with the ground beef. Let the ground beef stand for 20 minutes.

2. Heat wok or skillet on medium-high heat until it is nearly smoking. Add 2 teaspoons oil. When the oil is hot, add the ground beef. Stir-fry, stirring and tossing it in the pan, until there is no trace of pink and the ground beef is nearly cooked through. Remove the ground beef and drain in a colander or on paper towels.

3. Clean out the wok or skillet and add 2 tablespoons oil. When the oil is hot, add the garlic and ginger. Stir-fry for 10 seconds, then add the broccoli. Stir-fry the broccoli for 2 minutes, sprinkling with 1 teaspoon salt. Add ½ cup water, cover, and cook the broccoli for 4 to 5 minutes, until it is tender but still crisp. Remove the broccoli and drain in a colander or on paper towels.

4. Heat 1 tablespoon oil in the wok or skillet. When the oil is hot, add the rice. Stir-fry the rice in the oil for about 1 minute or until it begins to brown. Add the ground beef and broccoli back into the pan. Add the brown sauce, stirring quickly to thicken. Stir in the sugar. Stir-fry for 1 to 2 more minutes. Serve hot.

Fried Rice Fundamentals When making fried rice, use previously cooked rice if possible. The rice should be at least one day old (two- or even three-day-old rice is even better). Sprinkle a few drops of water on the rice, and use your fingers or a spatula to break up the clumps.

Arroz con Pollo

This is Latin America's take on a nourishing chicken and rice dish. For a more authentic touch, add 6 to 8 soaked yellow saffron threads to the rice while it is cooking.

1 pound boneless, skinless chicken thighs

1 teaspoon salt

½ teaspoon black pepper

5 tablespoons olive oil, divided

2 cloves garlic, chopped

2 teaspoons chopped red chili peppers

1 onion, chopped

1 tablespoon paprika

1½ cups cooked rice

½ red bell pepper, seeded and cubed

½ orange bell pepper, seeded and cubed

¾ cup chicken broth

¼ cup tomato sauce

1. Cut the chicken thighs into thin strips about 1½ inches long and ⅛ inch wide. Place the chicken strips in a bowl and stir in the salt and black pepper.

2. Heat a wok or skillet over medium-high heat until it is nearly smoking and add 2 tablespoons oil. When the oil is hot, add the chicken. Let the chicken brown briefly, then stir-fry until it turns white and is nearly cooked through. Remove and drain in a colander or on paper towels.

3. Heat 2 tablespoons oil in the wok or skillet and add the garlic and red peppers. Stir-fry for 10 seconds and add the onion. Stir-fry the onion until it begins to soften (about 2 minutes), sprinkling the paprika over the onion while you are stir-frying.

4. Add 1 tablespoon oil in the middle of the pan. Add the rice and stir-fry, stirring it in the oil for a minute until it begins to turn golden brown. Add the bell peppers and stir-fry for 1 minute or until the peppers are tender but still crisp, adding 1 or 2 tablespoons of the chicken broth if the vegetables begin to dry out.

5. Add the chicken broth and bring to a boil. Stir in the tomato sauce. Return the chicken to the pan. Continue stir-frying for 2 to 3 minutes to mix all the ingredients together. Taste and adjust seasoning if desired. Serve hot.

Super-Sticky Glutinous Rice Glutinous rice is famous for its sticky texture, earning it the nickname "sticky rice." The unusually sticky texture of glutinous rice comes from a starch called amylopectin. Amylopectin comprises over 80 percent of the starch in glutinous rice, compared to only 70 percent in regular long-grain white rice.

½ teaspoon salt

¼ teaspoon black pepper

1½ teaspoons cornstarch

¾ pound ground beef

3 tablespoons plus 2
    teaspoons olive oil,
    divided

2 cloves garlic, minced

2 thin slices ginger, minced

1 onion, chopped

1 tablespoon paprika

1½ cups cooked white rice

1 cup frozen corn

1 cup beef broth

1 tablespoon Worcestershire
    sauce

1 tablespoon brown sugar

Salt and black pepper to
    taste

Super-Easy Beef in Rice

*To add extra flavor to this dish, try cooking the
rice in chicken broth or beef broth instead of water.*

1. In a bowl, mix the salt, pepper, and cornstarch in with the ground beef. Let the ground beef stand for 20 minutes.

2. Heat wok or skillet on medium-high heat until it is nearly smoking. Add 2 teaspoons olive oil. When the oil is hot, add the ground beef. Stir-fry, stirring and tossing it in the pan, until there is no trace of pink and the ground beef is nearly cooked through. Remove the ground beef and drain in a colander or on paper towels.

3. Clean out the wok or skillet and add 2 tablespoons olive oil. When the oil is hot, add the garlic and ginger. Stir-fry for 10 seconds and add the onion. Stir-fry the onion until it begins to soften (about 2 minutes), sprinkling the paprika over the onion while you are stir-frying.

4. Add 1 tablespoon oil in the middle of the pan. Add the rice and stir-fry, stirring it in the oil for a minute until it begins to turn golden brown. Add the frozen corn and stir-fry for a minute, mixing the corn with the onion and seasonings.

5. Add the beef broth and bring to a boil. Stir in the cooked ground beef. Stir in the Worcestershire sauce and brown sugar. Continue stir-frying for 2 to 3 minutes to mix all the ingredients together and until most of the liquid is absorbed. Taste and adjust seasoning, adding salt and pepper if desired. Serve hot.

Curried Beef Fried Rice

*Although it is traditional, there's no rule that says you need to add egg to
a fried-rice dish. As always, feel free to adjust the amount of seasoning
according to your own tastes, adding more or less curry powder as desired.*

1. Cut the beef across the grain into thin strips. Place the beef in a bowl, and add the light soy sauce, rice wine or sherry, sesame oil, and cornstarch. Marinate the beef for 15 minutes. Combine the chicken broth and dark soy sauce in a small bowl. Set aside.

2. Heat a wok or skillet over medium heat until it is nearly smoking. Add 2 tablespoons oil. When the oil is hot, add half the garlic and ginger. Stir-fry for 10 seconds, then add half the beef, laying it flat in the pan. Let sear (brown) briefly, then stir-fry the meat, stirring and tossing until it is nearly cooked. Remove the meat and drain in a colander or on paper towels. Repeat with the other half of the beef. If the beef begins to dry out, splash with 1 tablespoon of rice wine instead of adding more oil.

3. Add 2 tablespoons oil. When the oil is hot, add the remainder of the garlic and ginger. Stir-fry for 10 seconds, then add the onion. Stir-fry the onion for about 2 minutes, until it starts to soften, sprinkling the curry powder over the top. Add the frozen peas and stir-fry for a minute.

4. Push the vegetables to the side and add 1 tablespoon oil in the middle. Add the rice and stir-fry in the oil for a minute until the rice begins to turn golden. Sprinkle the salt over the rice.

5. Add the chicken broth mixture. Stir in the sugar and black pepper. Add the beef back into the pan. Stir-fry for another 1 to 2 minutes and serve hot.

Serves 3 to 4

1 pound sirloin steak

2 tablespoons light soy sauce

1 tablespoon Chinese rice wine or dry sherry

1 teaspoon Asian sesame oil

2 teaspoons cornstarch

½ cup chicken broth

1½ tablespoons dark soy sauce

5 tablespoons vegetable or peanut oil, divided

2 cloves garlic, chopped

2 thin slices ginger, chopped

1 tablespoon rice wine or sherry, optional

1 onion, chopped

3 tablespoons curry powder

1 cup frozen peas

1½ cups cold cooked rice

½ teaspoon salt

1 teaspoon granulated sugar

¼ teaspoon black pepper, or to taste

2 tablespoons pure olive oil

1 medium yellow onion, chopped

1 cup Arborio rice

3½ cups low-sodium chicken broth

1¾ teaspoons salt, or to taste

Basil, oregano, and thyme to taste

Basic Stir-Fried Risotto

With its smooth, creamy texture, risotto is the perfect comfort food. Feel free to jazz up this basic risotto recipe by adding vegetables as desired.

1. Heat the olive oil in a skillet on medium heat. Add the onion. Stir-fry the onion for about 2 minutes to soften.

2. Add the rice. Stir-fry, moving the rice around the pan to mix it in with the olive oil, until the grains are shiny and translucent.

3. Slowly add ½ cup of chicken broth, stirring continually. Add ¼ teaspoon salt. When the chicken broth is nearly absorbed into the rice, pour in ½ cup broth and repeat the process. After adding the last ½ cup of broth, stir in the basil, oregano, and thyme.

4. Continue stirring until the rice grains are tender but still firm. Do a taste test and add additional seasonings if desired. Serve immediately.

Stir-Frying, Italian Style   While it doesn't make use of the high heats normally associated with stir-frying, risotto is often referred to as the Italian version of stir-fried rice because of the large amount of stirring involved.

Fast and Feisty Arroz con Pollo

Feisty Fajita Marinade lends a spicy Mexican flavor to this popular Latin dish. If you prefer, you can substitute chicken breasts for the chicken thighs called for in this recipe.

Serves 3 to 4

¾ pound boneless, skinless chicken thighs

Feisty Fajita Marinade (page 24)

4 tablespoons olive oil, divided

2 cloves garlic, chopped

1 tablespoon hot sauce

½ onion, chopped

1 cup cooked rice

²/₃ cup diced tomatoes with juice

¼ cup pimentos

Salt and pepper to taste

1. Cut the chicken thighs into thin strips about 1½ inches long and ⅛ inch wide. Place the chicken strips in a bowl and stir in the Feisty Fajita Marinade. Marinate the chicken for 20 to 30 minutes.

2. Heat a wok or skillet over medium-high heat until it is nearly smoking and add 2 tablespoons oil. When the oil is hot, add the garlic and hot sauce. Stir-fry for 10 seconds, then add the chicken. Let the chicken brown briefly, then stir-fry until it turns white and is nearly cooked through.

3. Push the chicken to the sides and heat 2 tablespoons oil in the middle of the wok or skillet. Add the onion and stir-fry for 2 minutes, or until it begins to soften. Add the cooked rice and stir-fry for a minute, mixing it in with the onion, until it begins to turn golden.

4. Add the diced tomatoes and bring to a boil. Stir in the pimentos. Stir-fry for 1 to 2 more minutes to combine all the ingredients. Taste and adjust seasoning, adding salt or pepper if desired. Serve hot.

Garlic Health Benefits Garlic adds more than a powerful aroma to stir-fry dishes. Modern research shows that the same chemical reaction that gives garlic its characteristic odor is also responsible for the numerous health benefits that are derived from eating it, including lower blood pressure and inhibition of the free radical cells that can cause cancer.

4½ cups chicken broth

½ ounce dried porcini mushrooms

2 tablespoons olive oil

½ medium white onion, chopped

1½ cups Arborio rice

½ cup dry white wine

2 teaspoons salt, or to taste

½ cup peas

Freshly ground black pepper to taste

½ cup grated Parmesan cheese

2 tablespoons chopped fresh parsley

Rustic Vegetable Risotto

Serve this flavorful vegetable and rice dish with the Quick and Easy Chicken Stir-Fry (page 30) for a complete meal.

1. Bring the broth to a boil. Add the dried mushrooms and simmer for 5 minutes or until they are softened. Remove the mushrooms and thinly slice. Reserve the broth.

2. Heat the olive oil in a skillet on medium heat. Add the onion. Stir-fry the onion for about 2 minutes to soften.

3. Add the rice. Stir-fry, moving the rice around the pan to mix it in with the olive oil, until the grains are shiny and translucent.

4. Slowly add the wine, stirring continually. When the wine is nearly evaporated, add the mushrooms and 1 cup of the chicken broth and ½ teaspoon salt. Continue stirring until the broth has been absorbed. Repeat the process until you have added the last ½ cup of broth, then stir in the peas. Do a taste test and add salt and pepper to taste.

5. Continue stirring until the rice grains are cooked tender but still firm. Turn off the heat and add the Parmesan and parsley. Serve immediately.

Risotto Rice Types Super-absorbent Arborio rice is the perfect rice for making Italian risotto. The short, plump grains are loaded with amylopectin, a type of starch that helps the rice absorb more liquid. But while Arborio is the rice of choice for making risotto, you can substitute any other short-grain rice if it is unavailable.

One Dish Chicken and Rice Stir-Fry

*Hoisin sauce adds a sweet-and-spicy flavor to this simple
chicken and rice stir-fry that is a great cold-weather dish.*

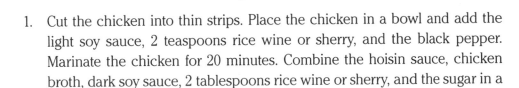

¾ pound chicken meat

1½ tablespoons light soy
   sauce

2 tablespoons plus 2
   teaspoons Chinese rice
   wine or dry sherry,
   divided

¼ teaspoon black pepper, or
   to taste

4 tablespoons hoisin sauce

4 tablespoons chicken broth

4 tablespoons dark soy sauce

1 teaspoon granulated sugar

4 tablespoons vegetable or
   peanut oil, divided

2 thin slices ginger, minced

2 cloves garlic, minced

1 green onion, finely
   chopped

1 onion, chopped

1½ cups cooked white rice

1 cup canned baby corn,
   drained

½ teaspoon salt

1. Cut the chicken into thin strips. Place the chicken in a bowl and add the light soy sauce, 2 teaspoons rice wine or sherry, and the black pepper. Marinate the chicken for 20 minutes. Combine the hoisin sauce, chicken broth, dark soy sauce, 2 tablespoons rice wine or sherry, and the sugar in a bowl. Set aside.

2. Heat a wok or skillet over medium-high heat until it is nearly smoking and add 2 tablespoons oil. When the oil is hot, add half the ginger and garlic. Stir-fry for 10 seconds, then add the chicken. Let sit briefly, then stir-fry the chicken until it turns white and is nearly cooked through. Remove the chicken and drain in a colander or on paper towels.

3. Heat 2 tablespoons oil in the wok or skillet. Add the green onion, and the remaining ginger and garlic. Stir-fry for 10 seconds, then add the onion. Stir-fry the onion for about 2 minutes or until it begins to soften. Add the rice and stir-fry for 1 minute, until it begins to turn golden brown. Add the baby corn and stir-fry for 1 minute, sprinkling with the salt.

4. Add the hoisin sauce mixture and bring to a boil. Stir in the cooked chicken. Continue stir-frying for 2 to 3 minutes to mix all the ingredients together and until most of the liquid is absorbed. Taste and adjust seasoning if desired. Serve hot.

Serves 4

1 cup basmati or jasmine
  rice, uncooked

¾ cup chicken broth

¾ cup coconut milk

2 tablespoons olive oil

3 tablespoons raisins

2 shallots, chopped

2 cloves garlic, chopped

3 tablespoons tomato paste

1 tablespoon fish sauce

1 tablespoon brown sugar

Freshly ground white pepper
  to taste

Southeast Asian Spanish Rice

*This flavorful rice side dish would go nicely with Easy Chicken with
Snow Peas (page 36) or Thai-Style Cashew Chicken (page 40).*

1. Bring the rice, chicken broth, and coconut milk to a boil in an uncovered saucepan on medium heat.

2. When the liquid is boiling, partially cover and lower the heat to medium-low. Cook until most of the liquid is absorbed.

3. When the broth is nearly absorbed, completely cover and cook over low heat until the broth is completely absorbed.

4. Heat a wok or skillet over medium heat until it is nearly smoking. Add the olive oil. When the oil is hot, add the rice, stirring it in the oil until it turns golden brown. Stir in the raisins.

5. Stir the shallots and garlic into the rice. Continue stir-frying for about 3 minutes or until the shallots are softened.

6. Stir in the tomato paste. Stir in the fish sauce and the brown sugar. Add white pepper to taste. Mix everything together and serve hot.

Scented Rice Also called fragrant rice, scented rice refers to several varieties of rice that have a pleasant aroma. Basmati and jasmine are the two most well-known types of scented rice. Originally grown in the Himalayan foothills, basmati rice is famous for its pleasant nutty flavor and fine texture. While not as flavorful, jasmine rice also has a nutty flavor and is much cheaper than basmati.

Hoppin' John

There are numerous versions of this popular Southern dish, but they all contain black-eyed peas and rice. While Hoppin' John is traditionally made with bacon or ham hock, chicken can be used as well.

1. Cut the chicken into thin strips. Place the chicken strips in a bowl and add the soy sauce, white wine or sherry, black pepper, and cornstarch. Marinate the chicken for 20 minutes.

2. Heat a wok or skillet over medium-high heat until it is nearly smoking. Add 2 tablespoons olive oil. When the oil is hot, add half the garlic and ginger. Stir-fry for 10 seconds, then add the chicken. Let it brown briefly, then stir-fry the chicken until it turns white and is nearly cooked through. Remove and drain in a colander or on paper towels.

3. Heat 1 tablespoon oil in the wok or skillet. When the oil is hot, add the remainder of the garlic and ginger. Stir-fry for 10 seconds, then add the onion. Sprinkle the paprika over the mixture, and stir-fry until the onion begins to soften (about 2 minutes). Add the celery and stir-fry for a minute, until the celery turns a darker green, mixing it with the onion and seasonings.

4. Stir in the black-eyed peas and diced tomatoes with juice. Bring to a boil. Add the chicken back into the pan. Stir in the ground cumin. Taste and adjust seasoning, adding salt and pepper if desired. Continue stir-frying for 2 to 3 minutes to mix all the ingredients together. Serve hot over the cooked rice.

Serves 2 to 4

2 boneless, skinless chicken breasts, 7–8 ounces each

1 tablespoon soy sauce

1 tablespoon dry white wine or dry sherry

Black pepper to taste

2 teaspoons cornstarch

3 tablespoons olive oil, divided

1 teaspoon minced garlic

1 teaspoon minced ginger

1 cup chopped Vidalia onion

1 tablespoon paprika

2 ribs celery, thinly sliced

1 cup black-eyed peas

1 cup diced tomatoes, undrained

½ teaspoon ground cumin

Salt to taste

Black pepper to taste

Basic Cooked Rice (page 228)

4 ounces shrimp, shelled and deveined

¼ teaspoon salt

2 tablespoons chicken broth

1 tablespoon oyster sauce

1 tablespoon soy sauce

2 large eggs

¹⁄₈ teaspoon black pepper, or to taste

3 tablespoons vegetable or peanut oil, divided

2 thin slices ginger

2 green onions, finely chopped

½ onion, chopped

1 red bell pepper, cut into bite-sized chunks

3 cups cooked rice

Fried Rice with Shrimp

This recipe calls for a relatively small amount of shrimp to keep the shrimp flavor from overpowering the other ingredients. If you want more protein, add 4 ounces of either cooked ham or cooked pork, or 2 Chinese sausages that have been thinly sliced.

1. Rinse the shrimp under cold running water and pat dry with paper towels. Toss with the salt.

2. Combine the chicken broth, oyster sauce, and soy sauce in a bowl. Set aside. Lightly beat the eggs, stirring in the black pepper.

3. Heat a wok or skillet over medium-high heat until it is nearly smoking. Add 2 tablespoons oil. When the oil is hot, add the sliced ginger and green onions. Stir-fry for 10 seconds, then add the shrimp. Stir-fry the shrimp briefly until it turns bright pink.

4. Push the shrimp to the sides and add the onion in the middle of the wok or skillet. Stir-fry for 2 minutes or until it begins to soften. Add the red bell pepper. Stir-fry for 1 minute or until it is tender but still crisp. Remove the shrimp and vegetables from the pan.

5. Heat 1 tablespoon oil in the wok or skillet. When the oil is hot, add the rice. Stir-fry the rice for 1 minute or until it begins to turn golden. Add the lightly beaten eggs and scramble, mixing them in with the rice. Add the chicken broth mixture. Add the shrimp and vegetables back into the pan. Stir-fry for 1 to 2 minutes to mix everything together. Serve hot.

Fried Rice Origins   While the Chinese were the first to come up with the idea of adding stir-fried vegetables to leftover cooked rice, the precise origins of this popular restaurant dish have been lost to history. However, fried rice was probably invented in the eastern province of Yangzhou, during the Sui dynasty (A.D. 581–617).

Pork in Rice

To add extra flavor to this dish, you can try cooking the rice in beef broth instead of water.

Serves 2 to 3

½ teaspoon salt

¼ teaspoon black pepper

1½ teaspoons cornstarch

¾ pound ground pork

3 tablespoons plus 2 teaspoons olive oil, divided

2 cloves garlic, minced

2 thin slices ginger, minced

1 onion, chopped

1 tablespoon paprika

1½ cups cooked white rice

1 cup chopped red bell pepper

1 tablespoon light soy sauce

1 tablespoon ketchup

1 cup chicken broth

1 tablespoon brown sugar

Salt and black pepper to taste

1. In a bowl, mix the salt, pepper, and cornstarch in with the ground pork. Let the ground pork stand for 20 minutes.

2. Heat wok or skillet on medium-high heat until it is nearly smoking. Add 2 teaspoons olive oil. When the oil is hot, add the ground pork. Stir-fry, stirring and tossing it in the pan, until there is no trace of pink and the ground pork is nearly cooked through. Remove the ground pork and drain in a colander or on paper towels.

3. Clean out the wok or skillet and add 2 tablespoons olive oil. When the oil is hot, add the garlic and ginger. Stir-fry for 10 seconds and add the onion. Stir-fry the onion until it begins to soften (about 2 minutes), sprinkling the paprika over the onion while you are stir-frying.

4. Add 1 tablespoon oil in the middle of the pan. Add the rice and stir-fry, stirring it in the oil for 1 minute, until it begins to turn golden brown. Add the bell pepper and stir-fry for 1 minute, mixing with the onion and seasonings. Stir in the soy sauce.

5. Stir the ketchup into the chicken broth. Add into the pan and bring to a boil. Stir in the cooked ground pork. Stir in the brown sugar. Continue stir-frying for 2 to 3 minutes to mix all the ingredients together, until most of the liquid is absorbed. Taste and adjust seasoning, adding salt and pepper if desired. Serve hot.

Healthy Rice While low-carb dieters may shun it, rice provides a high degree of nutritional bang for the caloric buck. Besides being low in fat and cholesterol, rice contains no sodium and is a good source of iron and the B vitamins thiamin, riboflavin, and niacin. Rice also contains pantothenic acid, believed to help ward off signs of aging, such as gray hair and wrinkles!

Serves 2

2½ tablespoons pure olive oil

1 medium yellow onion, chopped

½ cup Arborio rice

1 medium tomato, chopped

1¾ cups chicken broth

¾ teaspoon salt, or as needed

1 (7-ounce) can flaked turkey, drained

1 tablespoon chopped fresh parsley, or to taste

Black pepper to taste

Weeknight Turkey Risotto for Two

This simple but comforting dish is a great choice for cold winter days. It makes a filling lunch or a light dinner for two people.

1. Heat the olive oil in a skillet on medium heat. Add the onion and stir-fry for about 2 minutes to soften.

2. Add the Arborio rice. Stir-fry, moving the rice around the pan to mix it in with the olive oil, until the grains are shiny and translucent. Add the chopped tomato, gently pushing it down with the back of the spatula so that it releases its juices.

3. Slowly add ½ cup chicken broth, stirring continually. Stir in ¼ teaspoon salt. Continue adding the broth, ½ cup at a time, and stirring until it is absorbed into the rice. When all the broth is nearly absorbed into the rice, stir in the canned turkey. Stir for another minute, then remove from the heat. Stir in the parsley and black pepper. Serve immediately.

Simple Beans and Rice

This simple dish is a great way to use up leftover cooked rice. To add extra flavor,
use crushed tomatoes that have been flavored with herbs and seasonings.

Serve 2 to 4

3 tablespoons vegetable or peanut oil, divided

2 cloves garlic, minced

1 onion, chopped

1 tablespoon paprika

1 green bell pepper, cut into bite-sized chunks

1 tablespoon soy sauce or water, optional

1½ cups cooked rice

1 (14-ounce) can kidney beans, drained

½ cup chicken broth

1½ cups crushed tomatoes

Salt and pepper to taste

1. Heat a wok or skillet over medium-high heat and add 2 tablespoons oil. When the oil is hot, add the garlic. Stir-fry for 10 seconds, then add the onion. Stir-fry until the onion has softened (about 2 minutes), stirring in the paprika.

2. Add the pepper and stir-fry until it is tender but still crisp. Add 1 tablespoon soy sauce or water if the bell pepper begins to dry out during stir-frying.

3. Push the vegetables to the sides of the wok or skillet. Heat 1 tablespoon oil in the middle. Add the rice and stir-fry until it begins to turn golden brown. Add the beans. Stir-fry for a minute, then add the chicken broth and crushed tomatoes. Bring to a boil. Season with the salt and pepper. Cook for another 1 to 2 minutes to blend all the flavors. Serve hot.

Healthy Beans Beans are high in protein and dietary fiber. Scientists recommend a diet rich in kidney, pinto, garbanzo, and other types of beans for people trying to lower their cholesterol levels. Their high fiber content also makes beans a good choice for people with diabetes, as it helps stabilize blood-sugar levels by preventing them from rising too rapidly after a meal has been consumed.

2 large eggs

1/8 teaspoon salt

1/8 teaspoon black pepper

1 tablespoon hoisin sauce

2 teaspoons water

3 tablespoons vegetable or peanut oil, divided

3 cups cooked wild rice

1 tablespoon soy sauce

1 cup sliced portobello mushrooms

½ cup frozen peas, thawed

2 green onions, finely chopped

1 teaspoon Asian sesame oil

Mushroom Fried Rice

For extra flavor, try using scented basmati or jasmine rice in this recipe.

1. Lightly beat the eggs, stirring in the salt and pepper. In a small bowl, combine the hoisin sauce with the water.

2. Heat a wok or skillet over medium-high heat until it is nearly smoking. Add 2 tablespoons oil. When the oil is hot, add the eggs. Stir the eggs until they are lightly scrambled. Remove the scrambled eggs and clean out the pan.

3. Heat 1 tablespoon oil. When the oil is hot, add the rice. Stir-fry for 2 minutes, stirring and tossing the rice. Stir in the soy sauce.

4. Stir in the mushrooms. Stir-fry for a minute, then add the peas. Stir to mix the rice and the vegetables. Stir in the scrambled eggs. Stir in the hoisin sauce mixture and green onions. Cook for another minute to blend the flavors. Remove from the heat and stir in the sesame oil. Serve hot.

Pineapple Fried Rice

In Thailand, a more elaborate version of Pineapple Fried Rice calls for the fried rice to be served in a carved-out pineapple.

1. One day ahead of time, prepare the Coconut-Scented Rice. Store the rice in a sealed container in the refrigerator.

2. Rinse the shrimp under cold running water and pat dry with paper towels. Lightly beat the eggs, stirring in the salt and pepper.

3. Heat a wok or skillet over medium-high heat and add 1 tablespoon oil. When the oil is hot, reduce the heat to medium and add the egg mixture. Lightly scramble the eggs. Remove them from the pan and clean out the pan.

4. Heat 2 tablespoons oil in the wok or skillet. When the oil is hot, add the garlic. Stir-fry for 10 seconds, then add the onion and the shrimp. Stir-fry for about 2 minutes, until the shrimp turns pink and the onion begins to soften. Add the red bell pepper. Stir-fry for a minute, stirring in the soy sauce. Stir in the pineapple.

5. Push the vegetables to the sides or remove from the wok (whether you need to do this will depend on the size of your wok) and heat 1 tablespoon oil. Add the cooked rice to the hot oil and stir-fry briefly. Either add the vegetables back into the pan or stir to mix the rice in with the vegetables. Stir in the scrambled eggs and the green onions. Stir in the oyster sauce. Stir-fry briefly to heat through, and serve hot.

Rice—the Staff of Life Rice is the primary source of energy for over half of the world's population, largely because it is an excellent source of energy and has a high calorie count, and is relatively inexpensive to grow. Also, rice can be directly consumed after harvesting, without any further processing (unlike cereal crops such as wheat, which need to be processed into cereal, flour, or another food before being consumed).

Serves 2 to 3

Coconut-Scented Rice (page 228)

¼ pound shrimp, shelled, deveined

2 eggs

1 teaspoon salt

Black or white pepper to taste

4 tablespoons vegetable or peanut oil, divided

1 teaspoon chopped garlic

½ cup chopped onion

1 red bell pepper, cut into bite-sized chunks

1 tablespoon Chinese light soy sauce or fish sauce

1 cup pineapple chunks, drained

2 green onions, cut into 1-inch pieces

1 tablespoon oyster sauce

Indonesian Fried Rice (Nasi Goreng)

Made from fermented shrimp, shrimp paste is available in Asian grocery stores. You can adjust this recipe to use only chicken or shrimp or to use uncooked chicken and shrimp if desired (just stir-fry the ingredients first and then use as called for in the recipe).

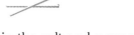

1. Lightly beat the eggs, stirring in the salt and pepper. Heat a wok or skillet over medium-high heat and add 1 tablespoon oil. When the oil is hot, reduce the heat to medium and pour in the beaten eggs. Cook until the eggs are firm, turning over once. Remove the cooked eggs and cut into thin strips. Clean out the pan.

2. Heat 2 tablespoons oil in the wok or skillet over medium-high heat. When the oil is hot, add the garlic and onion. Sprinkle the chili powder over the mixture and stir-fry for about 2 minutes, until the onion begins to soften. Add the shrimp paste and continue stir-frying until the onion has softened.

3. Add the rice and stir-fry for 1 to 2 minutes, until it begins to turn golden. Stir in the cooked chicken and shrimp. Stir in the kecap manis or dark soy sauce. Stir-fry for 1 to 2 more minutes, to blend the ingredients.

4. Before serving, remove the fried rice from the wok or skillet and lay the strips of fried egg on top.

Chapter 10

Vegetable Dishes

Stir-Fried Zucchini

*Zucchini is the perfect vegetable for quick
stir-frying, as it is high in moisture and not too tough.*

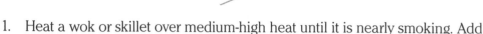

Serves 2 to 4

1 tablespoon vegetable oil

1 large zucchini, cut on the
    diagonal into 1-inch slices

¼ teaspoon salt, or to taste

1 tablespoon soy sauce

1. Heat a wok or skillet over medium-high heat until it is nearly smoking. Add the oil.

2. When the oil is hot, add the zucchini. Sprinkle the salt over the zucchini. Stir-fry for a minute, then stir in the soy sauce.

3. Stir-fry the zucchini until it turns dark green and is tender but still crisp (about 3 minutes). Serve hot.

Vegetable Sweet and Sour "Pork"

*This easy version of the popular restaurant dish takes only
minutes to make. To speed things up even further, wash and
drain the vegetables and prepare the sauce earlier in the day.*

Serves 4

2 tablespoons vegetable or
    peanut oil

1 teaspoon minced ginger

1 teaspoon minced garlic

2 carrots, peeled and cut on
    the diagonal into thin
    slices

1 green bell pepper, seeded and
    cut into bite-sized chunks

Salt to taste

1 red bell pepper, seeded and
    cut into bite-sized chunks

Pineapple Sweet and Sour
    Sauce (page 25)

1 cup canned pineapple
    chunks

Black pepper to taste

1. Heat a wok or skillet over medium-high heat until it is nearly smoking. Add the oil. When the oil is hot, add the minced ginger and garlic. Stir-fry for 10 seconds, then add the carrots and green bell pepper. Stir-fry for 1 minute, adding a bit of salt if desired.

2. Add the red pepper. Stir-fry for 1 more minute or until the vegetables are tender but still crisp.

3. Add the sauce and bring to a boil, stirring quickly to thicken. Add the pineapple chunks. Stir-fry for 2 more minutes or until all the ingredients are heated through. Taste and adjust seasoning, adding pepper if desired. Serve hot.

Stir-Fried Celery

Celery is another high-moisture vegetable that is perfect for stir-fries. Stir-frying celery deepens its natural green color.

Serves 2 to 4

2 teaspoons vegetable oil

2 slices ginger, minced

2 ribs celery, cut on the diagonal into thin slices

¼ teaspoon salt, or to taste

$1/8$ teaspoon nutmeg, or to taste

$1/8$ teaspoon cinnamon, or to taste

¼ teaspoon granulated sugar

1. Heat a wok or skillet over medium-high heat until it is nearly smoking. Add the oil. When the oil is hot, add the ginger. Stir-fry for 10 seconds and add the celery. Sprinkle the salt over the celery and stir-fry until it begins to turn a brighter green (about 1 minute). Add the nutmeg, cinnamon, and the sugar. Stir-fry for another minute, mixing the celery with the spices. Serve hot or cold.

Simple Sprouts Stir-Fry

The trick to stir-frying mung bean sprouts is to go light on the seasonings and not to overcook them.

Serves 3 to 4

3 cups mung bean sprouts

1 tablespoon vegetable or peanut oil

2 thin slices ginger

1 tablespoon soy sauce

¼ teaspoon salt

½ teaspoon granulated sugar

½ teaspoon Asian sesame oil, optional

1. Rinse the mung bean sprouts and drain thoroughly.

2. Heat a wok or skillet over medium-high heat until it is nearly smoking and add the oil. When the oil is hot, add the ginger. Brown for 2 to 3 minutes and then remove from the pan.

3. Add the mung bean sprouts. Stir-fry for a minute, stirring in the soy sauce. Stir-fry for a bit longer, stirring in the salt, sugar, and sesame oil if using. Serve hot.

Celery and Bamboo Shoots

If you live near an Asian market, feel free to use a fresh bamboo shoot in this recipe.
Boil the shoot for 15 minutes to soften, and then cut into ¼-inch-thick slices.

Serves 4

1 cup sliced bamboo shoots

1½ tablespoons dark soy
sauce

1½ tablespoons chicken
broth

1 teaspoon granulated sugar

1½ tablespoons vegetable or
peanut oil

2 slices ginger

2 ribs celery, cut into ½-inch
pieces on the diagonal

¼ teaspoon salt

½ teaspoon sesame oil

1. If using canned bamboo shoots, rinse under warm running water. Drain thoroughly.

2. Combine the dark soy sauce, chicken broth, and sugar in the bowl. Set aside.

3. Heat a wok or skillet on medium-high heat. Add the oil, swirling it around the wok or skillet so that it covers the sides. When the oil is hot, add the ginger. Stir-fry for 10 seconds and add the celery. Sprinkle the salt over the celery and stir-fry until it begins to turn a brighter green (about 1 minute).

4. Add the bamboo shoots. Stir-fry for another minute, then add the sauce. Stir for a few more seconds to mix the vegetables with the sauce; turn down the heat. Cover and simmer for 3 minutes or until the vegetables are tender.

5. Remove the wok or skillet from the heat. Stir in the sesame oil. Remove the ginger slices or leave in as desired. Serve immediately.

Preparing Canned Vegetables Fresh is always best, but it's often easier to find canned versions of Chinese vegetables such as water chestnuts, bamboo shoots, and baby corn. To get rid of any taste of tin from the can, rinse the vegetables under running water or blanch them briefly in boiling water.

Spicy Fries

For an interesting contrast in texture and flavor, serve this spicy dish with Chicken with Bean Sprouts (page 38).

...Chicken with Bean Sprouts (page 38).

1. Cut the potato lengthwise into thin strips. Lay flat and slice lengthwise again into very thin strips (about ⅛ inch thick).

2. Heat a wok or skillet on medium-high heat until it is nearly smoking. Add the oil. When the oil is hot, add the ginger and the chile paste. Stir-fry for about 30 seconds.

3. Add the sliced potato. Stir-fry, stirring and tossing the potato strips around the pan. Stir in the salt and the five-spice powder. Splash the potato with the rice wine and continue stir-frying for 6 minutes or until the strips firm up and begin to brown. Serve immediately.

Fabulous Five-Spice Powder An intriguing mix of sweet, sour, salty, bitter, and pungent flavors, five-spice powder is an indispensable tool in any Chinese cook's culinary repertoire. Cooks rely on five-spice powder to lend flavor to everything from meat marinades and rubs to stuffings. Thanks to its rising popularity, five-spice powder is available in the spice section of most supermarkets, as well as Asian groceries and specialty shops.

Serves 2 to 4

1 large potato, peeled

3 tablespoons vegetable oil

2 slices ginger, minced

1–2 tablespoons chile paste, as desired

1 teaspoon salt

1½ teaspoons five-spice powder

1 tablespoon Chinese rice wine or dry sherry

---

4 tortillas

2 portions Feisty Fajita
  Marinade (page 24)

2 Japanese eggplants,
  quartered and cut on
  the diagonal into 1-inch
  pieces

½ cup chicken broth

2 tablespoons vegetable or
  peanut oil

2 teaspoons minced garlic

2 green onions, cut on the
  diagonal into thirds

Vegetarian "Fajitas"

*You can load up this basic vegetarian filling with raw vegetables,
such as sliced tomato, avocado, or raw sweet red onion.*

1. Heat the flour tortillas according to the package directions. Keep warm in a 250°F oven while preparing the filling.

2. Brush one portion of the marinade on the eggplant. Let sit for 15 minutes. Stir the remainder of the marinade into the chicken broth. Set aside.

3. Heat a wok or skillet over medium-high heat until it is nearly smoking. Add 2 tablespoons oil. When the oil is hot, add the minced garlic. Stir-fry for 10 seconds, then add the eggplant. Stir-fry until the eggplant begins to brown (about 3 minutes). Pour the chicken broth mixture over the eggplant. Turn down the heat, cover, and simmer until the eggplant is tender. Stir in the green onions.

4. Lay a tortilla out flat. Spoon a portion of the stir-fried vegetable mixture onto the tortilla, making sure the filling isn't too close to the edges. Fold in the left and right sides of the tortilla and tuck in the edges. Repeat with the remainder of the tortillas until the filling is used up.

What Is a Diagonal Cut? Recipes frequently call for vegetables to be cut on the diagonal prior to stir-frying. Diagonal cutting exposes more of the vegetable's surface area, allowing it to cook more quickly. To cut vegetables on the diagonal, hold the knife or cleaver at a 60-degree angle and cut the vegetable crosswise.

Veggie Loaded Egg Foo Yung

For extra flavor, add 1 or 2 teaspoons oyster sauce to the egg mixture with the other seasonings. Vegetarians can use a vegetarian version of oyster sauce made with mushrooms.

Serves 2 to 4

2 tablespoons vegetable or peanut oil, divided

½ medium onion, chopped

¼ pound button mushrooms, thinly sliced

1 medium carrot, shredded

1 red bell pepper, seeded and diced

1 cup mung bean sprouts

6 eggs

¼ teaspoon salt

Freshly ground white pepper to taste

1 teaspoon Asian sesame oil

1. Heat a wok or skillet on medium-high heat until it is nearly smoking. Add 1 tablespoon oil. When the oil is hot, add the onion and the mushrooms. Stir-fry for about 2 minutes or until the onion begins to soften. Stir in the shredded carrot and red bell pepper. Stir-fry for 1 minute, then add the bean sprouts. Remove the vegetables from the pan.

2. Beat the eggs lightly, stirring in the salt, pepper, and sesame oil. Stir in the cooked vegetables.

3. Heat 1 tablespoon oil in the wok or skillet. When the oil is hot, add the egg mixture. Cook until golden brown on both sides, turning over once during cooking. Serve hot.

Vegetable Stir-Fry Times Softer vegetables like zucchini and bell peppers need to be stir-fried for only a couple of minutes, while thicker, harder vegetables like broccoli and carrots take longer. If you're planning to combine several types of vegetables in a stir-fry and aren't sure about cooking times, simply stir-fry them all separately and combine them in the wok in the final stages of cooking.

Quick Fried Green Tomatoes

*Picked from the vine before they have fully ripened,
firm green tomatoes are a great addition to stir-fries.*

½ teaspoon salt

Freshly ground black pepper to taste

½ teaspoon dried oregano

¼ cup cornmeal

3 green tomatoes, cut in slices ½ inch thick

2 tablespoons olive oil

1. Combine the salt, black pepper, oregano, and cornmeal in a bowl.

2. Dredge the tomato slices with the cornmeal mixture.

3. Heat a wok or skillet on medium heat until it is nearly smoking. Add the oil. When the oil is hot, add the green tomatoes. Stir-fry for about 2 minutes or until the tomatoes turn golden brown. Serve hot.

Lucky Three Vegetables

The number 3 symbolizes success in Chinese culture. However, the Cantonese believe the number 4 is very unlucky, so think twice before adding one more vegetable to this dish!

Serves 2

1 red bell pepper

4 Napa cabbage leaves

1 cup canned straw mushrooms

1½ tablespoons vegetable or peanut oil

2 teaspoons minced ginger

½ teaspoon salt

1–2 tablespoons chicken broth or water

1. Cut the bell pepper in half, remove the seeds, and cut into thin strips. Cut the cabbage leaves crosswise into thin strips. Cut the straw mushrooms in half.

2. Heat a wok or skillet on medium-high heat until it is nearly smoking. Add the oil. When the oil is hot, add the ginger. Stir-fry for 10 seconds, until aromatic.

3. Add the Napa cabbage and the red bell pepper. Sprinkle with the salt. Stir-fry for a minute, then add the mushrooms. Stir in the chicken broth or water. Stir-fry for 1 more minute, then remove from the pan. Serve hot.

Stir-Fried Cabbage

*Many people don't realize that Napa cabbage, which is named
after the Napa Valley region of California where it is cultivated, is
actually a type of Chinese cabbage, also called celery cabbage.*

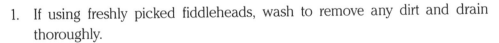

Serves 4

1½ tablespoons vegetable or peanut oil

3 cloves garlic, crushed

1 pound Napa cabbage, cored and cut crosswise into thin strips

½ teaspoon sugar

¼ cup chicken broth

1. Heat a wok or skillet over medium-high heat until it is nearly smoking. Add the oil. When the oil is hot, add the garlic and the Napa cabbage. Sprinkle with the sugar. Add the chicken broth. Stir-fry the cabbage for 3 to 4 minutes, until it is tender but still crisp. Remove the garlic before serving.

Double Nutty Fiddlehead Greens with Sesame

*Toasting sesame seeds gives them a pleasant nutty flavor, which
nicely complements the natural nutty flavor of fiddlehead greens.*

Serves 2 to 4

1 pound fiddlehead greens, fresh or frozen

2 tablespoons olive oil

2 teaspoons minced ginger

½ teaspoon salt, or to taste

2 teaspoons Asian sesame oil

2 tablespoons toasted sesame seeds

1. If using freshly picked fiddleheads, wash to remove any dirt and drain thoroughly.

2. Heat a wok or skillet over medium-high heat until it is nearly smoking. Add the olive oil. When the oil is hot, add the ginger. Stir-fry for 10 seconds, then add the fiddlehead greens. Stir-fry for 1 minute, then stir in the salt.

3. Stir-fry for 1 to 2 more minutes, until the fiddlehead greens are tender but still firm. Remove from the heat and stir in the sesame oil. Garnish with the toasted sesame seeds before serving.

4 ears corn

1 teaspoon cornstarch

4 teaspoons water

2 tablespoons palm oil

3 cloves garlic, crushed

2 tablespoons fish sauce

½ cup coconut milk

1 tablespoon palm sugar

1 teaspoon white pepper, or
to taste

Thai-Inspired Creamed Corn

Made from the fruit of the tropical palm tree, palm oil is the oil of choice for Thai stir-fry dishes. If unavailable, substitute peanut oil or a vegetable oil such as canola.

1. To shuck the corn, remove the outer husk and the silky threads covering the kernels. Use a sharp knife to cut off the kernels. Rinse the corn kernels under warm running water. Drain thoroughly.

2. In a small bowl, dissolve the cornstarch into the water. Set aside.

3. Heat a wok or skillet over medium-high heat until it is almost smoking. Add the palm oil. When the oil is hot, add the crushed garlic. Stir-fry for 10 seconds, then add the corn. Stir-fry the corn for 1 minute, stirring in the fish sauce. After 1 minute, add the coconut milk. Stir in the palm sugar.

4. Bring the coconut-milk mixture to a boil. Stir in the cornstarch and water mixture and keep stirring until thickened. Stir in the white pepper. Remove the crushed garlic before serving.

Storing Canned Vegetables If you have leftover straw mushrooms, water chestnuts, bamboo shoots, or baby corn, place the vegetables in a sealed container with enough water to cover, and store in the refrigerator. Stored in this manner, the canned vegetables will last for 3 to 4 days. For a fresher taste, change the water daily.

Burgundy Mushrooms

*Stir-frying mushrooms releases their moisture, allowing them to soak up
the burgundy and seasonings. If using reduced-sodium beef broth, you may want
to add a bit of salt or salt substitute to the mushrooms in addition to the pepper.*

1. In a small bowl, combine the burgundy and beef broth. Set aside.

2. Heat a wok or skillet over medium-high heat until it is nearly smoking. Add the oil. When the oil is hot, add the minced ginger and garlic. Stir-fry for 10 seconds, then add the chopped shallots. Sprinkle the dried parsley and basil over the shallots and stir-fry for 1 minute, until the shallots begin to soften.

3. Add the mushrooms. Stir-fry for about 2 minutes, until they have browned. Stir in the black or white pepper. Add the burgundy mixture.

4. Cook, stirring occasionally, until the liquid has almost evaporated (4 to 5 minutes). Serve hot.

Serves 2 to 4

¼ cup burgundy wine

¼ cup beef broth

1½ tablespoons vegetable or peanut oil

1 teaspoon minced ginger

1 teaspoon minced garlic

2 shallots, chopped

½ teaspoon dried parsley

½ teaspoon dried basil

½ pound fresh mushrooms, thinly sliced

Black or white pepper to taste

1 pound cauliflower

1½ tablespoons white wine vinegar

2½ tablespoons water

1½ teaspoons granulated sugar

2 tablespoons olive oil

2 teaspoons minced ginger

Stir-Fried Cauliflower

If you like, you can substitute Chinese or Japanese white rice vinegar for the white wine vinegar in this recipe. Stay away from regular white vinegar, though—it will overpower the cauliflower's flavor.

1. Remove the outer leaves and the stalk from the cauliflower. Cut off the florets, leaving part of the stem attached. Soak the florets in cold water. Drain thoroughly.

2. Fill a large saucepan with enough water to cover the cauliflower, and bring to a boil. Blanch the cauliflower in the boiling water for 2 minutes. Remove the cauliflower, rinse under cold running water, and drain thoroughly.

3. Combine the white wine vinegar, water, and sugar in a bowl. Set aside.

4. Heat a wok or skillet over medium-high heat until it is nearly smoking. Add the oil. When the oil is hot, add the ginger. Stir-fry for 10 seconds, then add the cauliflower florets. Stir-fry for 1 minute, then pour the white wine vinegar mixture over the top. Stir-fry for another 2 minutes or until the cauliflower is tender but still crisp, stirring vigorously to keep the cauliflower from browning. Serve immediately.

Cucumbers with Oyster Sauce

*Serve this spicy vegetable dish with Asian Garlic Chicken (page 58) or
Italian-Inspired Garlic Chicken (page 52) and cooked rice for a complete meal.*

1. Dissolve the cornstarch into 2 teaspoons water and set aside.

2. Heat a wok or skillet over medium-high heat until it is nearly smoking. Add the oil. When the oil is hot, add the minced garlic. Stir-fry for 10 seconds, then add the cucumber. Sprinkle the salt over the cucumber. Stir-fry the cucumber slices for about 3 minutes, until they have darkened and are fork-tender but still crisp. Move cucumbers to the sides of the wok/skillet.

3. Stir in the oyster sauce, ¼ cup water, and granulated sugar. Stir-fry briefly, then add the cornstarch and water mixture into the liquid, stirring quickly to thicken. When the mixture has thickened, stir to mix it in with the cucumber.

4. Make a space in the middle of the pan and add the chopped red chilies. Stir-fry the chilies for a few seconds until aromatic, then mix in with the cucumber. Serve hot.

Serves 2 to 3

½ teaspoon cornstarch

¼ cup plus 2 teaspoons water, divided

1 tablespoon vegetable or peanut oil

1 teaspoon minced garlic

1 large cucumber, cut lengthwise into quarters, seeded, and cut into ½-inch-thick slices

¾ teaspoon salt

1 tablespoon oyster sauce

1 teaspoon granulated sugar

2 teaspoons chopped jarred red jalapeño peppers

Glazed Carrots

Glazed carrots make an excellent side dish for family dinners and special occasions. They also add a bit of color to the spread.

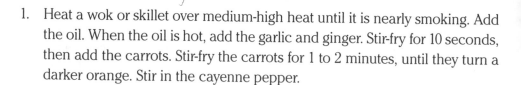

Serves 4

2 tablespoons olive oil

1 tablespoon minced garlic

2 teaspoons minced ginger

4 carrots, peeled and thinly sliced on the diagonal into ½-inch slices

¼ teaspoon cayenne pepper

½ cup chicken broth

2 tablespoons brown sugar

1. Heat a wok or skillet over medium-high heat until it is nearly smoking. Add the oil. When the oil is hot, add the garlic and ginger. Stir-fry for 10 seconds, then add the carrots. Stir-fry the carrots for 1 to 2 minutes, until they turn a darker orange. Stir in the cayenne pepper.

2. Add the chicken broth and the brown sugar. Bring to a boil. Cover and cook the carrots for 4 minutes.

3. Uncover and cook, stirring, until the carrots are tender but still crisp and nicely glazed with the broth and sugar mixture, which has been reduced (total cooking time is about 8 minutes). Serve hot.

Indian Spiced Okra

In India this spicy vegetable dish would be cooked in a kadhai, the Indian version of the Chinese wok. Feel free to use a kadhai if you have one!

Serves 2 to 4

2 tablespoons peanut or vegetable oil

3 cloves garlic, minced

¼ teaspoon cumin

1 teaspoon red pepper flakes

1 shallot, chopped

1 pound okra, cut on the diagonal into slices ¼–½ inch thick

1 tomato, cut into 6 wedges, each wedge halved

1 teaspoon curry powder

1 teaspoon brown sugar

1. Heat a wok or skillet over medium-high heat until it is nearly smoking. Add the oil. When the oil is hot, add the garlic, cumin, red pepper flakes, and the shallot. Stir-fry until the shallot begins to soften.

2. Add the okra. Stir-fry, stirring and moving the okra around the pan for about 4 minutes or until it is just starting to turn golden brown.

3. Add the tomato. Add the curry powder and the brown sugar and stir-fry for 1 minute. Serve hot or cold.

Spicy Cucumbers

*Chile paste with garlic can be found at Asian markets. If it is
unavailable, feel free to use regular chile paste or chopped red chilies,
or sprinkle the cucumber with red pepper flakes during stir-frying.*

1. Place the cucumber slices in a colander and sprinkle the salt over them. Let the cucumber pieces sit for 30 minutes. Pat dry with paper towels to remove the excess water.

2. Heat a wok or skillet over medium-high heat until it is nearly smoking. Add the oil. When the oil is hot, add the chile paste with garlic, minced ginger, and green onion. Stir-fry until aromatic, then add the cucumber slices. Stir-fry for about 3 minutes, until the cucumber is tender but still crisp.

3. Splash cucumber slices with the red wine vinegar. Serve hot.

Serves 2 to 4

1 large cucumber, cut lengthwise into quarters, seeded, and cut into ½-inch-thick slices

1 teaspoon salt

1 tablespoon vegetable or peanut oil

½ teaspoon chile paste with garlic

2 teaspoons minced ginger

1 green onion, finely chopped

1 tablespoon red wine vinegar

Indian Creamed Spinach

*Indispensable to northern Indian cuisine, garam masala is a fragrant
mixture of cumin, coriander, cardamom, and other spices. Garam
masala can be found in the spice section of many supermarkets.*

1. Heat a wok or skillet over medium-high heat until it is nearly smoking. Add the oil. When the oil is hot, add the minced garlic, ginger, and the curry paste.

2. Add the chopped shallot. Stir-fry until the shallot begins to soften, then add the spinach and the salt. Stir-fry for 1 minute or until the spinach turns a dark green.

3. Add the heavy cream and the garam masala. Bring to a boil, then cook for another minute until the cream and spinach are heated through. Serve hot.

Serves 4

2 tablespoons olive oil

2 tablespoons minced garlic

1 tablespoon minced ginger

2 teaspoons curry paste

1 shallot, chopped

20 ounces frozen spinach, thawed, drained, and chopped

½ teaspoon salt

½ cup heavy cream

1 teaspoon garam masala

Serves 3 to 4

1 pound bok choy

1 tablespoon oyster sauce

3 tablespoons chicken broth

2 tablespoons vegetable or
   peanut oil

2 cloves garlic, crushed

½ teaspoon salt

Stir-Fried Bok Choy

*If you like, thicken the sauce by stirring in 1 teaspoon cornstarch
mixed with 2 teaspoons water at the end of cooking. Stir quickly
until the sauce has thickened and serve immediately.*

1. Separate the leaves of the bok choy from the stalks. Cut the stalks diagonally into 2-inch pieces. Cut the leaves crosswise into 2-inch pieces.

2. Stir the oyster sauce into the chicken broth. Set aside.

3. Heat a wok or skillet over medium-high heat until it is almost smoking. Add the oil. When the oil is hot, add the crushed garlic. Stir-fry for 10 seconds, then add the bok choy stalks. Add the salt. Stir-fry for 1 minute, then add the leaves. Stir-fry for 1 more minute or until the bok choy turns bright green.

4. Add the chicken broth/oyster sauce mixture into the wok. Bring to a boil. Stir-fry for another minute and serve hot.

Beautiful Bok Choy The most popular vegetable in Chinese cooking, bok choy has white stalks and beautiful emerald leaves. Normally, bok choy stalks are separated from the leaves and stir-fried for a bit longer. However, if you're lucky enough to find baby bok choy, a smaller version of regular bok choy with a more delicate flavor, simply cut it in half lengthwise before stir-frying.

Vegetarian Cashew Chili

Roasted cashews add flavor and healthy monounsaturated fats to this vegetarian version of chili. Feel free to replace the zucchini with a green bell pepper if desired.

Serves 2 to 4

½ cup raw, unsalted cashews

2 tablespoons olive oil

1 teaspoon minced ginger

1 teaspoon minced garlic

½ onion, chopped

1 tablespoon chili powder, or to taste

½ teaspoon cumin

1 cup frozen corn

1 zucchini, cut on the diagonal into 1-inch slices

¼ teaspoon salt

1 tablespoon Worcestershire sauce

1 cup kidney beans, drained

1 cup diced tomatoes with juice

1 tablespoon brown sugar

Black pepper to taste

1. Roast the cashews in a wok or skillet over medium heat, shaking the pan continuously so that the nuts do not burn. Roast until the cashews are browned (about 5 minutes). Remove the cashews from the pan to cool.

2. Clean out the wok or skillet and add the oil. When the oil is hot, add the ginger and garlic. Stir-fry for 10 seconds, then add the onion. Sprinkle the chili powder and cumin over the onion mixture, and stir-fry the onion until it begins to soften (about 2 minutes). Add the corn and stir-fry for 1 minute, mixing the corn with the onion and seasonings.

3. Push the onion and corn to the side and add the sliced zucchini in the middle of the pan. Sprinkle the salt over. Stir-fry for 1 minute, then stir in the Worcestershire sauce. Stir-fry the zucchini for 3 minutes or until the zucchini is dark green and tender but still crisp.

4. Stir in the red kidney beans and diced tomatoes with juice. Bring to a boil. Stir in the brown sugar and black pepper. Stir in the roasted cashews. Continue stir-frying for 2 to 3 minutes to mix all the ingredients together. Taste and adjust seasoning if desired. Serve hot.

Kadhai—the Indian Wok With its deep sides and rounded bottom, the kadhai is the Indian version of a wok. Like the classic Chinese wok, the main advantages of using a kadhai are quick cooking times and the need for less oil since the food cooks primarily in its own juices. The sturdy kadhai frequently doubles as a serving dish, going straight from the stove to the dining table.

3 ribs celery

1 tablespoon vegetable or peanut oil

1 tablespoon minced ginger

½ teaspoon sugar

1 tablespoon lemon juice

1 tablespoon soy sauce

Three Flavor Celery

*Sweet, sour, and salty come together in this speedy stir-fry dish.
Serve with Tomato Beef (page 84) and lots of steamed rice.*

1. Rinse the celery and cut on the diagonal into thin slices.

2. Heat a wok or skillet over medium-high heat until it is nearly smoking. Add the oil. When the oil is hot, add the ginger. Stir-fry for 10 seconds, then add the celery. Stir in the sugar.

3. Stir-fry the celery for 2 minutes or until it turns a brighter green and is tender but still crisp. Splash the celery with the lemon juice and soy sauce while you are stir-frying.

Serves 3 to 4

2 (8-ounce) cans baby corn (rinse the corn to remove any tin taste)

2 tablespoons vegetable or peanut oil

2 teaspoons chopped fresh ginger

1 green onion, finely chopped

1 teaspoon salt

2 tablespoons liquid

Stir-Fried Baby Corn

There are no hard-and-fast rules about what type of liquid to splash on vegetables during stir-frying—soy sauce, water, Chinese rice wine, and chicken broth all work well.

1. Cut the baby corn in half.

2. Heat a wok or skillet over medium-high heat until it is nearly smoking. Add the oil. When the oil is hot, add the ginger. Stir-fry for 10 seconds, until the ginger is aromatic.

3. Add the green onion, salt, and baby corn. Stir-fry for 1 minute, then splash the baby corn with the liquid. Stir-fry for another 30 seconds to heat through. Serve hot.

Hot Spinach Salad

The same ingredients that form the basis of a spinach salad—fresh spinach leaves, mushrooms, and bacon—go together nicely in a stir-fry. If you prefer, replace the bacon with cooked Chinese sausage, called lop cheong.

1. Heat a wok or skillet over medium-high heat until it is nearly smoking. Add the oil. When the oil is hot, add the ginger. Stir-fry for 10 seconds, then add the spinach and sprinkle with the salt. Stir-fry for about 30 seconds.

2. Add the mushrooms, soy sauce, and lemon juice. Stir-fry for 1 minute or until the spinach turns a dark green and the mushrooms are heated through.

3. Stir in the cooked bacon. Remove the wok or skillet from the heat and stir in the sesame oil. Serve immediately.

Serves 4

2 tablespoons olive oil

1 tablespoon minced ginger

1 pound fresh spinach leaves

½ teaspoon salt

1 cup canned straw mushrooms, cut in half

1 tablespoon soy sauce

1 tablespoon lemon juice

4 slices cooked bacon, chopped

1 teaspoon Asian sesame oil

Easy Mixed-Vegetable Stir-Fry

The combination of baby corn, carrots, and bean sprouts provides an interesting contrast in color and texture. You can adapt this basic recipe to make chop suey or egg foo yung.

1. Heat a wok or skillet over medium-high heat until it is nearly smoking. Add the oil. When the oil is hot, add the garlic and ginger. Stir-fry for 10 seconds until aromatic.

2. Stir in the salt and the carrots. Stir-fry for 1 minute, then stir in the sugar and the baby corn. Stir-fry for 1 minute, then add the bean sprouts. Stir-fry for 30 seconds to 1 minute, taking care not to overcook the bean sprouts. Add more salt or sugar if desired.

3. Remove from the heat and stir in the sesame oil. Serve hot.

Serves 3 to 4

2 tablespoons vegetable or peanut oil

1 clove garlic, crushed

2 slices ginger

½ teaspoon salt, or to taste

2 medium carrots, peeled and cut on the diagonal into 1½-inch slices

1 teaspoon granulated sugar

1 (8-ounce) can baby corn, drained

1 cup mung bean sprouts

1 tablespoon Asian sesame oil

1 pound broccoli

¼ cup chicken broth

1½ tablespoons oyster sauce

1 tablespoon dark soy sauce

2 teaspoons cornstarch

2 tablespoons vegetable or peanut oil

2 teaspoons minced ginger

1 teaspoon salt, or to taste

½ cup water

Two-Step Broccoli

This tasty vegetable stir-fry is meant to have lots of extra sauce to mix in with cooked rice. Serve the broccoli and cooked rice with Beef in Stir-Fry Sauce (page 102) for a complete meal.

1. Cut off the broccoli florets and cut in half. Cut the spears on the diagonal.

2. Combine the chicken broth, oyster sauce, and dark soy sauce in a bowl. Whisk in the cornstarch.

3. Heat a wok or skillet over medium-high heat until it is nearly smoking. Add the oil. When the oil is hot, add the ginger. Stir-fry for about 10 seconds, then add the broccoli and sprinkle the salt over the top. Add the water, cover the broccoli, and cook for 4 to 5 minutes or until it is tender but still crisp.

4. Push the broccoli to the sides of the wok and add the sauce in the middle, stirring to thicken. When the sauce has thickened, stir-fry for a minute to mix the sauce with the broccoli. Serve hot.

Storing Soy Sauce Because soy sauce contains salt, a preservative, many people don't think to refrigerate it after opening. While it is true that the salt acts as a preservative, soy sauce will still maintain its flavor longer if it is stored in the refrigerator. The same holds true for Thai fish sauce, made with salted preserved fish.

Mushrooms and Bamboo Shoots

Don't want to use the soaking liquid from the mushrooms in the stir-fry? Feel free to substitute an equal amount of chicken broth.

Serves 2 to 4

6–8 dried black mushrooms

2 tablespoons vegetable or peanut oil

3 slices ginger, minced

1 (8-ounce) can sliced bamboo shoots (rinse the bamboo shoots to remove any tin taste)

1 teaspoon brown sugar

1 teaspoon Asian sesame oil

1. Soak the dried black mushrooms in hot water for 25 to 30 minutes, until they have softened. Reserve ¼ cup of the liquid used to soak the mushrooms (strain the liquid if it has any grit from the mushrooms in it). Cut the stems off the mushrooms and discard.

2. Heat a wok or skillet over medium-high heat until it is nearly smoking. Add the oil. When the oil is hot, add the ginger. Stir-fry for 10 seconds, until the ginger is aromatic, then add the dried mushrooms and the bamboo shoots. Stir-fry for 1 minute.

3. Add the reserved mushroom broth. Stir in the brown sugar. Cook for another minute to heat through. Remove from the heat and stir in the sesame oil. Serve immediately.

Chinese Dried Black Mushrooms Also known as flower mushrooms, Chinese dried black mushrooms lend a rich, savory flavor to stir-fries, soups, and other dishes. The mushrooms are soaked in hot water before using, both to soften and to remove any dirt or grit. Traditional Chinese medical practitioners believe eating black mushrooms helps lower blood pressure.

2 tablespoons olive oil

2 slices ginger

2 shallots, chopped

6 large portobello
    mushrooms, stems
    removed

½ teaspoon dried basil, or
    to taste

2 tomatoes, halved and
    thinly sliced

3 tablespoons white wine
    vinegar

3 tablespoons lemon juice

Freshly cracked black or
    white pepper to taste

6 hamburger buns

Mayonnaise to taste

Dijon mustard to taste

6 large lettuce leaves

2 tablespoons chopped
    capers, optional

Portobello Mushroom Burgers

*The strong, "meaty" flavor of portobello mushrooms makes them a
popular substitute for meat, particularly ground beef, among vegetarians.*

1. Heat a wok or skillet over medium-high heat until it is nearly smoking. Add the oil. When the oil is hot, add the ginger slices. Let brown for 2 to 3 minutes, then remove. Add the shallots and the portobello mushrooms. Stir-fry for 2 minutes or until the shallots begin to soften, sprinkling the dried basil over the top. Add the tomato. Stir-fry for 1 minute.

2. Splash the vegetables with the white wine vinegar and the lemon juice. Stir in the pepper. Cook for another minute to heat through.

3. Lay out the hamburger buns and spread with mayonnaise or Dijon mustard as desired. Add the lettuce leaves. Spoon one-sixth of the stir-fried vegetables into each burger. Garnish with 1 teaspoon chopped capers if desired.

Vegetarian Jambalaya

Imitation ground beef crumbles are a good choice for this recipe. Feel free to use white or brown rice as desired.

1. Heat a wok or skillet over medium-high heat until it is nearly smoking. Add 2 tablespoons oil. When the oil is hot, add the garlic and the cayenne pepper. Stir-fry for 10 seconds, then add the onion. Stir-fry the onion for about 2 minutes, until it begins to soften.

2. Add the okra. Continue stir-frying for 2 minutes, splashing with a bit of chicken broth if it begins to dry out. Add the green bell pepper and tomatoes. Continue stir-frying until the green vegetables are tender but still crisp (about 2 minutes). Add more chicken broth if needed while stir-frying and season the vegetables with salt if desired. Remove the vegetables from the pan.

3. Heat 1 tablespoon oil in the wok or skillet. When the oil is hot, add the rice. Stir-fry for a minute until the grains turn a light brown, stirring in the dried thyme and oregano. Stir in the meat substitute. Stir-fry for a minute, then add 1 cup chicken broth. Bring to a boil. Add the stir-fried vegetables. Stir in the black pepper.

4. Continue stir-frying for 2 to 3 minutes to mix all the ingredients together and until most of the liquid is absorbed. Taste and adjust seasoning if desired. Garnish with fresh parsley.

Serves 2 to 4

3 tablespoons olive oil, divided

2 cloves garlic, crushed

1 teaspoon cayenne pepper, or to taste

1 medium white onion, chopped

2 okra, cut on the diagonal into thin slices

1¼ cups chicken broth, or as needed

1 green bell pepper, seeded, cut into bite-sized chunks

2 tomatoes, halved and thinly sliced

1 teaspoon salt, or as needed

1½ cups cooked rice

¼ teaspoon dried thyme, or to taste

¼ teaspoon dried oregano, or to taste

1 cup vegetarian meat substitute

Black pepper to taste

1 bunch fresh parsley, optional

½ cup vegetable broth

2 tablespoons soy sauce

1 teaspoon cornstarch

2 tablespoons vegetable or
peanut oil

4 thin slices ginger, minced

1 medium onion, chopped

3 cups packaged stir-fry
vegetable mix, fresh or
frozen

1 cup mung bean sprouts

¼ teaspoon salt

½ cup cashews

1 teaspoon granulated sugar

Black pepper to taste

Speedy Vegetarian Chop Suey

Instead of adding the cashews in the final stages of cooking, you can stir-fry them separately. Stir-fry 1 minute, taking care not to burn the cashews, and then remove from the pan. Add the cashews to the chop suey just before serving.

1. Combine the vegetable broth and soy sauce in a small bowl. Whisk in the cornstarch.

2. Heat a wok or skillet over medium-high heat until it is nearly smoking. Add the oil. When the oil is hot, add the sliced ginger. Stir-fry for about 10 seconds, then add the onion. Stir-fry the onion until it begins to soften (about 2 minutes). Add the stir-fry vegetable mix. Stir-fry according to the package directions or until the vegetables are tender but still crisp.

3. Add the mung bean sprouts and the salt. Stir-fry for about 30 seconds, then add the vegetable broth mixture. Bring to a boil, stirring continually. Stir in the cashews and the sugar. Add black pepper to taste. Serve hot.

Got a Cold? Eat Some Celery! Medieval doctors had so much faith in celery's curative powers that it was used primarily for medicinal purposes. Modern scientific research supports the wisdom of these ancient practitioners—celery is a rich source of vitamin C, proven to help reduce cold symptoms.

Spring Vegetable Medley

You can create your own combination of spring vegetables to use in this simple stir-fry. Bell peppers, green beans or French haricots verts, and zucchini are all good choices.

Serves 2 to 4

¼ cup chicken broth

1½ tablespoons red wine vinegar

2 teaspoons granulated sugar

½ cup cauliflower florets

2 tablespoons vegetable or peanut oil

½ teaspoon minced garlic

½ teaspoon minced ginger

1 cup shredded red cabbage

1 teaspoon salt

1 carrot, julienned

1. Combine the chicken broth, red wine vinegar, and sugar in a bowl. Set aside.

2. Fill a large saucepan with enough water to cover the cauliflower and bring to a boil. Blanch the cauliflower in the boiling water for 2 minutes. Remove the cauliflower, rinse under cold running water, and drain thoroughly.

3. Heat a wok or skillet over medium-high heat until it is nearly smoking. Add the oil. When the oil is hot, add the garlic and ginger. Stir-fry for 10 seconds, then add the shredded cabbage. Stir-fry for 2 minutes, sprinkling with the salt; then add the carrot. Stir-fry for another minute, then add the cauliflower.

4. Stir-fry for a minute, then add the chicken broth mixture. Bring to a boil and continue cooking until the vegetables are tender but still crisp.

Serves 2 to 4

1 head cauliflower

2 tablespoons vegetable or peanut oil

2 cloves garlic

Cauliflower Fried "Rice"

Use this basic recipe in Shrimp Fried "Rice" (page 137) or any fried-rice recipe. Besides being low in carbohydrates, an added plus for dieters is that cauliflower is low in calories but very filling.

1. Break off the florets from the cauliflower and chop into chunks. Chop the core into chunks. Process the florets and core in a food processor, a few pieces at a time, using the "grate" function. Scrape out the bottom of the blender or food processor as needed. Continue until you have 3 cups of grated cauliflower.

2. Heat a wok or skillet over medium-high heat until it is nearly smoking. Add the oil. When the oil is hot, add the garlic. Stir-fry for 10 seconds, then add the cauliflower.

3. Stir-fry the cauliflower, stirring and turning it over in the pan for 4 to 5 minutes, until it is tender but still crisp. (If you're uncertain about when the cauliflower is done, do a taste test—stir-fried cauliflower does not change noticeably in color, but it will taste cooked.)

Low-Carb "Rice" Cauliflower is not a good substitute for rice in recipes with a high liquid content as cauliflower doesn't absorb liquid in the same way that rice does. However, it makes a handy stand-in for rice in fried-rice recipes, which normally use only a small amount of liquid seasoning such as soy sauce.

Thai-Style Mixed Vegetables

Seasonings take center stage in this quick and easy Thai stir-fry dish. If you need to use regular basil in place of holy basil, try adding a small amount of freshly ground black or white pepper for extra flavor.

Serves 2 to 4

- 2 tablespoons vegetable or peanut oil
- 3 cloves garlic, chopped
- 2 small fresh red Thai chilies
- 1 cup chopped broccoli
- 1½ teaspoons granulated sugar, or to taste, divided
- 1 cup chopped bok choy
- ½ teaspoon salt
- 2 plum tomatoes, thinly sliced
- 1 cup baby corn, halved
- ¼ cup water
- 1 tablespoon fish sauce
- 1 tablespoon oyster sauce
- 1 tablespoon Chinese rice wine or dry sherry
- ¼ cup chopped holy basil leaves

1. Heat a wok or skillet over medium-high heat until it is nearly smoking. Add the oil. When the oil is hot, add the garlic and chilies. Stir-fry for 20 seconds, then add the broccoli. Sprinkle ½ teaspoon sugar over the mixture. Stir-fry for a minute, then add the bok choy. Stir in the salt. Stir-fry until the vegetables turn a darker green and are tender but still crisp (2 to 3 minutes).

2. Add the plum tomatoes. Stir-fry for 1 minute, then add the baby corn. Stir-fry for another minute, then add the water. One at a time, stir in the fish sauce, oyster sauce, and the rice wine or dry sherry. Stir in 1 teaspoon sugar, or to taste.

3. Add the holy basil into the wok or skillet. Stir-fry for about 30 seconds, until the leaves have just wilted. Taste and adjust seasoning if desired. Serve hot.

What Is Baby Corn? As the name implies, baby corn are tiny ears of corn that are picked before they have fully matured. Their miniature length (2 to 3 inches) makes baby corn perfect for stir-frying. When using canned baby corn, be sure to rinse it under running water to remove any "tinny" taste.

Terrific Tofu Dishes

Spicy Stir-Fried Tofu

Serves 3 to 4

1 tablespoon vegetable or peanut oil

1 teaspoon minced ginger

1 teaspoon red pepper flakes

1 pound firm tofu, drained and cut into ¾-inch cubes

3 tablespoons chicken broth

1 tablespoon red wine vinegar

2 tablespoons chopped green onions

Vegetarians can replace the chicken broth in this dish with water or vegetarian broth. Pair this simple stir-fry with Glazed Carrots (page 262) and rice for a complete meal.

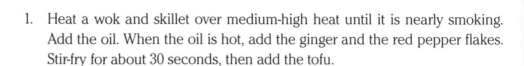

1. Heat a wok and skillet over medium-high heat until it is nearly smoking. Add the oil. When the oil is hot, add the ginger and the red pepper flakes. Stir-fry for about 30 seconds, then add the tofu.

2. Stir-fry the tofu for 1 to 2 minutes, until it begins to brown. Add the chicken broth and the red wine vinegar. Stir in the chopped green onions. Simmer for about 5 minutes or until heated through. Serve immediately.

Five-Spiced Tofu

Serves 2 to 4

1 tablespoon five-spice powder

¼ cup cornstarch

1 pound firm tofu, drained and cut into ¾-inch cubes

2 tablespoons olive oil

2 tablespoons finely chopped green onion

Adding five-spice powder to the cornstarch in this recipe gives the fried tofu a brown coating and a unique spicy flavor.

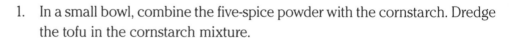

1. In a small bowl, combine the five-spice powder with the cornstarch. Dredge the tofu in the cornstarch mixture.

2. Heat a wok or skillet over medium heat. Add the olive oil. When the oil is hot, add the dredged tofu. Stir-fry, gently moving the tofu around the wok, until it is crispy and browned on all sides (about 5 minutes per side).

3. Garnish the tofu with the chopped green onion before serving.

Sweet and Sour Tofu

Always be sure to quickly stir the cornstarch and water mixture before adding it into the sauce—the mixture tends to separate when left sitting for too long.

Serves 3 to 4

1 teaspoon cornstarch

2 teaspoons water

2 tablespoons vegetable or peanut oil

1 teaspoon minced ginger

1 teaspoon minced garlic

14–16 ounces firm tofu, drained and cut into 1-inch cubes

Simple Sweet and Sour Sauce (page 28)

1. In a small bowl, dissolve the cornstarch into the water.

2. Heat a wok or skillet over medium-high heat until it is nearly smoking. Add the oil. When the oil is hot, add the ginger and garlic. Stir-fry for 10 seconds, then add the tofu cubes. Stir-fry the tofu for 1 minute, gently stirring and moving the cubes around the pan.

3. Add the Simple Sweet and Sour Sauce, and bring to a boil. Cook for 1 minute, stirring the tofu cubes in the sauce. Add the cornstarch and water solution, stirring to thicken. Stir for another minute to mix the ingredients together. Serve hot.

French-Inspired Fried Tofu

Gruyère, the cheese of choice for classic Swiss cheese fondue, lends a sharp bite to this tofu recipe.

Serves 2 to 4

1 pound firm tofu, drained and cut into ½-inch cubes

¼ teaspoon dried thyme

¼ cup red wine vinegar

2 large eggs

1/8 teaspoon nutmeg, or to taste

Salt and black pepper to taste

¼ cup grated Gruyère cheese

2 tablespoons olive oil

2 cloves garlic, crushed

2 tablespoons chopped fresh parsley, optional

1. Place the tofu cubes in a medium bowl and add the dried thyme and red wine vinegar. Marinate the tofu for 15 minutes.

2. Lightly beat the eggs, stirring in the nutmeg, salt, and pepper. Stir in the Gruyère cheese. Dip the tofu cubes into the egg and cheese mixture.

3. Heat a wok or skillet over medium-high heat until it is nearly smoking. Add the oil. When the oil is hot, add the crushed garlic. Stir-fry for 10 seconds, then add the tofu cubes. Stir-fry, gently moving the tofu cubes through the pan, until they are browned. Garnish with the chopped fresh parsley before serving, if desired.

½ cup vegetable broth

1 tablespoon vegetarian oyster sauce

1 tablespoon dry sherry

3½ tablespoons vegetable or peanut oil, divided

1 teaspoon minced ginger

1 red onion, cut into rings

2 ribs celery, cut on the diagonal into ½-inch pieces

½ teaspoon salt

½ pound fresh mushrooms, thinly sliced

1 red bell pepper, cut into bite-sized chunks

1 tablespoon water, optional

1 pound firm tofu, drained and cut into ¾–1-inch cubes

1 teaspoon granulated sugar

Black pepper to taste

Easy Vegetarian Stir-Fry

Made with mushrooms instead of oysters, the vegetarian version of oyster sauce is available at Asian markets or can be purchased online (see Appendix B, "Online Shopping Resources").

1. Combine the vegetable broth, oyster sauce, and sherry in a bowl. Set aside.

2. Heat a wok or skillet on medium-high heat until it is nearly smoking. Add 1½ tablespoons oil, swirling so that it covers the sides. When the oil is hot, add the ginger and stir-fry for 10 seconds. Add the onion, celery, and the salt. Stir-fry for about 2 minutes, until the onion begins to soften, then add the mushrooms. Stir-fry for a minute, then add the red bell pepper. Add 1 tablespoon water if the vegetables begin to dry out during stir-frying.

3. Push the vegetables to the sides, and add 2 tablespoons oil in the middle. Add the tofu cubes. Stir-fry for 1 to 2 minutes, until they firm up and begin to brown.

4. Stir in the sauce and bring to a boil. Stir in the sugar, and add the black pepper if using. Stir until heated through. Serve hot.

How to Drain Tofu   Draining tofu enhances its ability to absorb the flavors of the food it is cooked with. To drain a block of tofu, wrap it completely in absorbent paper towels. Place the wrapped tofu on a plate and place a heavy object (such as a book) on top. Let the tofu drain for at least 15 to 20 minutes.

Marinated Tofu

Some people find that the strong and unique taste of cilantro is too overwhelming. If you're not a fan of cilantro, substitute chopped fresh parsley.

1. In a bowl, combine the orange juice, tamari, red wine vinegar, 2 table-spoons olive oil, and cilantro.

2. Place the tofu cubes in a resealable plastic bag. Pour the orange juice mixture over the tofu cubes. Marinate the tofu in the refrigerator all night, turning the bag occasionally to make sure all of the tofu is coated in the marinade.

3. Heat a wok or skillet over medium-high heat until it is nearly smoking. Add 2 teaspoons olive oil. When the oil is hot, add the tofu cubes. Stir-fry the tofu for 2 minutes or until it is browned. Serve hot.

Types of Tofu Tofu is divided into two main categories, based on its texture. Regular tofu is fairly solid, with fibers running throughout, while the texture of silken tofu is similar to gelatin. Regular tofu comes in several degrees of firmness, ranging from soft to extra-firm.

Serves 2

¼ cup orange juice

1½ tablespoons tamari

1½ tablespoons red wine vinegar

2 tablespoons plus 2 teaspoons olive oil, divided

1 tablespoon chopped fresh cilantro leaves

½ pound firm tofu, drained and cut into ½-inch cubes

2 cups macaroni

1 tablespoon butter or margarine

6 ounces medium-firm tofu, drained

1½ teaspoons fresh parsley, chopped

4 large eggs

½ teaspoon salt

⅛ teaspoon black pepper

4 ounces drained tuna

½ cup milk

¼ cup cream of mushroom soup

2 tablespoons olive oil

1 clove garlic, crushed

1 onion, chopped

¾ cup shredded cheese

2 tablespoons soy sauce, optional

Tuna Tofu Casserole

Feel free to use your favorite type of shredded cheese in this recipe. If you find the total amount of ingredients too large to manage in your wok or skillet, feel free to use only 3 eggs and reduce the tofu to 3 ounces. Use only ¼ cup milk combined with 2 tablespoons cream of mushroom soup.

1. Cook the macaroni according to the package directions. Drain the macaroni and stir in the butter or margarine.

2. Mash the tofu in a bowl, mixing in the fresh parsley. In a large bowl, lightly beat the eggs, stirring in the salt and black pepper.

3. Combine the cooked macaroni with the mashed tofu, eggs, and the tuna. Combine the milk with the cream of mushroom soup in a bowl. Set aside.

4. Heat a heavy skillet over medium-high heat until it is nearly smoking. Add the oil, moving the skillet so that the oil covers the bottom of the pan. Add the garlic and the onion. Stir-fry for about 2 minutes, until the onion begins to soften.

5. Add the tuna/egg/tofu mixture. Stir-fry for about 3–4 minutes, until it begins to turn brown and the eggs are cooked.

6. Add the milk and mushroom soup mixture. Bring to a boil. Stir-fry for 1 minute, then add the shredded cheese and stir-fry for another minute. Stir in the soy sauce if desired.

Why Is It Important to Drain Tofu? Think of tofu as a large white sponge. Draining the tofu (also called pressing the tofu) removes all the water, leaving it free to soak up the flavors of the food it is cooked with. Stir-fries made with tofu that has been drained before cooking have a much fuller flavor.

Stuffed Tofu Triangles with Pork

*Feel free to adjust the filling by reducing the pork and adding
vegetables. Water chestnuts and Chinese dried mushrooms
that have been softened in water are both good choices.*

Serves 3 to 4

4 blocks firm tofu (14–16
   ounces total), drained
½ cup ground pork
1 tablespoon soy sauce
1 teaspoon brown sugar
Black pepper to taste
4 teaspoons cornstarch,
   divided
2 tablespoons water
1 cup chicken broth
2 tablespoons oyster sauce
3 tablespoons vegetable or
   peanut oil, divided
1 green onion, finely
   chopped
1 tablespoon chopped garlic

1. Cut each block of tofu in half, diagonally. You should now have 8 triangle-shaped pieces of tofu. Take 1 of the tofu triangles and use a knife to carefully make an insert along the cut edge, being careful not to cut through the sides or the back. This will be the pocket for the stuffing. Repeat with the remaining tofu triangles.

2. In a medium bowl, combine the ground pork with the soy sauce, brown sugar, black pepper, and 1 teaspoon cornstarch. Marinate the pork for 15 minutes. In a small bowl, dissolve 3 teaspoons cornstarch in the water. In a separate small bowl, combine the chicken broth and oyster sauce.

3. Heat a wok or skillet over medium-high heat until it is nearly smoking. Add 1 tablespoon oil. When the oil is hot, add the chopped green onion and half the chopped garlic. Stir-fry for 10 seconds, then add the ground pork. Stir-fry the pork until it is no longer pink and is nearly cooked through. Remove and drain in a colander or on paper towels.

4. Take a tofu triangle and place it on the cutting board. Carefully spoon a portion (about 1 tablespoon) of the stir-fried pork into the pocket. Continue with the remainder of the tofu triangles.

5. Heat 2 tablespoons oil in the wok or skillet. When the oil is hot, add the remainder of the chopped garlic. Stir-fry for 10 seconds, then add the stuffed tofu. Let cook until browned on the bottom (about 2 minutes), then add the chicken broth mixture. Simmer for 5 minutes or until the pork is cooked through. Stir the cornstarch and water mixture and add into the pan, stirring to thicken. Serve hot.

Pad Thai with Tofu

Made with tofu instead of chicken, this recipe is perfect for pescetarians (people who follow a vegetarian diet but will eat fish).

8 ounces flat rice stick noodles

½ cup vinegar

4 teaspoons lime juice

¼ cup soy sauce

2 tablespoons ketchup

4 teaspoons granulated sugar

2 large eggs

2 tablespoons vegetable or peanut oil

2 shallots, chopped

8–10 jumbo shrimp, shelled, deveined

1 pound firm tofu, drained, cut into 1-inch cubes

1 tablespoon water, if needed

2 cups mung bean sprouts

2 teaspoons chopped red chilies, or to taste

½ cup roasted peanuts, crushed

1. Soak the rice noodles in warm water for 20 minutes or until they have softened.

2. While the rice noodles are softening, prepare the other ingredients. Combine the vinegar, lime juice, soy sauce, ketchup, and sugar in a bowl. In a separate small bowl, lightly beat the eggs.

3. Heat a wok or skillet on medium-high heat until it is nearly smoking. Add the oil. When the oil is hot, add the chopped shallots and stir-fry for about 1 minute, until they begin to soften. Add the shrimp, stir-frying quickly until they turn pink.

4. Push the cooked shrimp to the sides and add the tofu in the middle of the pan. Stir-fry for 1 minute, adding more water to the pan if needed.

5. Add the lightly beaten eggs in the middle and gently scramble. Stir-fry briefly to mix the bits of scrambled egg with the other ingredients. Add the sauce and bring to a boil. Add the noodles, stirring continually. Cook for a minute, then stir in the mung bean sprouts and the chopped chilies. Stir-fry for another minute to mix everything through. Taste and adjust seasonings, adding salt, pepper, or soy sauce if desired. Garnish with the crushed peanuts before serving.

The Nutritional Benefits of Tofu Besides being a rich source of protein, tofu is high in calcium and vitamin B, is low in calories, and has no cholesterol. The only potential drawback to eating tofu is the fat content, which is higher than many types of meat. However, tofu is a good source of healthy omega-3 fatty acids, which help prevent heart disease. A 4-ounce serving of tofu has 86 calories.

Tofu Stew

Extra-firm tofu has a firmer, meatier texture than medium or firm tofu does, making it an excellent substitute for meat in a stew recipe.

1. Toss the tofu with ½ teaspoon salt.

2. Heat 2 tablespoons oil in the wok or skillet. When the oil is hot, add the garlic. Stir-fry for 10 seconds and add the red onion. Sprinkle the dried parsley and oregano over the garlic and onion and stir-fry for 2 minutes or until it begins to soften. Add the zucchini, stir-fry for 1 minute, and then add the carrots. Stir fry for 1 minute, sprinkling with ½ teaspoon salt, then add the tomatoes. Splash the vegetables with a bit of water or beef broth if they begin to dry out during stir-frying.

3. Add the tofu. Stir-fry for 1 minute, gently moving the tofu around the pan.

4. Add the beef broth. Stir in the Worcestershire sauce. Bring to a boil. Reduce the heat, cover, and simmer for 5 minutes or until heated through. Taste and adjust the seasoning, adding black pepper if desired. Serve hot.

Worcestershire Sauce Invented by two British chemists trying to reproduce the unique flavor found in Indian curries, Worcestershire sauce is a spicy mixture made with tamarind, anchovies, dark soy sauce, vinegar, onions, and other seasonings. Use Worcestershire sauce whenever you want to lend flavor to a stir-fry—just add 1 to 2 tablespoons to the marinade or sauce.

Serves 4

1 pound extra-firm tofu, drained and cut into ½-inch cubes

1 teaspoon salt, divided

3 tablespoons olive oil, divided

2 cloves garlic, chopped

1 large red onion, chopped

1 teaspoon dried parsley

½ teaspoon dried oregano

1 zucchini, cut on the diagonal into ½-inch pieces

2 medium carrots, cut on the diagonal into ½-inch pieces

2 tomatoes, halved and quartered

1 cup beef broth

1 tablespoon Worcestershire sauce

Black pepper to taste

Twice-Fried Tofu with Stir-Fry Sauce

In this recipe the tofu is deep-fried and then stir-fried with a flavorful sauce. Deep-frying tofu increases its absorbency, but you can stir-fry the tofu instead if desired.

1. Heat oil for deep-frying in a deep-fat fryer or wok to 360°F to 375°F, making sure you have enough oil to cover the tofu. Carefully add the tofu cubes. Deep-fry the tofu cubes, turning them occasionally, until they are browned (about 2 minutes). Remove the tofu cubes and drain in a colander or on paper towels.

2. Heat a wok or skillet over medium-high heat until it is nearly smoking, and add 2 tablespoons oil. (If you used a wok to deep-fry the tofu, remove all but 2 tablespoons of the oil used for deep-frying from it.) When the oil is hot, add the sliced ginger. Stir-fry until aromatic, then add the sauce. Bring to a boil, then add the tofu. Stir gently to mix the tofu with the sauce. Serve hot.

Sesame Tofu

Sesame Sauce lends a rich flavor to this basic tofu stir-fry. Feel free to prepare the sauce up to 3 days ahead of time and store in the refrigerator until ready to use.

1. Heat a wok or skillet over medium-high heat until it is nearly smoking. Add the oil. When the oil is hot, add the ginger and garlic. Stir-fry for 10 seconds, then add the tofu cubes.

2. Stir-fry the tofu for 1 to 2 minutes, until it is beginning to brown. Add the sauce and bring to a boil. Stir in the green onion. Cook for another minute, stirring gently, to heat everything through. Garnish with the sesame seeds before serving.

Simple Japanese Tofu Stir-Fry

*The Japanese version of rice wine, sake, is made
by fermenting a mixture of rice and water.*

1. Dredge the tofu cubes in the flour.

2. Heat a skillet over medium-high heat until it is nearly smoking, and add the oil. When the oil is hot, add the tofu cubes. Stir-fry the tofu, moving it around the pan, until it is browned on both sides (4 to 5 minutes).

3. Stir in the soy sauce, sake, sugar, and sesame oil. Stir in the green onions. Stir-fry for another minute and serve hot.

Serves 3 to 4

1 block (about ½ pound) tofu, drained, cut into ¾-inch cubes

¼ cup flour, or as needed

2 tablespoons vegetable or peanut oil

1½ tablespoons Japanese soy sauce

2 teaspoons sake

1 teaspoon granulated sugar

1 teaspoon Asian sesame oil

2 green onions, finely chopped

Vegetarian Kung Pao "Chicken"

*Red pepper flakes lend spice to this simple tofu stir-fry. Serve with a less
highly-seasoned vegetable dish such as Stir-Fried Zucchini (page 250) and cooked rice.*

1. In a small bowl, combine the red pepper flakes with the cornstarch. Dredge the tofu in the cornstarch. In a separate small bowl, combine the light soy sauce, dark soy sauce, and water.

2. Heat a wok or skillet over medium-high heat until it is nearly smoking. Add the oil. When the oil is hot, add the garlic and ginger. Add the Szechuan peppercorn if using. Stir-fry for about 10 seconds, then add the tofu. Stir-fry the tofu for 1 minute, gently stirring and moving it around the pan.

3. Add the soy sauce mixture and bring to a boil. Stir in the sugar. Stir in the peanuts and green onions. Stir-fry for 2 minutes or until the ingredients are thoroughly heated and mixed together. Serve hot.

Serves 2 to 4

2 teaspoons red pepper flakes

¼ cup cornstarch

12 ounces firm tofu, drained and cut into 1-inch cubes

1 tablespoon light soy sauce

2 tablespoons dark soy sauce

2 tablespoons water

2 tablespoons vegetable or peanut oil

1 clove garlic, chopped

2 thin slices ginger, chopped

1 teaspoon ground roasted Szechuan peppercorn, optional

1 teaspoon granulated sugar

½ cup unsalted peanuts

2 green onions, quartered

Serves 2 to 3

6 ounces extra-firm tofu,
   drained, cut into ½-inch
   cubes

½ teaspoon salt

¼ teaspoon black pepper, or
   to taste

½ teaspoon turmeric

½ teaspoon paprika, or to
   taste

1 tablespoon nutritional
   yeast

1 green onion, finely
   chopped

1½ tablespoons vegetable or
   peanut oil

2 thin slices ginger

1 tablespoon soymilk or soy
   sauce

Easy Tofu Scramble

*While it doesn't exactly resemble the yellow color of scrambled eggs,
the turmeric in this recipe gives the scrambled tofu a nice golden color.*

1. Place the tofu cubes in a bowl. Use your fingers to break up the tofu until it has the texture of scrambled egg. Stir or use your fingers to mix in the salt, pepper, turmeric, paprika, nutritional yeast, and green onion.

2. Heat a wok or skillet over medium-high heat until it is nearly smoking, and add the oil. When the oil is hot, add the ginger slices. Let brown for 2 to 3 minutes, then remove from the pan.

3. Add the tofu to the wok or skillet. Stir-fry for about 1 minute, then stir in the soymilk or soy sauce. Stir-fry for about 1 or 2 more minutes or until the scrambled tofu is light and fluffy. Serve immediately.

Veggie Fajitas

For extra color and flavor, you may use a flavored tortilla,
such as spinach or red pepper, to make your fajitas.

Yields 4 fajitas

3½ ounces pressed tofu

Feisty Fajita Marinade (page 24)

2 tablespoons olive oil

1 teaspoon minced garlic

2 teaspoons chopped red chili peppers

2 shallots, chopped

1 green bell pepper, cubed

1 tablespoon soy sauce, optional

1 red bell pepper, cubed

1 tomato, diced

2 green onions, finely chopped

4 tortillas

3 lettuce leaves, shredded

4 tablespoons shredded cheese, or to taste

1. Cut the tofu into matchsticks about 2¼ inches long, ½ inch thick, and ½ inch wide. Place the tofu in a resealable plastic bag and add the Feisty Fajita Marinade. Seal the bag and shake it so that all the tofu is coated in the marinade. Marinate the tofu overnight in the refrigerator.

2. Heat a wok or skillet over medium-high heat until it is nearly smoking. Add the olive oil. When the oil is hot, add the garlic and chilies. Stir-fry for 10 seconds, then add the shallots. Stir-fry the shallots until they begin to soften. Add the green bell pepper. Stir-fry for 1 minute, stirring in 1 tablespoon soy sauce if the vegetables begin to dry out. Add the red bell pepper and the diced tomato. Stir-fry for another minute or until the vegetables are tender but still crisp.

3. Add the tofu and the green onions. Stir-fry the tofu matchsticks for about 2 minutes, until they are browned.

4. Lay a tortilla on a plate and add a portion of the shredded lettuce. Spoon one-quarter of the stir-fry mixture onto the bottom section of the tortilla. Sprinkle 1 tablespoon shredded cheese over the top and roll up the tortilla. Continue with the remaining 3 tortillas. Serve immediately.

Which Tofu to Use for Stir-Frying For best results, use medium to extra-firm tofu in stir-fries. Soft tofus can fall apart during the stirring and tossing needed for stir-frying, while firmer tofus hold their shape. If a recipe calls for tofu without specifying which type, use regular, firm tofu.

Tofu with Broccoli

Serves 3 to 4

If you're lucky enough to live near an Asian market that sells pressed tofu that's been seasoned with spices such as star anise, try adding it to this recipe.

1/3 cup chicken broth

1½ tablespoons oyster sauce

1 tablespoon Chinese rice wine or dry sherry

1 teaspoon granulated sugar

1 teaspoon cornstarch

4 teaspoons water

3 tablespoons vegetable or peanut oil

4 thin slices ginger, minced

2 cups chopped broccoli

¼ pound fresh mushrooms, thinly sliced

2 green onions, cut into thirds

½ pound pressed tofu, cut into small cubes

1. Combine the chicken broth, oyster sauce, rice wine or sherry, and sugar in a bowl. In a separate small bowl, dissolve the cornstarch into the water.

2. Heat a wok or skillet until it is almost smoking. Add the oil. When the oil is hot, add the ginger slices. Stir-fry for about 10 seconds, then add the chopped broccoli and the mushrooms. Stir-fry for about 1 minute, until the mushrooms have darkened and the broccoli has turned a bright green. Stir in the green onions.

3. Add the tofu and gently stir it around the pan for about 1 minute. Push the tofu and vegetables to the sides of the pan. Add the sauce in the middle and bring to a boil. Add the cornstarch and water mixture into the sauce and stir quickly to thicken. Serve hot.

Hassle-Free Pressed Tofu Purchasing pressed tofu means the work of pressing and draining the liquid out of the tofu has already been done for you. The process used to make pressed tofu renders it even firmer and meatier in texture than extra-firm tofu. Pressed tofu can frequently be found in local supermarkets. If unavailable, extra-firm tofu makes an acceptable substitute—just be sure to drain it before using.

Sesame Tofu with Vegetables

The tofu in this dish provides plenty of protein, and the vegetables
supply a variety of necessary vitamins. Serve this protein-packed
dish with plenty of cooked rice for a nutritious meal.

Serves 2

2 tablespoons vegetable or
   peanut oil

½ teaspoon chile paste

½ teaspoon minced ginger

½ teaspoon minced garlic

½ cup chopped onion

½ green bell pepper, cubed

¼ teaspoon salt

½ red bell pepper, cubed

1–2 tablespoons water,
   optional

¾ pound firm tofu, drained
   and cut into ¾-inch cubes

2 portions Sesame Sauce
   (page 19)

1 green onion, chopped

2–3 tablespoons toasted
   sesame seeds, optional

1. Heat a wok or skillet over medium-high heat until it is nearly smoking. Add the oil. When the oil is hot, add the chile paste. Stir-fry for 10 seconds, then add the minced ginger and garlic. Stir-fry for another 10 seconds, then add the onion. Stir-fry the onion until it begins to soften (about 2 minutes).

2. Add the green bell pepper. Stir-fry briefly, sprinkling the salt over the mixture. Add the red bell pepper. Stir-fry until the vegetables are tender but still crisp (about 2 minutes). Splash the peppers with 1 to 2 tablespoons of water if they begin to dry out during stir-frying.

3. Push the vegetables to the sides of the pan and add the tofu cubes in the middle of the pan. Stir-fry the tofu for 1 to 2 minutes, gently stirring and moving it around the pan. Add the sauce and bring to a boil. Stir in the green onion. Cook for another minute, stirring gently, to heat everything through. Garnish with the sesame seeds before serving.

1 pound firm tofu, frozen

1 tablespoon chili powder

¼ cup cornstarch

3 tablespoons vegetable or peanut oil

2 cloves garlic, chopped

1 green onion, finely chopped

1 onion, chopped

¼ teaspoon ground allspice

¼ teaspoon ground cinnamon

1 cup frozen corn

1 cup canned red kidney beans, drained

1 cup canned diced tomatoes with juice

1 tablespoon brown sugar

Salt and black pepper to taste

Tofu Chili

Freezing tofu gives it a meatier texture. Feel free to substitute other vegetables, such as bell pepper or zucchini, in place of the frozen corn.

1. Thaw the tofu at room temperature, drain, and cut into 1-inch cubes. In a bowl, combine the chili powder with the cornstarch. Dredge the tofu cubes in the mixture.

2. Heat a wok or skillet over medium-high heat until it is nearly smoking. Add the oil. When the oil is hot, add the garlic and the green onion. Stir-fry for 10 seconds, then add the chopped onion. Sprinkle the allspice and cinnamon over the top. Stir-fry for about 2 minutes, until the onion begins to soften.

3. Add the frozen corn. Stir-fry for 1 minute, mixing with the onion. Add the tofu. Stir-fry gently for 1 minute, moving it around the pan.

4. Stir in the red kidney beans and diced tomatoes with juice. Bring to a boil. Stir in the brown sugar. Continue stir-frying for 2 to 3 minutes to mix all the ingredients together. Taste and adjust seasoning, adding salt and black pepper if desired. Serve hot.

Spicy Szechuan Peppercorn Not really a peppercorn at all, Szechuan peppercorn is a reddish-brown berry famous for the numbing effect it has on the tongue. In 2005, the United States Food and Drug Administration lifted a longtime ban on importations of Szechuan peppercorn, meaning cooks can once again enjoy their favorite spicy Szechuan dishes.

Mediterranean Tofu

*Using tofu as the protein source in this recipe means you don't have to
worry about the marinade being contaminated by meat juices. This
flavorful tofu dish would go very nicely with a green salad or a fresh fruit salad.*

Serves 3 to 4

2/3 pound firm tofu, drained
and cut into ¾–1-inch
cubes

Citrusy Mediterranean
Marinade (page 24)

½ teaspoon cornstarch

1 teaspoon water

2 tablespoons olive oil

1 clove garlic, chopped

1. Place the tofu cubes in a resealable plastic bag. Pour the Citrusy Mediterranean Marinade over the cubes. Seal the bag. Marinate the tofu in the refrigerator overnight, turning the bag over occasionally to make sure all of the tofu is coated in the marinade.

2. Remove the tofu from the bag, reserving the marinade. In a small bowl, dissolve the cornstarch into the water and set aside.

3. Heat a wok or skillet over medium-high heat until it is nearly smoking. Add the olive oil. When the oil is hot, add the garlic. Stir-fry for 10 seconds, then add the tofu cubes. Stir-fry the tofu cubes until they begin to brown (1 to 2 minutes).

4. Add the reserved marinade. Stir-fry the tofu cubes in the marinade for 2 minutes. Add the cornstarch and water mixture in the middle of the pan, stirring it into the liquid. Stir-fry for another minute, until the liquid is nearly absorbed. Serve hot.

Marinades—Bag It Up! Most stir-fry recipes call for a small amount of marinade and short marinating times. When you're marinating food overnight in a larger quantity of marinade, a resealable plastic bag is the perfect choice. It's easy to pour the marinade into the bag, and the bag can be turned frequently, ensuring that all of the food is coated.

2 cakes bean curd, drained

¼ teaspoon salt

4 Chinese dried mushrooms

2 tablespoons chicken broth

1 tablespoon dark soy sauce

1 tablespoon Chinese rice
wine or dry sherry

1 teaspoon granulated sugar

1½ teaspoons cornstarch

4 teaspoons water

3½ tablespoons vegetable or
peanut oil, divided

1 teaspoon minced garlic

1 teaspoon minced ginger

1/3 cup sliced canned bamboo
shoots, drained

1 tablespoon water or
chicken broth, optional

1 green onion, quartered

Bear's Paw Bean Curd

This Szechuan specialty gets its name from the color of the browned tofu, which resembles a bear's paw. Instead of browning the tofu, you can also deep-fry it until it turns golden brown, or use premade deep-fried tofu (available at Asian grocery stores).

1. Cut each block of bean curd diagonally into 4 triangles. In a bowl, sprinkle the salt over the triangles.

2. Place the Chinese dried mushrooms in a bowl with hot water to cover. Soak the dried mushrooms for 20 to 30 minutes, until they are softened. Squeeze out the excess water and cut the mushrooms into thin slices. In a small bowl, combine the chicken broth, dark soy sauce, Chinese rice wine or dry sherry, and the sugar. In a separate small bowl, dissolve the cornstarch into the water.

3. Heat a wok or skillet over medium-high heat until it is nearly smoking and add 2 tablespoons oil. When the oil is hot, add the garlic. Stir-fry for 10 seconds, then add the bean curd triangles. Stir-fry the bean curd, gently stirring and moving it around the pan, until it is golden brown on both sides (about 4 to 5 minutes). Remove from the pan.

4. Heat 1½ tablespoons oil in the wok or skillet. When the oil is hot, add the ginger. Stir-fry for 10 seconds, then add the dried mushrooms. Stir-fry for 1 minute, then add the bamboo shoots. Stir-fry for 30 seconds to 1 minute, adding a bit of water or chicken broth if the vegetables begin to dry out.

5. Add the bean curd back into the pan. Add the sauce. Stir in the green onion. Cook for another 1 to 2 minutes, then add the cornstarch and water mixture, stirring to thicken.

Curried Tofu for Two

*This spicy dish can easily be doubled to serve
four people. Garnish with toasted coconut flakes.*

Serves 2

1½ tablespoons curry powder

1 teaspoon brown sugar

1 teaspoon minced ginger

½ pound firm tofu, drained,
  cut into ¾-inch cubes

3 tablespoons coconut milk

3 tablespoons chicken broth

2 tablespoons vegetable or
  peanut oil

2 cloves garlic

2 tablespoons raisins

Salt and black pepper to taste

1. In a bowl, combine the curry powder, brown sugar, and minced ginger. Add the tofu cubes and coat with the mixture. Let the tofu stand for 5 minutes.

2. In a small bowl, combine the coconut milk and chicken broth and set aside.

3. Heat a wok or skillet over medium-high heat until it is nearly smoking. Add the oil. When the oil is hot, add the garlic and the tofu cubes. Stir-fry, gently moving the tofu cubes around the pan until they are golden brown (about 5 minutes).

4. Add the coconut milk mixture. Bring to a boil. Stir in the raisins. Taste and add salt and pepper if desired. Serve hot.

Spicy Tofu and Spinach

*Thicker than regular Japanese soy sauce, tamari is similar in texture and flavor to Chinese
dark soy sauce. If tamari is unavailable, Chinese dark soy sauce can be substituted.*

Serves 4

2 tablespoons vegetable or
  peanut oil

½ teaspoon chile paste, or
  to taste

1 tablespoon chopped garlic

1 pound spinach leaves,
  trimmed

2 tablespoons tamari

¾ pound medium-firm to
  firm tofu, drained, cut into
  ½-inch cubes

¼ cup chicken broth

1 teaspoon granulated sugar

1. Heat a wok or skillet over medium-high heat until it is nearly smoking, and add the oil. When the oil is hot, add the chile paste and the garlic. Stir-fry for 10 seconds, then add the spinach.

2. Stir-fry the spinach for 1 minute, splashing with the tamari. Add the tofu cubes. Stir-fry for 1 minute, moving the tofu cubes around the pan.

3. Add the chicken broth into the pan and bring to a boil. Stir in the sugar. Stir-fry for another 2 to 3 minutes, to heat through. Serve hot.

6 ounces extra-firm tofu, drained, cut into ½-inch cubes

1/8 teaspoon salt, or to taste

Black pepper to taste

½ teaspoon curry powder

1 teaspoon granulated sugar

1 tablespoon milk

1½ tablespoons vegetable or peanut oil

2 thin slices ginger

1 tablespoon Worcestershire sauce

Spicy Tofu Scramble

You can add extra flavor to this dish by adding ¼ cup of chopped onion and 1 teaspoon of chopped red chilies.

1. Place the tofu in a bowl. Use a spatula to gently mash the tofu until it resembles bits of scrambled egg. Stir in the salt, pepper, curry powder, sugar, and milk.

2. Heat a wok or skillet over medium-high heat until it is nearly smoking, and add the oil. When the oil is hot, add the ginger slices. Let brown for 2 to 3 minutes, then remove from the pan.

3. Add the tofu to the wok or skillet. Stir-fry for about 2 minutes, then stir in the Worcestershire sauce. Stir-fry for about 4 minutes or until the scrambled tofu is fluffy but has not browned. Serve immediately.

Serves 2 to 3

¾ pound extra-firm tofu, drained, cut into ½-inch cubes

1 teaspoon salt

1 teaspoon black pepper, divided

½ teaspoon turmeric

2½ tablespoons nutritional yeast

1 green onion, finely chopped

1½ tablespoons vegetable or peanut oil

2 thin slices ginger

2 shallots, chopped

2 tomatoes, halved and cut into wedges

2 tablespoons soymilk

Vegan Tofu and Tomato Scramble

Tomato and shallots add extra flavor to this hearty breakfast dish. Serve with toast and garnish with fresh tomato slices.

1. Place the tofu cubes in a bowl. Use your fingers to break up the tofu until it has the texture of scrambled egg. Stir or use your fingers to mix in the salt, ½ teaspoon black pepper, turmeric, nutritional yeast, and green onion.

2. Heat a wok or skillet over medium-high heat until it is nearly smoking, and add the oil. When the oil is hot, add the ginger slices. Let brown for 2 to 3 minutes, then remove from the pan.

3. Add the shallots to the wok or skillet. Stir-fry until they begin to soften, then add the tomatoes. Stir-fry the tomatoes for a minute, sprinkling with ½ teaspoon black pepper.

4. Add the tofu to the wok or skillet. Stir-fry for about 1 minute, then stir in the soymilk. Stir-fry for about 1 to 2 more minutes, until the scrambled tofu is light and fluffy. Serve immediately.

Sweet and Sour Tempeh

This is a great dish for the summer months when bell peppers and vine-ripened tomatoes are in season.

1. Heat a wok or skillet over medium-high heat until it is nearly smoking and add the oil. When the oil is hot, add the minced ginger and garlic. Stir-fry for 10 seconds, then add the tempeh cubes. Stir-fry the tempeh about 4 minutes, until it is browned.

2. Push the tempeh to the sides of the pan, and add the green bell pepper in the middle. Stir-fry for a minute, splashing the pepper with the soy sauce. Add the tomato and stir-fry for 1 minute, sprinkling with the black pepper.

3. Stir the Pineapple Sweet and Sour Sauce and pour over the tempeh. Bring to a boil. Stir-fry for a minute, mixing the tempeh into the sauce. Serve hot.

Tempeh or Tofu? While both tempeh and tofu are made from soybeans, in the case of tempeh, the soybeans are fermented with a mold for several hours, giving it a nuttier flavor and much firmer texture. Extra flavor makes tempeh a good choice for persons who find tofu tastes too bland, while a firmer texture means it can be stirred and tossed more during stir-frying.

Serves 3 to 4

2 tablespoons vegetable or peanut oil

1 teaspoon minced ginger

1 teaspoon minced garlic

1 pound tempeh, cut into 1-inch cubes

1 green bell pepper, chopped

1 tablespoon soy sauce

1 tomato, halved and cut into wedges

¼ teaspoon black pepper

Pineapple Sweet and Sour Sauce (page 25)

2 tablespoons plus 1 teaspoon water, divided

1½ tablespoons hoisin sauce

1 tablespoon Chinese rice wine or dry sherry

¼ teaspoon chile paste, or to taste

½ teaspoon cornstarch

1 tablespoon vegetable or peanut oil

1 clove garlic, chopped

1 block pressed tofu (about 3½ ounces), cut into ½-inch cubes

1 green onion, quartered

1 cup cooked white or brown rice

Mongolian Tofu for Two

Tofu takes the place of marinated flank steak in this variation on Mongolian beef, a popular dish from northern China. This recipe is designed to make extra sauce for mixing in with the rice.

1. In a small bowl or measuring cup, combine 2 tablespoons water, hoisin sauce, rice wine or sherry, and the chile paste. In a separate small bowl, dissolve the cornstarch into 1 teaspoon water.

2. Heat a wok or skillet over medium-high heat until it is nearly smoking and add the oil. When the oil is hot, add the garlic. Stir-fry for 10 seconds, then add the tofu and the green onion. Stir-fry the tofu for 1 to 2 minutes, until it is browned.

3. Stir the sauce and pour it in the middle of the wok or skillet. Bring to a boil. Stir-fry for a minute, mixing the tofu in with the sauce.

4. Push the tofu to the sides of the pan. Stir the cornstarch and water mixture and add it into the middle of the sauce, stirring to thicken. When the sauce has thickened, stir briefly to mix everything together. Serve hot over the cooked rice.

Tangy Hoisin Sauce Sweet and spicy hoisin sauce is the secret ingredient in many northern Chinese dishes, including mu shu pork (see Restaurant-Style Mu Shu Pork, page 184). Like other types of Chinese bean sauces, hoisin sauce is made with soybeans. In this case, the fermented soybeans are made into a paste and seasoned with garlic, vinegar, sugar, and frequently chilies.

Mongolian Tofu with Noodles

*This recipe is very adaptable—feel free to add bamboo
shoots or baby corn and to replace the tofu with beef or pork.*

4 ounces dried rice vermicelli

¼ cup water

3 tablespoons hoisin sauce

2 tablespoons Chinese rice wine or dry sherry

½ teaspoon chile paste, or to taste

2 tablespoons vegetable or peanut oil

1 teaspoon minced garlic

1½ carrots, cut into ½-inch slices

1 teaspoon minced ginger

1 green bell pepper, cut into bite-sized chunks

2 blocks pressed tofu (about 7 ounces), drained and cut into ½-inch cubes

1 tablespoon soy sauce

1. Fill a bowl with enough boiling water to cover the noodles. Soak the noodles in the hot water for about 20 minutes or until they are softened. Drain thoroughly. Cut the noodles crosswise into three sections.

2. In a small bowl or measuring cup, combine the water, hoisin sauce, rice wine or sherry, and the chile paste.

3. Heat a wok or skillet over medium-high heat until it is nearly smoking and add the oil. When the oil is hot, add the garlic. Stir-fry for 10 seconds, then add the carrots and ginger. Stir-fry for 1 minute, then add the green pepper. Stir-fry for 1 more minute or until the carrots have turned a darker orange and the vegetables are crisp but still tender.

4. Add the tofu to the wok or skillet. Stir-fry the tofu for 1 to 2 minutes, stirring and moving it around the pan, until it begins to firm up and turn brown. Splash 1 tablespoon of soy sauce over the tofu while stir-frying. Add the rice noodles, stirring to mix them in with the tofu.

5. Add the sauce and bring to a boil. Stir-fry for 1 to 2 minutes to mix the sauce in with the tofu and noodles. Serve hot.

How Tofu Is Made For centuries, tofu has been made through a complex process that has a lot in common with making cheese. After soaking, soybeans are ground and combined with water to make soymilk. A coagulant is added, which curdles the soymilk, producing the soybean curd that is called tofu.

¼ pound flank or sirloin steak, cut across the grain into thin strips

1 tablespoon light soy sauce

Black pepper to taste

1¾ teaspoons cornstarch, divided

½ cup plus 1 tablespoon water, divided

1½ tablespoons oyster sauce

1 tablespoon dark soy sauce

2 teaspoons granulated sugar

½ teaspoon chile paste, or to taste

2 tablespoons vegetable or peanut oil, divided

1 teaspoon minced garlic

½ teaspoon minced ginger

½ pound firm tofu, drained, cut into 1-inch cubes

2 green onions, finely chopped

Tofu with Beef

You can use this sauce whenever you're preparing a beef stir-fry.
Serve this dish with basic stir-fried noodles (page 200) for a complete meal.

1. Place the beef strips in a bowl and add the light soy sauce, black pepper, and ¼ teaspoon cornstarch. Marinate the beef for 15 minutes.

2. Combine ½ cup water, oyster sauce, dark soy sauce, granulated sugar, and chile paste in a bowl. In a separate bowl, dissolve 1½ teaspoons cornstarch into 1 tablespoon water. Set aside.

3. Heat a wok or skillet over medium-high heat until it is nearly smoking. Add 1 tablespoon oil. When the oil is hot, add half the garlic and ginger. Stir-fry for 10 seconds, then add the beef. Let sear briefly, then stir-fry the beef until it is no longer pink and is nearly cooked through.

4. Push the beef to the sides of the pan. Heat 1 tablespoon oil in the middle. Add the remainder of the garlic and ginger. Stir-fry for 10 seconds, then add the tofu cubes. Stir-fry the tofu cubes for 1 to 2 minutes, until they begin to brown.

5. Push the tofu to the sides and add the sauce in the middle. Bring to a boil. Stir the cornstarch and water mixture and add to the sauce, stirring to thicken. Stir in the green onions. Stir-fry for 1 to 2 more minutes to mix together all the ingredients. Serve hot.

Pairing Tofu with Meat Don't feel you need to limit your use of tofu to vegetarian dishes. In Asia, tofu is frequently paired with meat to provide an interesting contrast in texture. A well-known dish combining the two is Grandmother Bean Curd, or Mapo Doufu (page 189), where tofu and ground pork are stir-fried with fermented black beans, chile paste, and other spicy seasonings.

Glossary of Basic Cooking Terms Used in Stir-Frying

Al dente

An Italian term literally meaning "to the teeth." *Al dente* is used to describe the state to which pasta should be cooked. Pasta that is cooked al dente has no taste of flour remaining, but there is still a slight resistance when bitten and it is still slightly chewy. Like Italian pasta, Chinese egg noodles should be cooked al dente.

Aromatics

In stir-frying, garlic and ginger are frequently added to the hot oil before the other ingredients, in order to flavor the oil.

Blanch

Blanching is a means of cooking food by immersing it in boiling water. In Chinese cooking, thicker, denser vegetables such as broccoli are often briefly blanched prior to being added to a stir-fry. This helps ensure that all the vegetables in the stir-fry finish cooking at the same time. After blanching, the cooked food is immediately placed in cold water to stop the cooking process. Always drain blanched foods thoroughly before adding to a stir-fry.

Chop

Chopping consists of cutting food into small pieces. While chopped food doesn't need to be perfectly uniform, the pieces should be roughly the same size.

Deep-fry

Deep-frying is a means of cooking food by immersing it briefly in hot oil. Along with stir-frying and steaming, deep-frying is one of the three main Chinese cooking techniques. In Chinese cuisine, some recipes call for food to be deep-fried first before it is added to the other ingredients in a stir-fry.

Deglaze

Deglazing the pan consists of using liquid to clean out the browned bits of drippings left over from cooking meat in a pan. Adding liquid (usually broth or alcohol) to the pan makes it easier to lift up the browned bits with a spatula. The flavored liquid is then used in a sauce or gravy. While deglazing the pan isn't a standard Chinese technique, it can be used in stir-fry recipes such as Speedy Beef Stew (page 92) and Pork Chops with Burgundy Mushrooms (page 162).

Dice

Dicing consists of cutting food into small cubes, usually ¼ inch in size or less. Unlike chopping, the food should be cut into even-sized pieces.

Drain

Draining consists of drawing off the liquid from a food. In stir-frying, washed vegetables are drained thoroughly before stir-frying so that excess water is not added to the pan, while meat is drained after stir-frying to remove any excess oil. Either a colander (a perforated bowl made of metal or plastic) or paper towels can be used to drain food.

Dredge

Dredging consists of coating food with a dry ingredient such as flour, bread crumbs, or potato starch before frying. Spices are frequently added to the coating for extra flavor. Dredging food before frying gives it a nice, crispy coating.

Julienne

To julienne food (also called matchstick cutting) consists of cutting it into very thin strips about 1½ to 2 inches long, with a width and thickness of about ⅛ inch. Both meat and vegetables can be julienned.

Marinate

Marinating food consists of coating it in a liquid prior to cooking. Stir-fry recipes with meat, seafood, and poultry nearly always include a marinade, both to tenderize the food and lend extra flavor. Cornstarch is frequently added to help seal in the other ingredients—always add the cornstarch last unless the recipe states otherwise.

Matchstick Head

To prepare matchstick heads, julienne the food and then cut it crosswise into small cubes the approximate size of matchstick heads.

Mince

Mincing consists of cutting food into very small pieces. In general, minced food is cut into smaller pieces than chopped food.

Sauce

A sauce is a liquid that is added to lend flavor to a dish. In stir-fries, a sauce is frequently added in the final stages of cooking.

Sear

Searing meat consists of quickly browning it over high heat before finishing cooking it by another method. Searing meat browns the surface and seals in the juices. In stir-fry dishes, the meat is briefly seared after it is added to the pan, and then finished by stir-frying.

Shred

Shredding food consists of cutting it into thin strips that are usually thicker than a julienne cut. Meat, poultry, cabbage, lettuce, and cheese can all be shredded.

Simmer

Simmering food consists of cooking it in liquid at a temperature just below the boiling point.

Stir-fry

Stir-frying consists of cooking food by placing it in a small amount of heated oil and moving it around quickly at high heat. The main difference between sautéing and stir-frying is that food for stir-fries is cut up into uniform pieces to make it cook more quickly.

Online Shopping Resources

Pacific Rim Gourmet

✑ *www.pacificrimgourmet.com*

Launched in 1998, Pacific Rim Gourmet specializes in providing harder-to-find ingredients used in Asian cooking. They carry a full range of woks and wok accessories, from carbon steel and cast iron woks to wok covers, rings, tempura racks, and bamboo wok brushes for cleaning your wok. Pacific Rim Gourmet also carries an extensive selection of Asian cooking ingredients, including sauces, marinades, noodles, exotic rices and flours, and batter mixes.

Oriental Pantry

✑ *www.orientalpantry.com*

Based in the United States, Oriental Pantry has an excellent supply of ingredients commonly used in stir-frying, from sauces to beans, noodles, and vegetables. They carry a number of prepackaged mixes for popular Asian specialties such as hot and sour soup and Philippine adobo sauce for those nights when you're really in a hurry.

Wing Yip

✑ *www.wingyip.com*

Based in the United Kingdom, Wing Yip has recently launched an online shopping site to accompany its stores located throughout Britain. They carry a wide variety of ingredients used in stir-frying, including their own line of products. Although they carry a few specialty items such as shiitake mushrooms and sushi ginger, the focus is primarily on Chinese cuisine.

Earthy Delights

✑ *www.earthy.com*

Based in Michigan, Earthy Delights specializes in supplying specialty foods, from mushrooms and gourmet cheeses to fine oils. They supply a wide range of sauces and seasonings used in Asian stir-fries, from soy sauce to sesame seeds and dried chili peppers.

The Wok Shop

✑ *www.wokshop.com*

Located in the heart of San Francisco's Chinatown district, this family-run business has been in operation for over thirty-five years. Their store is an invaluable resource for anyone who doesn't have easy access to an Asian market. In addition to their line of carbon steel woks, cleavers, and other basic equipment, they carry a number of harder-to-find utensils such as tempura racks, Chinese spatulas, and wire mesh skimmers.

Index

The EVERYTHING Series!

BUSINESS & PERSONAL FINANCE

Everything® Accounting Book
Everything® Budgeting Book
Everything® Business Planning Book
Everything® Coaching and Mentoring Book
Everything® Fundraising Book
Everything® Get Out of Debt Book
Everything® Grant Writing Book
Everything® Guide to Personal Finance for Single Mothers
Everything® Home-Based Business Book, 2nd Ed.
Everything® Homebuying Book, 2nd Ed.
Everything® Homeselling Book, 2nd Ed.
Everything® Improve Your Credit Book
Everything® Investing Book, 2nd Ed.
Everything® Landlording Book
Everything® Leadership Book
Everything® Managing People Book, 2nd Ed.
Everything® Negotiating Book
Everything® Online Auctions Book
Everything® Online Business Book
Everything® Personal Finance Book
Everything® Personal Finance in Your 20s and 30s Book
Everything® Project Management Book
Everything® Real Estate Investing Book
Everything® Retirement Planning Book
Everything® Robert's Rules Book, $7.95
Everything® Selling Book
Everything® Start Your Own Business Book, 2nd Ed.
Everything® Wills & Estate Planning Book

COOKING

Everything® Barbecue Cookbook
Everything® Bartender's Book, $9.95
Everything® Cheese Book
Everything® Chinese Cookbook
Everything® Classic Recipes Book
Everything® Cocktail Parties and Drinks Book
Everything® College Cookbook
Everything® Cooking for Baby and Toddler Book
Everything® Cooking for Two Cookbook
Everything® Diabetes Cookbook
Everything® Easy Gourmet Cookbook
Everything® Fondue Cookbook
Everything® Fondue Party Book
Everything® Gluten-Free Cookbook
Everything® Glycemic Index Cookbook
Everything® Grilling Cookbook

Everything® Healthy Meals in Minutes Cookbook
Everything® Holiday Cookbook
Everything® Indian Cookbook
Everything® Italian Cookbook
Everything® Low-Carb Cookbook
Everything® Low-Fat High-Flavor Cookbook
Everything® Low-Salt Cookbook
Everything® Meals for a Month Cookbook
Everything® Mediterranean Cookbook
Everything® Mexican Cookbook
Everything® No Trans Fat Cookbook
Everything® One-Pot Cookbook
Everything® Pizza Cookbook
Everything® Quick and Easy 30-Minute, 5-Ingredient Cookbook
Everything® Quick Meals Cookbook
Everything® Slow Cooker Cookbook
Everything® Slow Cooking for a Crowd Cookbook
Everything® Soup Cookbook
Everything® Stir-Fry Cookbook
Everything® Tex-Mex Cookbook
Everything® Thai Cookbook
Everything® Vegetarian Cookbook
Everything® Wild Game Cookbook
Everything® Wine Book, 2nd Ed.

GAMES

Everything® 15-Minute Sudoku Book, $9.95
Everything® 30-Minute Sudoku Book, $9.95
Everything® Blackjack Strategy Book
Everything® Brain Strain Book, $9.95
Everything® Bridge Book
Everything® Card Games Book
Everything® Card Tricks Book, $9.95
Everything® Casino Gambling Book, 2nd Ed.
Everything® Chess Basics Book
Everything® Craps Strategy Book
Everything® Crossword and Puzzle Book
Everything® Crossword Challenge Book
Everything® Crosswords for the Beach Book, $9.95
Everything® Cryptograms Book, $9.95
Everything® Easy Crosswords Book
Everything® Easy Kakuro Book, $9.95
Everything® Easy Large Print Crosswords Book
Everything® Games Book, 2nd Ed.
Everything® Giant Sudoku Book, $9.95
Everything® Kakuro Challenge Book, $9.95
Everything® Large-Print Crossword Challenge Book

Everything® Large-Print Crosswords Book
Everything® Lateral Thinking Puzzles Book, $9.9
Everything® Mazes Book
Everything® Movie Crosswords Book, $9.95
Everything® Online Poker Book, $12.95
Everything® Pencil Puzzles Book, $9.95
Everything® Poker Strategy Book
Everything® Pool & Billiards Book
Everything® Sports Crosswords Book, $9.95
Everything® Test Your IQ Book, $9.95
Everything® Texas Hold 'Em Book, $9.95
Everything® Travel Crosswords Book, $9.95
Everything® Word Games Challenge Book
Everything® Word Scramble Book
Everything® Word Search Book

HEALTH

Everything® Alzheimer's Book
Everything® Diabetes Book
Everything® Health Guide to Adult Bipolar Disorder
Everything® Health Guide to Controlling Anxiety
Everything® Health Guide to Fibromyalgia
Everything® Health Guide to Postpartum Care
Everything® Health Guide to Thyroid Disease
Everything® Hypnosis Book
Everything® Low Cholesterol Book
Everything® Massage Book
Everything® Menopause Book
Everything® Nutrition Book
Everything® Reflexology Book
Everything® Stress Management Book

HISTORY

Everything® American Government Book
Everything® American History Book, 2nd Ed.
Everything® Civil War Book
Everything® Freemasons Book
Everything® Irish History & Heritage Book
Everything® Middle East Book

HOBBIES

Everything® Candlemaking Book
Everything® Cartooning Book
Everything® Coin Collecting Book
Everything® Drawing Book
Everything® Family Tree Book, 2nd Ed.
Everything® Knitting Book
Everything® Knots Book
Everything® Photography Book

Everything® Quilting Book
Everything® Scrapbooking Book
Everything® Sewing Book
Everything® Soapmaking Book, 2nd Ed.
Everything® Woodworking Book

HOME IMPROVEMENT

Everything® Feng Shui Book
Everything® Feng Shui Decluttering Book, $9.95
Everything® Fix-It Book
Everything® Home Decorating Book
Everything® Home Storage Solutions Book
Everything® Homebuilding Book
Everything® Organize Your Home Book

KIDS' BOOKS

All titles are $7.95

Everything® Kids' Animal Puzzle & Activity Book
Everything® Kids' Baseball Book, 4th Ed.
Everything® Kids' Bible Trivia Book
Everything® Kids' Bugs Book
Everything® Kids' Cars and Trucks Puzzle
  & Activity Book
Everything® Kids' Christmas Puzzle
  & Activity Book
Everything® Kids' Cookbook
Everything® Kids' Crazy Puzzles Book
Everything® Kids' Dinosaurs Book
Everything® Kids' First Spanish Puzzle and
  Activity Book
Everything® Kids' Gross Cookbook
Everything® Kids' Gross Hidden Pictures Book
Everything® Kids' Gross Jokes Book
Everything® Kids' Gross Mazes Book
Everything® Kids' Gross Puzzle and
  Activity Book
Everything® Kids' Halloween Puzzle
  & Activity Book
Everything® Kids' Hidden Pictures Book
Everything® Kids' Horses Book
Everything® Kids' Joke Book
Everything® Kids' Knock Knock Book
Everything® Kids' Learning Spanish Book
Everything® Kids' Math Puzzles Book
Everything® Kids' Mazes Book
Everything® Kids' Money Book
Everything® Kids' Nature Book
Everything® Kids' Pirates Puzzle and Activity Book
Everything® Kids' Presidents Book
Everything® Kids' Princess Puzzle and Activity Book
Everything® Kids' Puzzle Book
Everything® Kids' Riddles & Brain Teasers Book
Everything® Kids' Science Experiments Book
Everything® Kids' Sharks Book
Everything® Kids' Soccer Book
Everything® Kids' States Book
Everything® Kids' Travel Activity Book

KIDS' STORY BOOKS

Everything® Fairy Tales Book

LANGUAGE

Everything® Conversational Japanese Book with
  CD, $19.95
Everything® French Grammar Book
Everything® French Phrase Book, $9.95
Everything® French Verb Book, $9.95
Everything® German Practice Book with CD,
  $19.95
Everything® Inglés Book
**Everything® Intermediate Spanish Book with
  CD, $19.95**
**Everything® Learning Brazilian Portuguese
  Book with CD, $19.95**
Everything® Learning French Book
Everything® Learning German Book
Everything® Learning Italian Book
Everything® Learning Latin Book
**Everything® Learning Spanish Book with
  CD, 2nd Edition, $19.95**
Everything® Russian Practice Book with CD, $19.95
Everything® Sign Language Book
Everything® Spanish Grammar Book
Everything® Spanish Phrase Book, $9.95
Everything® Spanish Practice Book
  with CD, $19.95
Everything® Spanish Verb Book, $9.95
Everything® Speaking Mandarin Chinese Book
  with CD, $19.95

MUSIC

Everything® Drums Book with CD, $19.95
**Everything® Guitar Book with CD, 2nd
  Edition, $19.95**
Everything® Guitar Chords Book with CD, $19.95
Everything® Home Recording Book
Everything® Music Theory Book with CD, $19.95
Everything® Reading Music Book with CD, $19.95
Everything® Rock & Blues Guitar Book
  with CD, $19.95
**Everything® Rock and Blues Piano Book
  with CD, $19.95**
Everything® Songwriting Book

NEW AGE

Everything® Astrology Book, 2nd Ed.
Everything® Birthday Personology Book
Everything® Dreams Book, 2nd Ed.
Everything® Love Signs Book, $9.95
Everything® Numerology Book
Everything® Paganism Book
Everything® Palmistry Book
Everything® Psychic Book
Everything® Reiki Book

Everything® Sex Signs Book, $9.95
Everything® Tarot Book, 2nd Ed.
Everything® Toltec Wisdom Book
Everything® Wicca and Witchcraft Book

PARENTING

Everything® Baby Names Book, 2nd Ed.
Everything® Baby Shower Book
Everything® Baby's First Year Book
Everything® Birthing Book
Everything® Breastfeeding Book
Everything® Father-to-Be Book
Everything® Father's First Year Book
Everything® Get Ready for Baby Book
Everything® Get Your Baby to Sleep Book, $9.95
Everything® Getting Pregnant Book
Everything® Guide to Raising a One-Year-Old
Everything® Guide to Raising a Two-Year-Old
Everything® Homeschooling Book
Everything® Mother's First Year Book
**Everything® Parent's Guide to Childhood
  Illnesses**
Everything® Parent's Guide to Children
  and Divorce
Everything® Parent's Guide to Children
  with ADD/ADHD
Everything® Parent's Guide to Children
  with Asperger's Syndrome
Everything® Parent's Guide to Children
  with Autism
Everything® Parent's Guide to Children with
  Bipolar Disorder
**Everything® Parent's Guide to Children with
  Depression**
Everything® Parent's Guide to Children
  with Dyslexia
**Everything® Parent's Guide to Children with
  Juvenile Diabetes**
Everything® Parent's Guide to Positive Discipline
Everything® Parent's Guide to Raising a
  Successful Child
Everything® Parent's Guide to Raising Boys
Everything® Parent's Guide to Raising Girls
Everything® Parent's Guide to Raising Siblings
Everything® Parent's Guide to Sensory
  Integration Disorder
Everything® Parent's Guide to Tantrums
Everything® Parent's Guide to the Strong-Willed
  Child
Everything® Parenting a Teenager Book
Everything® Potty Training Book, $9.95
Everything® Pregnancy Book, 3rd Ed.
Everything® Pregnancy Fitness Book
Everything® Pregnancy Nutrition Book
Everything® Pregnancy Organizer, 2nd Ed., $16.95
Everything® Toddler Activities Book
Everything® Toddler Book

Everything® Tween Book
Everything® Twins, Triplets, and More Book

PETS

Everything® Aquarium Book
Everything® Boxer Book
Everything® Cat Book, 2nd Ed.
Everything® Chihuahua Book
Everything® Dachshund Book
Everything® Dog Book
Everything® Dog Health Book
Everything® Dog Obedience Book
Everything® Dog Owner's Organizer, $16.95
Everything® Dog Training and Tricks Book
Everything® German Shepherd Book
Everything® Golden Retriever Book
Everything® Horse Book
Everything® Horse Care Book
Everything® Horseback Riding Book
Everything® Labrador Retriever Book
Everything® Poodle Book
Everything® Pug Book
Everything® Puppy Book
Everything® Rottweiler Book
Everything® Small Dogs Book
Everything® Tropical Fish Book
Everything® Yorkshire Terrier Book

REFERENCE

Everything® American Presidents Book
Everything® Blogging Book
Everything® Build Your Vocabulary Book
Everything® Car Care Book
Everything® Classical Mythology Book
Everything® Da Vinci Book
Everything® Divorce Book
Everything® Einstein Book
Everything® Enneagram Book
Everything® Etiquette Book, 2nd Ed.
Everything® Inventions and Patents Book
Everything® Mafia Book
Everything® Philosophy Book
Everything® Pirates Book
Everything® Psychology Book

RELIGION

Everything® Angels Book
Everything® Bible Book
Everything® Buddhism Book
Everything® Catholicism Book
Everything® Christianity Book
Everything® Gnostic Gospels Book
Everything® History of the Bible Book
Everything® Jesus Book

Everything® Jewish History & Heritage Book
Everything® Judaism Book
Everything® Kabbalah Book
Everything® Koran Book
Everything® Mary Book
Everything® Mary Magdalene Book
Everything® Prayer Book
Everything® Saints Book, 2nd Ed.
Everything® Torah Book
Everything® Understanding Islam Book
Everything® World's Religions Book
Everything® Zen Book

SCHOOL & CAREERS

Everything® Alternative Careers Book
Everything® Career Tests Book
Everything® College Major Test Book
Everything® College Survival Book, 2nd Ed.
Everything® Cover Letter Book, 2nd Ed.
Everything® Filmmaking Book
Everything® Get-a-Job Book, 2nd Ed.
Everything® Guide to Being a Paralegal
Everything® Guide to Being a Personal Trainer
Everything® Guide to Being a Real Estate Agent
Everything® Guide to Being a Sales Rep
Everything® Guide to Careers in Health Care
Everything® Guide to Careers in Law Enforcement
Everything® Guide to Government Jobs
Everything® Guide to Starting and Running a Restaurant
Everything® Job Interview Book
Everything® New Nurse Book
Everything® New Teacher Book
Everything® Paying for College Book
Everything® Practice Interview Book
Everything® Resume Book, 2nd Ed.
Everything® Study Book

SELF-HELP

Everything® Dating Book, 2nd Ed.
Everything® Great Sex Book
Everything® Self-Esteem Book
Everything® Tantric Sex Book

SPORTS & FITNESS

Everything® Easy Fitness Book
Everything® Running Book
Everything® Weight Training Book

TRAVEL

Everything® Family Guide to Cruise Vacations
Everything® Family Guide to Hawaii
Everything® Family Guide to Las Vegas, 2nd Ed.
Everything® Family Guide to Mexico
Everything® Family Guide to New York City, 2nd Ed.
Everything® Family Guide to RV Travel & Campgrounds
Everything® Family Guide to the Caribbean
Everything® Family Guide to the Walt Disney World Resort®, Universal Studios®, and Greater Orlando, 4th Ed.
Everything® Family Guide to Timeshares
Everything® Family Guide to Washington D.C., 2nd Ed.

WEDDINGS

Everything® Bachelorette Party Book, $9.95
Everything® Bridesmaid Book, $9.95
Everything® Destination Wedding Book
Everything® Elopement Book, $9.95
Everything® Father of the Bride Book, $9.95
Everything® Groom Book, $9.95
Everything® Mother of the Bride Book, $9.95
Everything® Outdoor Wedding Book
Everything® Wedding Book, 3rd Ed.
Everything® Wedding Checklist, $9.95
Everything® Wedding Etiquette Book, $9.95
Everything® Wedding Organizer, 2nd Ed., $16.95
Everything® Wedding Shower Book, $9.95
Everything® Wedding Vows Book, $9.95
Everything® Wedding Workout Book
Everything® Weddings on a Budget Book, $9.95

WRITING

Everything® Creative Writing Book
Everything® Get Published Book, 2nd Ed.
Everything® Grammar and Style Book
Everything® Guide to Magazine Writing
Everything® Guide to Writing a Book Proposal
Everything® Guide to Writing a Novel
Everything® Guide to Writing Children's Books
Everything® Guide to Writing Copy
Everything® Guide to Writing Research Papers
Everything® Screenwriting Book
Everything® Writing Poetry Book
Everything® Writing Well Book